THE **BLACK** HAMMERS

THE VOICE OF WEST HAM UNITED'S EBONY HEROES

B R I A N   B E L T O N

FOREWORD BY CLYDE BEST MBE AND KRISS AKABUSI MBE

First published in hardback in Great Britain 2006
By Pennant Books
A division of Pennant Publishing Ltd

Text copyright © Brian Belton 2006

British Library Cataloguing-in-Publication Data:
A catalogue record for this book is available from
The British Library

ISBN 0-9550394-5-2

Design & Typeset by Envy Design Ltd

Printed and bound in Great Britain by
William Clowes Ltd, Beccles, Suffolk

Pennant Books Ltd
A division of Pennant Publishing Ltd
PO Box 5071
Hove, BN52 9BB

To 'The Two' of 2 April 1970
(Johnnie and Clyde — They lived a lot together and finally
together they played with pride)
The day the Black Hammers were born

'Black or white — we all have football under our skin'
Eusebio

Thanks to Shaun Neal of www.nccukexclusive.co.uk –
his help has been invaluable

CONTENTS

FOREWORD – THE PLAYER
CLYDE BEST MBE

It is a great honour to have been asked to write a foreword for a book about West Ham United Football Club. What makes it that much more special is that it is a book about West Ham's black footballers. It shows that we will have contributed to British football history.

I first met Brian Belton in March 1999 at a hotel in Chigwell, Essex. After talking with him, I knew he was a Hammers fan through and through. When he told me that he had written books about West Ham before, I thought that it was great of Brian to have asked me to write this foreword for *The Black Hammers*.

I was very fortunate to have played under two great coaches during my time at West Ham – Ron Greenwood and John Lyall. When I took up coaching myself, I used their training methods and philosophy, although I did put my own stamp on this, also utilising my experience in Holland and the USA. It was great playing for West Ham because we had a reputation for playing both entertaining and skilful football. Some of our games against the likes of Celtic, Spurs, Manchester United, Derby County, Chelsea and Liverpool, at the peak of their powers, were breathtaking.

I stayed at West Ham for eight years. I will never forget the friends I have made both inside and outside of football. West Ham will always hold a special place in my heart. I joined West Ham in August 1968 two years after England had won the World Cup. The Hammers trio of Bobby Moore, Geoff Hurst and Martin Peters played a prominent part in making history beating West Germany in 1966. Through Geoff, I learned the art of playing target man. Bobby taught me how to believe in my own ability. Billy Bonds was another great player I admired. From Billy I learned that you never give in and keep going until you win!

Worldwide, youngsters today have greater distractions than former generations and of course this had an effect on football. Anyone that knows football today at youth level realises too much emphasis is put on winning, but coaches who coach players up to the age of 11 need to emphasise that football should be fun and make it enjoyable.

Once again, I would like to thank Brian Belton very much for giving me the opportunity to write a foreword for this book. I would also like to congratulate him on all of the good books he has written before.

Clyde Best MBE

FOREWORD – THE FAN

KRISS AKABUSI MBE

I first became aware of West Ham when I was eight years old. Bobby Moore, Geoff Hurst and Martin Peters had just performed and England had won the World Cup. But it was a few years later in 1969 while on holiday in Clacton that I became a West Ham United supporter. During my stay at the holiday resort, I made friends with a guy of a similar age to me called Terry Fagg who was full-on claret and blue. As I entered his room in the caravan he was staying in, I saw that the inside of the trailer was festooned with all sorts of material celebrating the existence and triumphs of the Hammers. However, what struck me more than anything else when I looked at the team photographs was the presence of black players. I had seen team pictures of most of the top sides of the time – Spurs, Arsenal, Liverpool – but none of them could match the cosmopolitan ethos portrayed by the Irons. From that time on, West Ham were my team.

I have watched the Hammers change and grow over the years. I'm a season-ticket holder and follow the Hammers 'over land and sea', in the company of my daughter from time to time too. She feels at home in the Bobby Moore Lower Stand behind the goal singing her head off, while I prefer the upper echelons of the West Stand overlooking the centre line, having had my fill of prawn sandwiches. But away we are together as one, Shakira, her dad and a few thousand Hammers – the West Ham United claret and blue army. West Ham, along with many clubs in British football, have grabbed the thorny issue of racism with the slogan 'Let's Kick Racism Out of Football'; however, as some of the Black Hammers themselves point out, there is still a glass ceiling in football for the black player. The executive makeup in the highest echelons of the game's organisation, as well as the coaching and management staff at club level, do not reflect the ethnic makeup of the playing ranks. This has much to do with the historical culture of British football, and I am sure, given time, when the current crop of footballers with ethnic roots away from these shores leave the playing arena, many will find their way into management and coaching.

The signs are there but we still have a long way to go before the numbers running the game are reflective of those who play it. Writing from the context of the modern game, this feels amazing given the rich multicultural makeup of contemporary football in Britain. I think that, in 10 to 15 years' time, we will look back on the current situation within the administration of the game with incredulity; culture is always moving so cultural change is inevitable. The pages that follow contain good examples of the second generation of black pioneers of the game, the likes of Leroy Rosenior, who are breaking new barriers in the same spirit that the first Black Hammers opened up possibilities for black professionals on the playing front. This continued progress provides all of us involved in football, at every level, with grounds for optimism.

One thing that has remained constant over the entire time I have supported the Irons is that the club has always reflected the community it is part of. In many ways, the area has defined what West Ham United is, but at the same time the club has had a tremendous influence on its birthplace, the docklands area of East London. Few authors have captured this part of the Hammers 'personality', but, in his many books looking at the colourful history of the Irons, Brian Belton has always placed this 'mutuality' at the centre of his focus. *The Black Hammers* continues and develops this emphasis.

The Black Hammers, in bringing together the biographies of all the black players to represent West Ham United, reflects on the contribution that these men have made to the progress of the club since the late 1950s, but in doing this it also shows how the district has come to embrace and appreciate the talents and gifts that Black British, Caribbean and African people have brought to the East End. The awareness of these sentiments in the vast majority of West Ham fans over the years is well expressed in this book by the reflections and memories of Bermudan Clyde Best, Canning Town boys John and Clive Charles and Ade Coker, born under African skies, who were at Upton Park together in the early 1970s; there is an enduring mutual affection and admiration between these men and the hundreds of thousands of Hammers fans who cheered them on through the good and not-so-good times. They, alongside the rest of *The Black Hammers*, paved the way for the multicultural game, on and off the pitch, we see today.

As such, not only is Brian's book a story of why and how young black men became professional footballers, it also demonstrates how cultures (East End or otherwise) do not stay the same, but grow and flourish as people merge and develop in community. At the same time, *The Black Hammers* gives living confirmation that positive feelings, such as love, solidarity, loyalty and care, can, in the last analysis, bring us together, causing a realisation that the things which separate us are, in reality, no more than skin deep and the only colours that matter are claret and blue.

Up the Hammers!

KRISS KEZIE UCHE CHUKWU DURU AKABUSI MBE MA

Olympic Silver (1984 4x400m) and Bronze (1992 400m Hurdles and 4x400m) medallist

World Champion 1991 (4x100m), Silver (1987 4x400m) and Bronze (1991 400m Hurdles) medallist

European Champion 1990 (400m Hurdles – beat David Hemery's 22-year-old British Record and 4x400m) and Bronze (1986 4x400m) medallist

Commonwealth Champion 1990 (400m Hurdles) and 1986 (4x400m)

INTRODUCTION

This book is a celebration of the contribution of a group from across the world to an East London sporting institution and cockney culture. What follows are the voices of and perspectives on lives lived of men that were affected by and helped create what we today understand to be West Ham United Football Club. Together, over generations, from a period just after the Hammers' return from their 26-year banishment from the elite of English football, to one of their proudest moments, the 2006 FA Cup final, wherein the Irons of the Docklands forced the Champions of Europe, in desperation, to claw their way to survival through extra-time and rely on the fates to carry them over the insanity of a penalty shoot-out.

The pages that follow provide not only a particular chronicle of a social and sporting phenomenon, but also something of a social history of an industry that has bled into the very soul of the 'manor of the Hammers', north of the river, east of the Tower and the people who abide there – wherever they might be in the world, for this place is a domicile of the spirit as much as a physical location. Yes, the words are about football and footballers, but the story is one of courage, development, success, failure and fun and how people come together to create their context and who they are.

I began to write *The Black Hammers* nearly 15 years ago now. I started it because I was sick of hearing, mostly from people who have never attended a game at the Boleyn Ground, how racist West Ham fans were and are. I have supported my team for the best part of half a century now. I come from a family with a number of ethnic, cultural and political affiliations. As a boy I was one of the skinhead 'originals'; the kids who, before the identity was hijacked by tossers with flags and no brains, took on the 'Rude Boy' culture of Reggae and two-tone that our schoolfriends gifted us from the warm and throbbing heart of the Caribbean. We filled the ranks of the first incarnation of the Anti-Nazi League (that, as a bonus, provided ample opportunities for chatting up pretty middle-class, Young Communist hippie girls in short skirts) but at night we danced to 'Prince Buster' and 'over Upten Parc' we sang 'North Bank supports West Ham!' to the tune of 'The Liquidator'.

The secondary modern school I attended, about a 10-minute walk from the Upton Park home of the Hammers boasted dozens of religions, races and ethnicities, in terms of pupils and staff. Not just 'some of my best friends were black' – my friends and my girlfriends were mostly not white. By the time I was 15 I'd experienced most and got pissed at many types of traditional ceremony and rites of passage a multicultural society has to offer.

My people fought Mosley's Fascist Brown Shirts and prevented them marching through the East End spreading their racist filth; my mother's uncle was one of the first East Londoners to die fighting Franco in Spain; my grandfather fought Nazis in Norway, helping undermine Hitler's attempts to develop a hydrogen bomb, and my uncles were amongst those who liberated the death camps of Europe.

As a youth worker, I have worked in China and Africa, East London and the Falkland Islands, Thailand and Israel. So, you can understand why I didn't like being called a racist and wanted to find out and tell others something closer to the truth than that provided by the discriminatory and prejudicial condemnations so often meted out by the popular media about the Hammers supporters, who have never had a voice to answer such accusations.

The most dangerous, powerful and ardent racists do not live in East London; they do not share in the radical tradition of the area; they have not been part of the multicultural socialisation it offers and they do not support West Ham United!

But who would I ask about all this? Who would speak for us, the vast majority of claret and blue supporters? Who would be the best judges of the situation? My conclusion was ... *The Black Hammers*.

However, as I started to speak to these men, much more came out of the process than I had at first imagined. I began to see a bigger story of identity and affinity; a tale of hope and clear messages not only about the state of football as a game, but also about the structure of British society. I was privileged to be a scribe to a collective wisdom and insight that I wanted others to share and add to.

The origins of *The Black Hammers* were in Africa, the West Indies, the Americas, Europe, East London and all over England and Wales. I have spoken to them in the USA, Europe, Essex, Norfolk, every part of London. They came from middle-class, working-class and poor families. They were brought up by single and foster parents, in extended or very conventional family situations. Fathers and mothers worked as (amongst other things) doctors, lawyers, teachers, cleaners, seafarers, social workers and homemakers; in many ways *The Black Hammers* are an authentic cross section of the world community. The contribution they have made to football across the world is astounding. Apart from their combined efforts as professionals for clubs and countries at every stage, from schoolboy to senior, they have coached and managed at club and international level with men and women, as well as playing significant parts in the non-League game and developing the sport at its roots in communities and with young people.

However, as members of the wider society, *The Black Hammers* who have left the game include individuals who have had influential and important roles in industries such as security, publishing, sales, information and communications technology. A number became businessmen or have gone into teaching in fields as diverse as special education, schools and university. Some have had to work in places like supermarkets and retail building outlets when they finished playing; others have become millionaires. But each and everyone has a story to tell, some overcoming incredible social obstacles and personal adversity, such as mental illness, physical injury, marriage breakdown, alcoholism, homophobia, racism and prison. Out of all this comes a collective account of hope, integrity, strength and success that spans the horizon of human achievement.

I set out to educate, but in the end *The Black Hammers* educated me. Of course, some were out of reach; prisoners of agents or, in just one case, it seems his own ego. But many of them agreed to meet with me; not one was less than extremely polite and affable. Some of them invited me into their homes to meet their families and friends; one or two became valued and good friends. I thank them all, these generous, intelligent, noble, hospitable, interesting, humorous, patient people, from the bottom of my Hammering heart.

Please note: The personal narratives included in this book have been recorded as closely as possible to reflect the course of conversations with the people concerned. There has been no attempt to change the order of topics covered during conversations. There has been some attempt to limit errors or lack of clarity, but not to arrange responses in terms of the 'correct' chronology of events discussed.

JOHN WILLIAM CHARLES

HAMMERS DEBUT: 4/5/63

'They didn't ask if you were black or white; they asked if you were West Ham.'

'Charlo' as his fellow players, friends and the Upton Park supporters christened him from his earliest days in football, or, as he occasionally called himself, 'Johnnie the One', was the first black player to break into West Ham United's first team, one of the first to play at the top level of the modern English game, and the first black player to represent England when he gained the first of his Youth caps. As such, he led the way for other black professionals to compete for selection at West Ham and the highest echelon of English, British and European football.

John was born in Canning Town, East London, on 20 September 1944. He was to become a pioneer of sport, albeit unwittingly, creating a path that others could follow during the early 1960s, the most difficult years in terms of football's and Britain's transition to multiculturalism. But the identity that John Charles was most proud of was that of his roots in Canning Town – part of the heartland of support for West Ham United, where the East End's football club had been born – and the qualities of this area: loyalty, protectiveness and an ability to experience joy in the face of adversity.

John was born into a big family. He told me,

I was number eight of nine children, all different colours. [John smiled.] There was Jessie, Josie, Bon, Len, Bonzo, Marge and Rita. Clive came later. One died. I just keep mainly in contact with me sister Rita and Clive and Bon and Marge. My dad, who originally came to

1

Britain from Grenada in the West Indies, was a seaman. They called him 'Gentleman Charles'. Mum was always a housewife. The four eldest were white (there were five, Michael got killed); then there was Bonzo and Margie, they were sort of tan, their dad was black but they didn't come out that way. [He chortled.] *They were olive colour, yeah. And then my dad was black but we come out black.* [John smiled.] *My sister, Rita, she was older than me (still is).* [Smiling again, he went on] *And then, seven years after me, there was Clive. So I was second from youngest, but the youngest up till I was seven. I was me dad's first son, so I was looked after and made a bit of a fuss of. Mum kept us pretty clean for a big family. Me and me sister were close, we still are. She's always round, 'How are yer?' and that.*

John told of some of the difficulties associated with a mixed-race marriage at the time:

My mum was from Silver Town. The old man was in digs down that way and that's how they met. My mum was white. She got called everything, from whatever to whatever. Even her family walked on the other side of the street, except for old Uncle Owen, me mum's brother, he was all right. He was at our wedding. All the others was dead I think. [John laughed.]

My mum was great, she was brilliant. She had three husbands! She died in May 1994. She was about 85. She was as tough as nails! She was as tough as boots that little old lady. Her name was Jessie. My dad was her third husband. He was the best one. [John laughed quietly.] *His name was Moister Leopold. I never saw me grandparents. Never been to Grenada, might go one day. I might have a plot of land out there.* [John chuckled cheerfully at the thought.] *They might have lived together somewhere in Silver Town before Ordinance Road, I don't know. Her first husband was a bastard to her. He'd beat her all over the place.*

Although the worst of wartime austerity had passed, John's family, like so many others in East London at that time, still needed to watch their finances:

JOHN WILLIAM CHARLES

My dad was quite a big man, he was very strict. I can remember my mum buying a brand-new pair of shoes off the tallyman. In them days, we all made bikes or scooters from all the old scrap, bits and pieces. I was on this bike with these brand-new shoes on and the pedals had spikes on 'em. They just ripped me shoes off completely. Me mum had to hide them till the following week till the tallyman came round again and sorted it out. But I got a belting for it. The old man used to take his belt off, cos he was a pretty big man and working in them docks and everything! He always said that he hit us with his belt because it would have been worse if he'd hit us with his hand. He could be heavy handed.

John entered full-time education as the world said goodbye to the 1940s:

My primary school was Clarkson Street. That was down Rathbone Street and just round the corner to us. I was the only black kid in my school [although John's sister Rita went to the school]. There was no problems with that. None at all. I left there, cos they were going to knock it down, then I went to Star Lane and did me last year at primary school. There were no black kids there other than my family. I didn't see any Asians when I was at school. I loved it at school. It was great!

In 1955, John moved on to secondary school:

Me and my sister Rita went to Pretoria Road School [now Eastlea]. Rita must have been the only black girl there. But it was never mixed there. It was boys this end and girls that end.

West Ham Boys was one of the main conduits that pumped local talent into the budding academy of football at Upton Park. For most of the 1950s, West Ham Boys were unbeaten, winning match after match from the under-11s onwards.

The West Ham Boys team was a good side. We used to win everything. We made the English Schools Cup final in 1959–60, but were thrashed 6–1 by Manchester. I was picked for Essex and London Boys.

THE BLACK HAMMERS

I went to England trials too. I did win five Youth caps for England in the end and we won the Junior World Cup – three lions on me chest. [John chuckled.]

This was the basis on which John was to claim international recognition. Although some have expressed the belief that it was prejudice that probably robbed him of a Schoolboy cap, John was to become the first black player to represent England at any level, but he didn't seem conscious of this point.

John certainly remembered his schooldays with affection and he seemed to be a good student. The school testimonial states that: 'His work is neat, careful and intelligent. Well up to standard … Top six in the class. Honest and trustworthy. Willing.'

It was during a difficult period that John got his first chance to break into professional sport, but the offer didn't come from football.

I was a pretty good cricketer. Essex phoned up when me dad died. I couldn't go and play for them because me father died.

The loss for Essex would be West Ham's gain. Following the club's first sighting of John by veteran goalkeeper-turned-coach and scout Ernie Gregory, Charlo told me how:

Before one game, a teacher told us that a West Ham scout was there and to do our best when we went out there to play. After that, Wally St Pier came up to me and said, 'I'd like to have you down at West Ham. I went home and told me mum and she had to go with me up the school because I didn't want to go to West Ham, I wanted to be a lorry driver's mate. [John laughed at the thought.] They were getting about £2 a week. But I went to West Ham straight from school. It was Christmas 1959.

When John joined the Upton Park staff, he soon forgot his lorry-driving ambitions:

My attitude changed when I actually got into West Ham and started training and everything. On my first day, I sowed the seeds on the

4

pitch. I cleaned all the stand out, scrubbed it out, washed it out, painted it, that's what we had to do. Paint the ground before you even kicked a ball. You didn't kick a ball until all that work was done. Underneath the stands stencilling 'A' block, 'B' block, all that and that's what I did.

Not long into Charlo's West Ham career, Ron Greenwood took over as manager of the club and, as the 60s really began to swing and the gloom of the 50s was lifting, West Ham's John Charles came of football age but he also made another big step in life.

In 1963, I signed pro. I was 17. I was married at 18. Carol was a mate of me sister, Rita, they worked together. I used to go round her house, she came round mine. Rita went out for a drink with her brother and his mates, I used to drink with Rita and that's how it happened. We were courting for about two years before we got married in St Mathias.

Carol was white and she and John married at a time when their union would have been know as a 'mixed marriage'. However, they told me they hardly ever felt out of place or conscious of discrimination.

John captained West Ham's first Youth Cup-winning side in 1963, the first black player to lead a first-class side to a major trophy. The young Hammers had achieved a fantastic victory. The Liverpool side that were beaten in the final were to be the seedbed of the team that would dominate Europe for years later in the century. West Ham's skipper that day had established himself as the hard man of the East End team, but Liverpool's own 'deterrent', the young Tommy Smith, the Anfield man-of-steel-to-be, was reduced to tears as John Charles led his team to collect the Cup. West Ham would not make the final again for a dozen years. John recalled,

I skippered the youth team because I was the most knowledgeable. I was the pro. They were all younger than me. The Youth Cup made history. About 17,000 turned out at Upton Park that night, the Friday before the Cup final. West Ham had lost the first leg at Anfield 3–1. Back at Upton Park we won 5–2.

THE BLACK HAMMERS

On 4 May 1963, Greenwood brought the 19-year-old Charlo into the first team. John recalled,

> *Blackburn won by the only goal of the game. I was playing against Ronnie Clayton that day, the England skipper.*

Although John missed out on West Ham's triumphant Cup campaign of 1964–65, it wasn't something he regretted. He told me,

> *I was just happy to be playing and be part of it all. Of course, I would have liked to have played, but it didn't really worry me.*

The Hammers victory at Wembley in the European Cup Winners' Cup final, defeating TSV Munich 1860 2–0, was the crowning glory of the 1964–65 season and the Irons' history up to that point. As in the FA Cup, John was obliged to watch his 11 compatriot Englishmen – including seven fellow East Enders – become the first club to use only English players on the road to European glory.

It was in the season 1965–66 that John Charles began to make the West Ham number 3 shirt his own. He told me,

> *I played most of my games with Bobby* [Moore].

Alongside England's captain, John would defend West Ham's honour for the rest of his football career. John played 132 games alongside Mooro in defence of West Ham's goal, a combination of finesse and force, of art and power, speed and guile.

Charlo was to notch up 25 League appearances in the 1965–66 season. As the Irons' schedule came to an end, John was not too far from getting full international recognition. His wife Carol recalled, 'Alf Ramsey phoned up for him.' John told me that he

> *... was told to report that evening. It was one of those out-of-season games. Like England 'A' vs. England 'B', England against 'The Rest'. It was at Highbury and I played for 'The Rest'. I must have done all*

right because I went with England to Jersey and played a Jersey XI.
I liked Alf Ramsey, he was very quiet, but a good manager.

Unfortunately, most reflections on the football career of John Charles portray him as a workmanlike player. However, although never given to boasting in any serious way, from time to time, he did demonstrate that he had much more talent than the traditional analysis of his capabilities might suggest. His youngest son Mitchell told me of the kind of finesse he was capable of: 'It was down Spitalfields. There was a salesman. He says, "I hear you used to play football, Charlo, was you any good?" Dad says, "Yeah, I was all right." So this bloke says, "Well how good was yer?" Dad put his hand in his pocket, pulled out a ten-pence piece and he flicked it up in the air. He caught it on his toe, on his shoe, kicked it back up high over his head, opened his jacket and it went straight in his inside pocket!'

John ran out for the Hammers 35 times during the 1966–67 season and it was during this campaign that he scored his first and last League goal. He told me,

I got two goals for the first team. The first was against Grimsby in the League Cup and the other against Manchester United, when they won the League in '67. They beat us 1–6.

West Ham called on John just 19 times during the 1967–68 campaign. However, the following season John made 35 League appearances helping his side back into the top half of the table (8th). But what seemed like being the high point of John's career quickly turned into its all-time low. From the autumn of 1969, he was plagued by injuries and was limited to just five games up to the start of spring 1970. John left West Ham in the summer of 1971. He was only 26. He turned down a chance to join Orient, then managed by former Hammer Jimmy Bloomfield. He told me,

I kept getting this hamstring problem. Carol's dad had the market stalls, he was a greengrocer.

THE BLACK HAMMERS

By this time, John had two children to support – Keith, who had been born on 12 May 1966, and Lesley, who came into the world on 8 May 1969 – and a third on the way (Mitchell, who arrived on 10 October 1971).

> *At West Ham, I was earning £65 a week. My first week as a barrow boy, I got £200. I started with Carol's dad. Once I got into that lark, I really loved it. I became me own guv'nor.*

John had spent most of his career playing under Ron Greenwood and he was quite clear about his relationship with his manager:

> *Greenwood was a bit careful, maybe sly even. For instance, he'd just leave you out and not tell you. I hardly ever spoke to him, as it happens, no one did really. People did have a go at Greenwood every now and then. I think him and Bobby had their rows.*
>
> *I was never one of Ron's boys … I think a good manager gets to know the boys who they've got. He'll mix with 'em. The more you mix with 'em the more you know.*

For all this, Greenwood recognised John's gifts; he once described him as 'a prince of a player; he was a good, strong, straightforward competitor whose influence was significant'.

At the same time, John was quite aware of his manager's qualities:

> *I was a good defender, good at winning the ball. I got it and passed it and, when Ron brought in the idea of overlapping, I could do that well, I got in a few good crosses. Ron was a great coach, he knew the game.*

Although he would refuse to see himself as any kind of a groundbreaker, it was only towards the end of John's career that other black players started to break into the First Division. From the very start of John's career at Upton Park, it seems there was some consciousness of potential racism. John told me how Ted Fenton made an early attempt at 'anti-racist practice':

JOHN WILLIAM CHARLES

When I was taken on the ground staff, Ted told me that I would get called a few names, but to keep kicking 'em.

There is little doubt that John did experience forms of racism, but he didn't seem to notice or more likely chose to ignore the more covert/institutional forms of discrimination. Charlie Green, a lifelong friend of John's from the days when they played together with West Ham Boys, told me, 'John definitely missed out on playing for England Boys. He was the best defender in the country. I think it was just his colour that went against him. It was the time. He was the best around.'

As John broke into the first team at Upton Park, there were very few black players in League football. It might be expected that, as the first black player to make West Ham's first team, and one of the first to break through in London football, John would have experienced a level of racism both from crowds and from other players. But this was not the case according to John:

> *I never remember any real racism, certainly not from other players at West Ham or our crowd. Maybe some players respond to it too quickly and become a target when everyone knows it winds them up. If they'd just keep playing they would stop.*
>
> *You got the odd 'black bastard', but that never worried me. But my mum would go mad if anyone called me a black bastard, she said she was the only one who could call me that. And she'd say, 'He's not a bastard!'* [John laughed at the memory.]

In one conversation with John, I brought up the accusation that some black players – for example, Les Ferdinand and John Barnes in their respective autobiographies – have accused West Ham fans of being racist. John's response was typically forthright:

> *I never had none of it at West Ham. I was a greengrocer then, there was no problem. It's a bit of a myth. I used to serve Bobby Barnes* [a member of the 'second generation' of black West Ham players] *on our stall. He never had a problem. Old Jimmy Frith*

9

[a long-serving coach at West Ham], *he's been there for a good 30 years, he's older than me, he's got to be 60-something. He never had any problems with that sort of thing. No. The idea that West Ham fans are racist is rubbish! They didn't ask if you were black or white; they asked if you were West Ham.*

It is, of course, possible that John and many other Black Hammers I have spoken with over the last 15 years who have confirmed John's perspective have got it wrong, or were just in some kind of state of denial. That kind of accusation has been made about some of those who broke the ground in professional football early on, Charlie Williams at Barnsley for example. But this is a very disparaging and disrespectful conclusion to reach; that players of this era were 'lacking' in some way. I worked for five years with John and his family on his life story (*Johnnie the One*). We shared social events and our families got to know each other well; I am still in touch with Carol and her children. I think they would call me a mate and I certainly would see them as friends. All the other players I spoke to were and are bright, intelligent and articulate people. They were clear about their feelings and memories and the major forms of racism that affect these people's lives seem, as in John's case, to have been institutional and related to the structure of football administration rather than the nature of the crowd behaviour.

It was not John's race or colour that would be the accompanying theme of his career and it wasn't racism that would impact most on his potential. According to Charlo,

We were always on the piss. We went from the club to the pub. I was part of a hard-drinking crowd.

John went on to elaborate on West Ham's and football's drinking culture of the 1960s:

Everyone liked a drink ... 'Win, draw or lose, we're on the booze!' You didn't even think about it. It was second nature.

It is certain that a drinking tradition was well established at West Ham by the early 60s. Alcohol was interwoven with the social side of the game in general at that time, but at Upton Park it seemed far more deeply entrenched than at other clubs in the top flight.

By the time he retired, John was standing on the border of alcoholism. His change of life after giving up football alongside the pressures of business pushed him over the boundary of booze addiction. But he was to slip into an even deeper psychological slough. Charlo recalled,

I soon had stalls all over Kent, but then they started to open the supermarkets and we went skint ... I was an alcoholic and in the end had a breakdown. I was so bad, once, in hospital, I dreamed I was eating my sister in a sandwich! [He laughed gently.]

Charlo had started drinking more heavily as his business failed. He admitted to being terrified when he was taken into what he called 'the cracker-factory', thinking that he was just going to have a check-up.

John's older son Keith told me about his experience of his father's health problems: 'I was away when he went in the mad house. He'd had his moments, shouting and rearing up, but he'd never got violent. I found out around August '94. Me mum phoned me up, said, "Dad's been taken away to the nut house."

'When he had his breakdown, the stalls were going down the pan. His mum had just died and, of course, he'd always been a boozer. He was away for about six months.'

Following his mental-health problems, John came out of hospital just before his 50th birthday, saying that the idea of ever touching a drink again was frightening. He was to be medicated for over a year after he was discharged from hospital.

The aftermath of the psychological trauma continued to have physical repercussions as John pointed out:

Three years after the breakdown I was 16-and-a-half stone. I just blew up. I was nearly as big as Clyde Best! [Best grew to almost 20

stone when he left football.] *I ended up in Tesco's through Carol. I'd been ill and it got to a stage where I had to do something. So she's says, 'Come on, John, me and you are going to go out and get a job.' I said, 'Where we going?' And she said, 'I don't know.' So we went shopping up Tesco's and she pointed out the jobs on the vacancies board and said, 'Look, go and get yourself a job.'*

When I was on me first night at Tesco's, the manager was introducing us to people and we got to this geezer, with his dreadlocks and everything, young black lad; the manager said, 'This is John Charles,' so he went, 'John Charles! John Charles! What, the footballer?' I said, 'Yeah.' He said, 'Where I was born, in East Ham, you're a hero amongst all the black kids.' And I thought, 'Am I?'

The first sign of John's final illness seemed sudden. He'd had chest problems for a while, but, having been a smoker most of his adult life, this wasn't totally out of the ordinary. But things got worse and cancer was diagnosed. This was around October 2001, shortly after John heard that his brother Clive had been suffering from a form of bone cancer.

John died peacefully on 17 August 2002 holding Carol's hand. Although John Charles had finished playing for West Ham more than 30 years before he passed away, there were many in the East End of London who remembered and recognised him. Probably more than anything we love the brave, the fighters and those we can call 'one of our own'. John's character, humour, courage and style made him one of the Hammers' all-time favourites.

From his own testimony, Charlo had no problems with racism from his home fans and dismissed the suggestion that there might have been as 'rubbish'. This is not the kind of thing headlines are made of, especially when one considers that, over the years, accusations about the racism of West Ham fans have helped fill newspaper columns and books, for example, see Les Ferdinand (1997, p. 117) and John Barnes (1999, p. 93). This begs the question why Ferdinand later joined West Ham and Barnes contradictorily and confusingly also nearly joined his friend Harry Redknapp at Upton Park in 1997 (1999, p. 257) but the money wasn't good enough. Barnes has since made himself a name under the anti-racism in football banner.

Charlo was a mould-breaker, not just in terms of his being the first black player to play for West Ham and make a mark in top-flight football in London, but also because he steadfastly refused to fit the predominant stereotype of 'the black footballer'. He almost belligerently lived his life on his own terms and formed his own values based on his impressions and experience. He was always a person first. He did not bow to the whims of the Tsars of the media nor to the national football establishment and the hierarchy of hangers-on it has produced. He stood up to the dictates of management at West Ham and was never in awe of the so-called 'stars' of the game. He never even came close to allowing himself to be identified only or mainly by his colour. His contribution to football, West Ham and humanity was perhaps best summed up by his good friend Brian Dear when he said at John's funeral: 'Charlo was a great teammate who always gave 100 per cent. Football is surely indebted to him as he undoubtedly paved the way for his black brothers who now enjoy the fame, riches and adulation, which he most certainly helped make possible. A true Hammer … you can all be assured that John treated the cancer that took him with the utmost contempt it deserved. As John would have said, "It turned out nice again."'

God Bless Charlo

Adapted from *Johnnie the One* by Brian Belton.

CLYDE CYRIL BEST

'The soccer ball doesn't care what colour you are.'

In the days when footballers from abroad were a rarity in the English game and no black player had been capped for England, Clyde Best was a hero at Upton Park. It was the late 60s, the Hammers were fresh from FA Cup and European success, with three players at the hub of the World Cup-winning team, and Clyde was rated by Ron Greenwood, the West Ham manager, as 'the best 17-year-old I've ever seen'.

Before his days at the Boleyn Ground, Clyde had represented his country and won a silver medal at the 1967 Pan Am Games. He had turned out for Bermuda in the Olympic-qualifying tournament in 1966–67 and the first ever World Cup preliminary tournament in 1968; he would also take part in the qualifying stages of the 1970 World Cup.

In the 1971–72 season, Clyde scored 23 times in 56 outings; he was the only black player playing regular first-team football in the English First Division. On 2 April 1970, the Irons hosted a Division One game against Leeds United. That day, Clyde took the field with his great friend, the defender John Charles. It was the full-back's final game for the club. This was the first time that the Hammers had included two black players in their line-up, and broke ground in terms of race and top-flight football in general. Best marked the occasion with a goal in the 2–2 draw.

Best was a powerful striker and he dwarfed everyone in the West Ham dressing room. But, despite his gigantic proportions, he was astonishingly fast. In fact, he was a graceful player. I saw him score a goal at Goodison Park, after he'd run from the halfway line with most of the Everton team hanging on to him. He had a potent shot and was a marvellous header of the ball.

In 218 appearances for West Ham, Clyde scored 58 times. He remains Bermuda's most famous footballer and was the highest-profile black player in British football during the late 60s/early 70s. He crossed the Atlantic to play Tampa Bay Rowdies in the USA and appeared alongside Pele, Moore, Beckenbauer and George Best in the summer of 1975. That year, Clyde was voted Most Valuable Player in the North American Soccer League.

Best came back to Upton Park for a few games in 1975–76 but, looking for a new challenge, he joined Feyenoord in the Dutch Eredivisie for two seasons before returning to the NASL with Toronto Blizzard and Portland Timbers.

Clyde took over the control of the Bermudan national side in 1997 as technical director. He and his wife Alfreida had given up their dry-cleaning business in California so that Clyde could return home, as he put it, 'to put something back into the country which shaped me'.

I first met Clyde during one of his occasional visits to East London, when he was bringing young players from the Bermuda Under-15s to work with the West Ham school of excellence.

In my time as an international I didn't even count the times I played for Bermuda. I played a lot. They didn't keep records. At that time, we didn't have a professional set-up.

In Bermuda when I was a kid, you didn't see much television, but I used to watch Spurs on the TV and that was the start of my ambition to play in England.

When I first came to London to play for West Ham, I arrived at Heathrow on a Sunday and there was nobody there to meet me. The club weren't expecting me until the Monday. Right then, I wished I'd never come [laughs]. I managed to get the tube to West Ham, not realising I needed Upton Park. It was getting late in the afternoon but a Hammers fan took this lonely, confused kid and directed me to a house owned by a lady called Michelle, in Plaistow. She provided lodgings for a few of the young players at West Ham and I stayed with her for a while, but after that I stayed at the family home of Clive and John Charles. When I arrived in England, now nearly 40 years ago, their mum was like a second mother to me. The Charles are my extended family. John took me under his wing. He and Clive were like my brothers.

Everybody at West Ham taught us the importance of acting like a family; everyone pulled together. There was a feeling of being a team and you took that out on the pitch.

I made my debut for West Ham in 1969, taking the number 7 shirt that had been the property of Harry Redknapp for much of the previous year. Arsenal were at Upton Park that day. The match ended in a 1–1 draw. Ron Greenwood came in on the Monday morning and he told me I was playing that evening. It was what you always wanted to do! But with the team we had it was easy to fit in. Ron Greenwood was like a father to me. He helped me through the initial feelings of homesickness and took a special interest in me. He had a feel for attacking football and worked with you on making your game better. All the time I was at West Ham, he continued working with me.

The first goal I scored for West Ham was one of two in a game against Burnley in October 1969. West Ham won 3–1 at Upton Park. As a striker, you've got to be able to put the ball in the back of the net or you don't play. That was my fifth game for West Ham.

We had three World Cup winners and just to be there with them was unbelievable. My first day at the training ground, Ron organised it so I had a picture taken with the three of them!

I was born in Somerset, Bermuda, on 24 February 1951. I played for Somerset. Graham Adams [an Englishman who knew Ron Greenwood], *who was in charge of the national team at the time, selected me to play for Bermuda when I was 15. The old West Ham skipper Phil Woosnam was in America then. He probably saw me play and recommended me to West Ham and Ron Greenwood invited me to come over for a trial.*

Looking back it didn't really scare me coming to London. But I was very young to come and live in the East End of London. In retrospect, it is hard to believe I managed to fit in and play alongside Bobby Moore and Geoff Hurst and everyone else – these were my heroes as a youngster. I watched the World Cup in 1966 and two years after that I was playing alongside these guys!

My dad was in charge of the prison at home. My mum was a housewife. I have five sisters and a brother. I've been married to Alfreida, who is also from Bermuda, since 1974. Our daughter, Kimberley, came along four years later. She studied law in Buckingham and is now working for the Bank of Bermuda in investments.

East London was a different world to me. Bermuda has a population of around 60,000. I played in front of more people at Old Trafford! John [Charles] let me know about the kind of problems I might get from supporters away from Upton Park and how not to let it affect my game.

Early in 1971, West Ham were knocked out of the FA Cup in the third round, by Blackpool. Following the game, the press was full of the news that Bobby Moore, Jimmy Greaves, Brian Dear, myself and club physio Rob Jenkins had spent the evening before the match at Brian London's Blackpool nightclub – he had been heavyweight boxing champion of Britain. The thing was blown out of all proportion by the club and then the press. I never touched a strong drink while I was playing, all I'd had was orange, the others only had a few beers and we were in bed by 1am. But Ron Greenwood wanted to sack all of us! He was only prevented from doing so when he was overruled by the board.

But the social life could have been our downfall sometimes [laughs]. It was good. We were a friendly club, we worked hard and we played hard. We socialised but, when the time came to play, we played. I was friendly with everybody. It was a very family-type club. Greenwood stressed that we should look after each other. Even when Ron went upstairs and John Lyall took over, he still had a large say in the way the team played, the style we wanted to play. John was a chip off the old block anyway. It was roughly the same thing when he took over as manager.

I first wore a West Ham shirt playing as a youth in the Metropolitan League. I was big for my age and had started shaving when I was in my early teens. I think some people thought I was older, but to me other *kids looked too young, thin and scrawny. I played wide and on the right, keeping Harry [Redknapp] out of the side for a while [laughs].*

A great memory was when we played Santos in New York, latish in 1970, it was a friendly game. I got both of our goals and it ended 2–2. Pele got the goals for Santos. Carlos Alberto skippered their team. Edu was a substitute. That was quite something at 19 for me.

In the 1971–72 season, I got 17 goals for West Ham, making me the top scorer at the club. I didn't miss a single Cup or League game. In the League Cup, Stoke City beat us over a four-game semi-final [two legs and two replays]. Bobby [Moore] went in goal during the last leg of that tie; he'd asked me to do it at first. I was nervous and still quite young and I wanted to try and score a goal to put the side into the final. The pitch was terrible, a lot of them were, including Upton Park, but Old Trafford was a mud patch that night. Everyone was just slipping and sliding. Later on, I did go in goal against Leeds. I was more mature and sure of myself and I put myself forward to take over from Fergie [Bobby Ferguson].

Whenever I went on the soccer field, I wanted to play. One of the best games was that first League Cup game at Stoke. I scored with a volley, beating Gordon Banks – that was special! Not too many people were able to do that. There are a few games that stick out in your mind, but Geoff Hurst couldn't beat Banks from the penalty spot in the second leg at Upton Park and that's the way it goes … that's soccer. That defeat meant that I missed out on becoming one of the first black players to be involved in a major Wembley final. That happened again in 1975, but this time it was John Lyall that blocked the way. Missing the FA Cup in '75 was what made me leave West Ham. I wanted to help the club win the Cup so badly. Not to be involved hurt me. Everything was resolved later, but it affected our relationship … when John Lyall put Bobby Gould in the side before me. I'm saying, 'What's going on?' I said, 'Hey, that's it!' I wasn't going to stay and put up with that! To me, that wasn't fair. Bobby Gould is not what I call a players' player. The crowd thought I was far better too [laughs]. Up to this day, I still think John made a mistake, but he was the boss. I had to live with it.

I spent the summer of 1976 playing in the North American Soccer

CLYDE CYRIL BEST

League for the Tampa Bay Rowdies. With Tampa, I won the championship in my first year. I played with some great players.

I was back in Europe for the 1977–78 season, playing for Feyenoord. This was a good move as far as building for the future was concerned. It was a terrifically technical league and it was great coming across the likes of Ruud Krol and Ari Haan. But in 1978 I decided to settle in America full-time.

I moved to Portland Timbers and for a time played in the same side as Clive Charles. I also played for Toronto Blizzard and indoors with Los Angeles Lazers. I hung up my boots in 1984. The NASL didn't provide me with enough stimulation. The USA was good, but it was easy for me. So I set up a dry-cleaning business in California, but football was in my blood and late in 1997 I took on the challenge of running the Bermudan side.

Bobby Moore will always stick out in my mind. He had it all. Grace on the field, a good passer of the ball, good mentality. Bobby was a giant of international football, but he was an ordinary person, he had time for everybody. He was a great man and great friend. When you had problems, you could always pull him aside and ask him for advice and he'd always give it. He was the best player in the world. I saw Franz Beckenbauer play and Bobby was better than him. You play soccer with your brain, and Bobby beat everyone in that department. He never played any differently, whether on a match day, practice matches or in training; he concentrated as if playing in a World Cup final. I am so grateful to have played with him. I have been able to achieve what I have because of him. I knew precisely what I would get from him. Billy Bonds is another player you'd always put in your side; he'd give nothing less than 100 per cent. Geoff Hurst and Martin Peters, Pop Robson and Patsy Holland were also excellent players.

The fans at West Ham, when you're playing well, they're with you; when you're not playing too good, they let you know [laughs]. Because the crowd were so close to the pitch at Upton Park, you tended to hear a bit more, but they were very knowledgeable. They knew what they wanted. Winning wasn't an end in itself. They just wanted to see attractive soccer. It was our responsibility to try to give them that and I think that we were very successful in that respect. For me, at the time, West Ham was just the best place in the world with the best people. They made me feel welcome and at home, which given the differences between the East End and Bermuda is quite an achievement [laughs]. I loved my time there.

At Upton Park on 20 September 1975, I became the first West Ham substitute to score a goal. It was my first appearance of the season. Sheffield United were the visitors. That was to be my final goal at Upton Park. Four days later, in the second round of the League Cup, a replay against Bristol City, I scored my last goal for the club, helping them into the next round. I got a handful of games before the end of 1975. In mid-January 1976, I was again brought off of the bench in a 3–0 defeat at Maine Road. I was never again to play for club.

I didn't see myself as a pioneer. At the time, it was a job. In later years, I learned that people looked up to you for making it into the side. I didn't set out with the intentions of being a 'groundbreaker', being the first or the second. I just wanted to play soccer. West Ham was the only place I could do that. I never saw racism at West Ham [laughs]. At times, playing away, especially up north, someone would shout 'nigger' from the terraces, but you've got to be mentally strong. As a professional, you had to block it out. For my teammates, the West Ham fans, the people that mattered to me, race was never an issue. You had to carry yourself in the right manner. Show them the soccer ball doesn't care what colour you are. Give your answer by sticking one in the back of their net.

When there are racist incidents, like there have been in Europe, the authorities, FIFA, UEFA, need to show a responsible attitude. But also players need to take responsibility too – not be intimidated and say when things are happening, if only for the sake of the next generation of players.

There was never racism in our dressing room. We didn't look at things that way – black or white, we were all mates. If it was ever at West Ham, I haven't seen it. But it was true that clubs in England were anxious about giving black players a chance at the time I arrived. Eusebio and Pele and other black players had proved themselves to be amongst the best in the world, but black players didn't get the same chances in the Football League. The old idea that black players have rhythm is true, but we didn't even get recognised for that in the late 1960s. In football, or anything else, a person should be judged by their ability and not their colour.

East London continues to feel like home. Or home from home maybe [laughs]. I miss the place and the comradeship of football.

Two days before Christmas 2000, Clyde was called in by the Bermuda FA president Neville Tyrrell and told his contract would not be renewed at the end of the month. Neither he nor the public was told why; few people who cared were less than astonished. Best had not yet served three years, nowhere near enough time to turn around a nation's footballing fortunes. Clyde's record had been good and a national radio debate polled 99 per cent support for him.

Clyde had probably been a bigger star in America than he had in Britain. His record in the USA was one of the best during the early years of the modern game there.

In 2004, Best was inducted into the Bermuda National Sports Hall of Fame, and on Thursday, 16 September 2004 Clyde was presented with the FIFA Order of Merit.

In recent years, Clyde has been involved with the Westgate Correction Centre, Bermuda, a place he has had a long involvement with since working there as an officer. According to Clyde, he treats 'people as I would want to be treated', and talking to individuals about football is a 'way in'. The fact that many of the people who Clyde works with do not reoffend gives him tremendous satisfaction.

Clyde was awarded an MBE in the January 2006 Honours for services to football and the community in Bermuda. One of his first thoughts was that, along with Bobby Moore, Geoff Hurst, Martin Peters, Ron Greenwood, Trevor Brooking and others, West Ham had possibly achieved some sort of record in terms of such honours. His reaction was typical of his modesty and gentlemanliness, seeing it as an honour to be bracketed with such individuals. He expressed thanks to West Ham for 'the opportunity to … make people happy'. He also saw the part his upbringing played in his achievements. Although his parents have passed away, he was sure they would be very proud. His father had received an MBE for his work in the prison service, and Clyde was pleased to have emulated his dad.

Some commentators have suggested that Best underachieved during his playing career, but his impact as the first black footballer to imprint himself on the national consciousness in British football's TV era should not be underestimated.

ADEWUNMI OLAREWAJU COKER

HAMMERS DEBUT: 30/14/71

'Blessed.'

I t was West Ham's legendary scout Wally St Pier who first alerted Ron Greenwood to the bubbly forward Ade Coker when the young Nigerian (born in Lagos on 19 May 1954) was playing for the Henry Gompton School and West London District and London Schoolboys. Other clubs were taking an interest in the talented 14-year-old but it was Wally, the man who discovered so many of the great Hammers players from the early 60s onwards, who spoke to Ade's father about him joining the Hammers.

His report to manager Ron Greenwood said, 'The boy is not big, but his close control of the ball looks exceptional, both when dribbling and while running. He has fast reactions and shows that he keeps his mind on who is around him.'

Ade's brother, Tony, and Isaac, his father, had come to the UK a year in advance of Ade. The young Coker arrived in London at the age of 11.

Coker could have signed for Fulham but chose to start his professional career at Upton Park, having some idea that it was seen as a good place for young players to start a career. He made his debut on 30 October 1971 in the First Division (then the top echelon of the English game) at Selhurst Park. A late injury to Geoff Hurst brought Coker into the reckoning at almost the last minute. He was more surprised than anyone else at his inclusion in the first team and it seems he was the last to be told, just half-an-hour before kick-off, that he was to be in the starting XI.

THE BLACK HAMMERS

For the majority of the West Ham fans at that game (and watching the highlights on the television the next day), it was the first time they had ever heard of Ade. The slight, sinewy, diminutive striker looked anything but a replacement for the strapping figure of Hurst. But the young African made the most of his opportunity, mesmerising the Palace defence with a dazzling display of dribbling and possessional skills.

With just six minutes played, the Glaziers were unable to deal with a corner slung in by Harry Redknapp, but Ade could; he lashed a left-foot volley into the top corner of the Palace net, giving John Jackson, an exceptionally talented goalkeeper, no chance. Coker's ingenious footwork in that game dominated the attention of both sets of claret and blue supporters of whom I was one. I saw Ade perform the 'stop the ball, spin 180 degrees, take it with you' move that, in recent years, has so often been portrayed as Joe Cole's creation. Well, Coker did it first!

A headed effort from Billy Bonds in the 14th minute and a third goal 20 minutes into the second half from Clyde Best, who took Ade under his wing while the lad was at Upton Park, gave West Ham a 3–0 win.

However, the long English winter, the pounding tackling and the relatively poor pitches of the time stymied the young man's creative prowess and Ade was not able to replicate that first stunning performance. But on 1 April 1972 he contributed to an historic milestone in the chronicles of West Ham United and the development of the English game when the Irons ran out on to the Upton Park pitch; the West Ham XI included Coker, Best and left-back Clive Charles. It was the first time that three black players had turned out for an English team in the top League of the game.

The newly elected 'Hammer of the Year' Trevor Brooking put his side into the lead with one of the best goals scored at Upton Park that season. But the icing on the cake for Ade was the second goal of the game that sealed a 2–0 defeat for deadly London rivals Tottenham Hotspur. Coker was waiting at the far post for Kevin Lock's cross from the left-wing.

ADEWUNMI OLAREWAJU COKER

Many years on, Ade recalled that he had only later understood the importance of that spring day in 1972 and how it would have impacted on young black players in Britain. He believed it motivated a feeling that there might be opportunities for young men of colour to break into major football. However, it is also telling that he saw West Ham as the one club where an occasion of such consequence could have taken place at that time. For Ade, Upton Park, under the sway of Ron Greenwood, was a place that looked to and shaped the future, seeing skin pigmentation as having no bearing on the endeavour to unearth skill and promise.

Coker was still in touching distance of inclusion in West Ham's plans at the beginning of the 1973–74 season, but the arrival of the expensive Ted MacDougall seemed to seal Ade's fate in the Docklands. His last run-out as a Hammer was in a 1–1 draw at home to Hereford in the FA Cup on 5 January 1974. The Hammers were disgraced in the replay, going down 2–1 to Hereford who played their League football two divisions below West Ham's position amongst the elite of the English game.

In Coker's 11 games as a Hammer, the net yielded to him on only three occasions, and that just could not compete with the other striking options at Greenwood's disposal. Ade was a stylish and talented player, a balanced and instinctive poacher in the Jimmy Greaves mould, but there was no room or time for him to flourish at the Boleyn Ground in the helter-skelter 70s; he would have needed to oust the likes of Best, Hurst and Robson, clearly too much of an ask for a teenager.

Ade had a month on loan with Lincoln City, and retrospectively saw that as another phase in his continuing education, working with and learning from the England manager-to-be Graham Taylor.

Starting his gradual departure from Upton Park, Coker played in the North American Soccer League during the summer of 1974. The NASL was growing apace, attracting hordes of players from South America and Europe, and it was a context in which Coker was practically guaranteed a place in starting XIs. What began as a stopgap opportunity became a permanent move when the NASL made him an offer he couldn't refuse.

THE BLACK HAMMERS

Ade was sad to turn his back on West Ham, but at the same time 'pro-soccer' in the USA was an exciting prospect for the young man and he was never to regret his decision to become a pioneer of the modern game in the USA.

In America, Coker became something of a star, turning out for the Boston Minutemen between 1974 and 1976. His teammates included Portuguese and Benfica superstars Antonio Simoes and Eusebio. Coker got on well with both these legends of the game.

From 1976 to 1978, Coker was with Minnesota Kicks. Ade moved on to the San Diego Sockers for the 1978 and 1979 seasons. However, his career seemed to be over in 1978 when an untimely tackle resulted in the tearing of anterior and posterior cruciate ligaments. A couple of days after, there seemed to be more prospect of amputation below the knee than hope that Coker would return to the professional ranks.

However, after 14 months of treatment, therapy and dogged determination on Ade's part, he returned to football with more enthusiasm than ever. This tale of overcoming of adversity climaxed with his selection for the American national team. Ade represented the USA half-a-dozen times during the World Cup-qualifying rounds of 1986. Defeating the Netherlands Antilles in COCCACAF first round, the USA finished runners-up in their second-round qualifying group behind Costa Rica and in front of 2006 qualifiers Trinidad and Tobago.

Coker was with Rochester Lancers in 1980 but he rejoined San Diego in 1982. He left the Sockers at the end of his NASL career in 1984.

Ade had been one of the most feared goal-getters in North America and this caused him to be rated amongst the top-20 US all-time players by the influential *Sports Illustrated*. His 74 goals and 38 assists in 156 games during his decade in the North American Soccer League places him 15th amongst the highest all-time scorers in the NASL. To put this achievement into context, George Best is in 23rd spot with 54 goals from 120 matches, while, with 55 nettings in 177 outings, Ade's erstwhile mentor at Upton Park, Clyde Best, is in 36th place.

ADEWUNMI OLAREWAJU COKER

Coker also distinguished himself in the Major Indoor Soccer Leagues (MISL). He ran out for the New York Arrows (1980), Baltimore Blast (1981–82), San Diego Sockers (1984–87) and St Louis Steamers (1987–88).

Ade retired from playing in 1988 and now works at Home Depot, the biggest home-improvement organisation in America. He lives in Seattle in Washington DC with his wife Debbie and two children. He spends a great deal of time giving Nickolas (born in 1992) and Alanna (who is three years younger) the benefit of his 'soccer' experience and know-how.

Ade's memories of West Ham, like many former players, are dominated by the impression that it was like a family, wherein he was nurtured and cared about. He recalled the kindness, approachability and encouragement of Bobby Moore and how the England skipper took time to introduce him to the culture and day-to-day workings of Upton Park. For Coker, West Ham was literally the place that enabled him to 'live the dream' from a very early point in his life, and he was able to see his presence there as preparing the way for other young black men to enrich themselves and invigorate first English and then European football. In his own words, he felt 'blessed' to have been given a chance to be part of the continued evolution of the game.

As a young player, Coker was perhaps a little too lightweight to take abuse from the likes of Ron Harris and Norman Hunter. John Charles laughed as he told me that, 'When someone got within a yard of him, he would go down as if he'd been hit by a train.'

But Ade became one of the great players in the mid-20th-century development of the game in North America. He was also one of those that broke the 'colour code' in the English game.

CLIVE MICHAEL CHARLES

'I just didn't think of myself as a black soccer player.'

Many European players migrated to the USA in the early 1970s, but Clive Charles was one of the few who stayed after the financial collapse of soccer in North America in the 1980s. He helped to rebuild the structure of the game in the USA from the grass roots and worked with many players who went on to play for the national teams of Canada, Mexico and the United States, and populate the professional ranks in America and Europe and Asia. He also played a great part in creating the women's US soccer team that became the most successful female side the world has ever known.

Those Clive worked with won Olympic gold medals, and were victorious in World Cup football; many of these people, touched by Clive's example, went on to become teachers and coaches themselves.

Clive can be considered one of the real pioneers and champions of the modern game in America. His biography is a 'rags to riches' story if ever there was one.

I first contacted Clive at his home in Maine, USA.

I played my first game for the West Ham first team on 21 March 1972. It was a 1–1 draw at Highfield Road. It was on the same night as Frank Lampard [Senior] played for England against Yugoslavia, that's why I got a game. I was lucky enough to help create the goal that gave West Ham the draw. I got three more League games that season.

I was in the team that played Tottenham Hotspur, that was 1 April

'72 – April Fools Day! [laughs] *That was first time three black players had played on the same side in the First Division. But probably more significant for us, after Kevin Lock came on as substitute for Johnny Ayris, Kevin laid on Ade Coker's goal. The average age of the 11 players on the field was just 21.*

I was born in Bow, East London, on 3 October 1951 and went straight to West Ham from school, having been associated with the club from the age of 12. West Ham was always my club. My school days were spent in Canning Town. My first real coach was John Lyall at West Ham. He was a wonderful teacher. He looked at the game intelligently and had a way of reading people. He always did what he saw as right for a player. I admired him for that and took a lot of his ways into my own coaching. He had a lot of patience but the one thing he didn't like was people who'd suck up to him.

I was good at cricket. I played for Newham and London Boys, but it was something I played in the summer, it was never going to compete with football. I was approached by some people from Essex to go down to Chelmsford, but I wasn't ever going to take it up. I kind of knew my future would be in football.

I was the last of nine children. John was the next eldest and seven years older than me. I wouldn't say the family was poor, not compared to some others around us. We never went short of anything that mattered, but I suppose we didn't want a lot. But yeah, compared to some we didn't have much in the way of material things and you had to work hard to get by in the East End at that time. You had to keep going. As you know, coming from the area yourself, Plaistow, Canning Town and that district have always been thought of as deprived areas. Some people had a hard time of it and, yes, life was never easy there, but we had a lot of fun as well.

When I was still living in my family home in Canning Town, Clyde [Best] lived with us, so he was like a brother. I'm still close to my family back in London, John, my brother, his wife Carol and their kids and grandkids. My mum, 50 years ago in Canning Town, could never have dreamed that her sons and grandchildren would have achieved so much.

My brother John did a good job of not spending any time with me [laughs]. *But that probably helped. It allowed me to develop my own style. I was a totally different player to John. He was a hard, tough tackling player. I was more of a footballer. I liked to get forward on the overlap. As such it wasn't too long before I attracted the interest of the England Youth set-up. I got four Youth caps. Getting into the England Youth side showed that I was good in my own right. It wasn't just about my brother being in the team. We never actually played together in the first team for West Ham, but we did play in the same Football Combination side during most of the 1970–71 season. I was potentially on a par with most of the people who could play at left-back at Upton Park, it was just that they had become established before I matured. Like a lot of things in life you have to make the most of what you've got.*

I signed pro forms in 1968. By the time I broke into the first-team squad I was a creative left-back, one of the forerunners of today's wing-backs. I was close to Frank Lampard. Frank took me under his wing a bit when I came to West Ham. Like me he had been at Star Lane school and was in the fourth year at Pretoria when I was a first year.

I was understudying McDowell and Lampard, two contenders for the English international defence. There's a time when it's right for you to come into the first team, a moment when you can blossom. Miss that and it gets harder to make your mark. John [McDowell] was ready to play and I didn't get a chance to establish myself, but that's the way things go in football. Today, at clubs like West Ham, the likes of Frank Lampard and Billy [Bonds] would maybe move on to bigger clubs, clearing the way for younger players to develop, but then players stayed with clubs longer and, unless a young player matured really early, they had to go down a division or two to get regular games, but I can't complain. It's a privilege to do something you love for a living.

I've never forgotten my roots and I have fond memories of being at Upton Park. I was friendly with Paul Grotier, Tony Carr and Patsy Holland, we were all in the same youth team together. I was with West Ham while Bobby Moore was club captain. Bobby was by far and away the best player I ever played with. No one was even near his class. He was a good passer, but was average at everything else, but put that together with a unique footballing brain and you got something else.

CLIVE MICHAEL CHARLES

I wish I had been more dedicated as a player. I always trained hard, and worked at my game, but we didn't earn much more than a dust man in my day. I was lucky though. I played against Bobby Charlton, the great Manchester United and Leeds sides – some good teams.

I played 14 times for the West Ham first team, but I only ever got one clear opportunity to break into the side. It was in the first game of the 1973–74 season. The first game I got in my own right, on the strength of my own form, not standing in for someone else. It was against Newcastle at Upton Park [25 August 1973]. Frank Lampard was playing at right back and John McDowell had been dropped. It was my chance to stake a claim for a regular place. I'd never had a bad game for West Ham, but we lost that game 1–2 and I had a stinker [laughs].

I didn't really know Ron Greenwood; I was a bit young, he was a bit aloof. I learned a lot from him though, but I learned most from John Lyall. Ron was a great coach, I'm not so sure about him as a man-manager though. Not a lot of people got close to Ron. I suppose I was a bit intimidated by him. John Lyall was the first one to make sense. He had something to say. He thought about the game and talked about it in an intelligent way. He articulated his ideas.

Everyone was always fair at West Ham. I never experienced any racism at Upton Park. I only really come across it in one game against Manchester United. Ron Greenwood had the balls to take me, Ade Coker and Clyde to Old Trafford. Although Ade didn't play, we took some stick that day. I didn't see myself as paving the way for others when I was playing, but I suppose we must have been. I just didn't think of myself as a black soccer player. I was just earning a living.

I don't see too many black managers. But it's a tight-knit circle anyway, even in terms of whites. It's the same names that get mentioned every time there's a top job going. It's the same in the States in grid iron and basketball. If Harry or George Graham got the sack at one club, they'd move on to another. It's a bit of a closed shop. As far as West Ham being a racist club, I can only say that they took me on and I think Ron Greenwood was the first Division One manager to play three black players in the same team. Jimmy Andrews, a former West Ham man, took me to Cardiff and Frank O'Farrell, who had also

31

been at Upton Park, made me club captain at Ninian Park. That was the first time I really thought about the fact that I was a black player. The local newspapers made a big thing about me being the first black player to captain a League side. Until that point I had thought about myself purely as a footballer rather than a black footballer.

Yes, problems with race are always a factor and they shouldn't be, but there is a bit of a bandwagon and one or two people make a living out of promoting anti-racism, so it is in their interests to look for and find racism, and, don't get me wrong, it's there. But I'm not sure how far saying 'don't be racist' gets rid of it. It goes deeper than that. People say racism is about ignorance, and that might be true, but it's more about fear. When I was in Canning Town as a kid we didn't get any noticeable racism, because everyone was more or less on the same level; no one had much of anything [laughs]. It's when you think you have something to lose to a group of people that you start to dislike that group. That's the bottom line. So if you are afraid of a group and they happen to be black you might express that fear and actually be racist. But if they were just a different religion you would fear them just as much and discriminate against them just as much. So if you want to get rid of that sort of thing you've got to get rid of the fear. And that's not so easy. You can say 'don't be afraid' but that is not going to stop anyone's fear. That won't make them feel less insecure about themselves.

You read some stuff that talks about how bad it was or is, but that's the thing to say now; they can't say anything else really. Just like years ago they said nothing, often the same people, that was the thing then, you didn't say anything 'cause it was seen as an expected thing. So the people who are saying 'this is bad' or 'that was bad', you don't know what they are actually thinking, all you know is that they are saying what they have to say now. Like you are right to stop people shouting out 'you black this or that', but just because you have stopped them shouting it out, expressing it, it don't mean they are OK with race. I suppose it is much harder now to find out who is racist, as anyone who was going to say anything has been educated just not to say it. That stops people being offended, but beyond that, who knows? That has to be done, but it goes deeper than just doing that. Can you make it so that no one ever gets offended about anything? I suppose if you did that would have a cost.

That defeat against Newcastle was to be my last game for West Ham. I didn't want to leave Upton Park, but I couldn't get in the first team. I had to think of the future; I got married in '73 to Clarena and we had a family on the way. She was an air hostess. The wedding took place in London but we had met while I was on loan to Montreal Olympics in NASL [1971–72] nearly three years earlier. I enjoyed the experience.

I asked Ron Greenwood for a transfer and went to Cardiff, at first on loan. They were in relegation trouble. I played in the last eight games of the season. I signed for them in March '74. I played just a hundred games there, 75 League matches, in three years, scoring five goals.

Don Megson, who had been at Bristol Rovers, got the coaching job at Portland and asked me to come over. Everybody was going at the time. It was the best thing I ever did. Clyde [Best] was already playing there of course.

I was with the Timbers from 1978 to 1981. Played around 70 games. In 1982 I was with Montreal. I played for Pittsburgh Spirit in the Major Indoor Soccer League and Los Angeles Lazers in '82. I went into coaching and just went from strength to strength. When I was playing for West Ham I was coaching in schools. I'm able to get information over to people in a way that seems to make sense to them and I enjoy that. I am not so much result-oriented as teaching-orientated. If it becomes all about winning, all you get is frustrated when you lose. I can't say results were secondary, but they were kind of linked up with everything else. I think you always look to the next game – how are we going to make it better, not perfect, but nearer perfect? I get a lot out of getting players to improve their game but also develop as people. I think the two things can be connected.

Living and working in America has made me a better coach. I think if I'd have stayed in England I'd probably have been quite restricted in what I could have learned. For every John Lyall there were a dozen who really didn't have much idea what coaching was about, and in the 70s no one in the English game was prepared to learn from other sports or the way things were done in South America or Europe. I know that is changing now, but, even at this time, the English game is a bit inward looking. In the United States you sort of get a bigger picture. If I sat down and chatted to people I played with in England and talked to them about coaching they probably wouldn't understand what I was talking about. Harry Redknapp would have no idea, and he played in the US for a bit. That's not having a go at him, it is just the environment he's in … when I was assistant manager with the US World Cup team I told him about a good player we had; he said to me, 'You've been away a long time. Things have changed.' We had just played Brazil and Argentina!!

In England it is getting to be a case of buy, buy, buy and, if you get one out of three or four right, that's OK. You can always sell the ones that didn't work, if not for what you paid for them. It's all a bit frantic, almost panicky at times. Players come and go in what seems like no time and there is no time to establish any kind of identity with a club. So you end up with three or four clubs dominating things and then about a dozen or so clubs with nothing to choose between them, as all the players are at about the same level; good enough to be where they are but not good enough to be playing for the very top clubs. Look at the game in England now and almost any team of about 15 could end up in fourth or fifth place in the League by the end of the season. That, up to a point, is good, but there is practically no chance of the same clubs winning the League or even a major trophy. So success is finishing 10th! Then, when the European or World Cup comes along, everyone thinks England are going to win it. But if you are brought up on the idea that coming 10th is good, how are you in the right frame of mind to actually win?

Winning is not everything, in fact it is just something, but the ambition, the want to do as well as you can is important, and that has to be based on an idea of what real success is. Young fans, young players who turn out for their schools, can take that sort of thing into their everyday lives. Why should anyone be satisfied by second best? Again, there is nothing wrong with coming second, but that shouldn't stop you from trying to be first or even a better second.

I wouldn't have had the opportunity to coach women in England, certainly not to the highest standard, and coaching women has taught me patience and as such made me a better coach. You have to be ready to learn things from your players to be the best possible coach. There comes a point when things are going really well when you are learning as much from each other and it isn't just one way. I'm not sure many coaches in England have a chance to get to that point. Probably there are too many demands to produce performances overnight. But you can only teach a player so much, after that your job as a coach is learning as much as you can about them; how you can put them in a place where they can be the best they can be and in a position that is most useful to the team. That is about collaboration, working together and that of course takes trust. Trust is something given and you are honoured when it is given. But to get trust you have to give it. I think that is kind of hard in the game in England right now. That's a shame because without trust there can be no respect — so fear and threat take over and eventually that gets destructive. Where I coach, at Portland University, we've been lucky to have some good people on the staff and some good people playing. Together we've managed to build something bigger than a football programme. It is a bit like West Ham used to be, there's a family atmosphere and people feel a loyalty to the place and each other. That goes beyond football really. In the end that is the biggest thing any sport can do — become the source of something that endures throughout your life.

I've coached Portland University and American national squads, and being with West Ham has a lot to do with that. I think if you learn from your experiences in the game it's all good. Not getting into the side might be seen, over a broader view of things, as being as good for me than say if I have gotten a consistent place in the first team. If you want you can learn as much from the knock-backs as anything else. In fact, I think we learn more from having to do what is hard. That's what I think a coach can do — help players see the wider implications of what is happening to them because of their involvement with the team. That way football can help you live your life and is not just an end in itself.

Unlike some other sports your place in a soccer squad is reliant on the decisions of others; you can do so much, do your best and so on, but at the end of the day you have to learn to manage the best you can with the cards you are dealt. If you can do that, make the most of whatever it is you're given, then you must be successful. At West Ham John Lyall and Bobby Moore showed me that you can make something out of nothing; how much more can you do with a bit more than nothing? Bob had not very much other than a good footballing brain, but look how he used it!

A difficulty young people have today, not just young people maybe, is that they always seem to need or want more. It seems harder to make the most of any little opportunity. A place in the side is not enough, it has to be a guarantee of a place. The reality of course is that we mostly just get the one chance and it is up to no one but us to make the most of it. You miss a chance on goal, no one is going to say, 'Shame, why don't you have another pop?' The next chance you get it will be up to you to make the best of. I think it is the job of a coach to teach this sort of thing. Sport gives opportunities to learn about this stuff in a very real way. We do that in Portland and I know it works. It's not that young people are just 'bad' or 'spoiled', that's too easy, although some undoubtedly are, but in the main it's because they haven't had the chance to learn the lessons. We all have to learn these things by experience – no one can just be told and then get it. It's like saying 'There aren't enough black managers' and that 'someone should do something about it'. Sure 'they' should, but you can't wait for 'them' to help you, you might wait forever! You should do something about it!

What's the good of being given something just because of the fact that you 'are something'? A woman, black? That is just as racist as not being given something because you are black. If you want something you've got to go out and get it, that's a rule of life, no matter what or who you are. You can't expect to be given chances, you've got to make the world give you a chance. There's plenty of examples, 'role models', of people doing just that, so it's not just a case of saying it's OK for me to say that.

The best thing to come out of my coaching in the US is the FC Portland youth club. I'm proud of that because of the successes of the players that came out of that.

Portland is now my home. I love it here. My kids are Americans. My son, Michael, he's a golf pro. My daughter Sarah studied for her Masters degree at Oregon State University. She played in defence for Portland in the Collegiate First Division [a very good standard] *from '94 to '97.*

It's a melting pot here. After turning out for Portland most of the players go on to become pros. I had three girls from my Portland women's side in the US Women's World Cup-winning team. They can earn between $0.5m and $1.5m a year here. Our women get bigger crowds than most lower-division matches and some as good as some of the better clubs in England.

I've been offered more money and an opportunity to coach in MLS. I've had chances to coach at bigger schools and I can't say I wasn't tempted because it meant a bigger office, prestige, better facilities and a much bigger budget. But I didn't really want to leave. I think it's easier to leave a place that was already established when you went there. But, after building the place yourself, it's tough to leave. It is a good place for me to be and give a little back. I owe a lot to the game, everything really. I will never be able to repay what it's given me, but Portland has been a good place to give what I can.

Clive always remained true to his West Ham roots as was made obvious when he was asked how the US 2000 Olympic team that he took charge of would play. His answer was short and clear:

The US is going to play an attacking, entertaining style of soccer.

In the interim Clive successfully guided the Americans through the qualification games to the 1998 World Cup finals in France.

In 2000 America got to the Olympic semi-final where they met Spain. The US did well to hold the score to 2–1 until three minutes from time when Spain made it 3–1. The US must have taken a lot out of the Spanish as they were beaten by Cameroon in the final.

The US soccerteers looked to be at a low ebb in the bronze-medal match. It seems their morale had been hit and this put them at a psychological and physical disadvantage. They were defeated 2–0 by Chile. This was a disappointing conclusion to a great display by the US. Charles and his team had good reason to walk away from the Olympics proud of what they had achieved, and that was, by far and away, America's best Olympics soccer tournament ever, and the most notable display by a US men's soccer team in history.

Clive found out that he had prostate cancer in 11 August 2000, just before departing for the Sydney Olympic Games with the US Under-23 team. He went home that day and told his family and together experienced the kind of numbness commonly felt by families on receiving such information. But, for Clive, Australia provided him as he said 'with another focus' and this helped.

Following the success of the Portland Women in 2002, Charles was invited, with the team, to the White House by President George Bush. Clive's response was typically disarming: 'It'll be the Queen of England asking us to Buckingham Palace next!'

On Tuesday, 26 August, surrounded by family, at his home in North West Portland, Oregon, Clive Charles passed away at the age of 51. He was a distinguished player and a great coach. He is just one of three former Hammers to take control of national football teams; Clyde Best and Bobby Gould are the others, but his achievements at Olympic and World Cup level were exceptional. Clive was a brilliant teacher and noble human being.

CLIVE CHARLES – CAREER HIGHLIGHTS

Men's Programme – University of Portland
10 NCAA play-off berths, 1988–93, 95, 99, 01, 02
NCAA Final Four, 1988, 1995

Five WCC titles, 1988, 1989, 1990, 1992, 2002

Far West Region Coach of the Year, 1988

WCC Coach of the Year, 1988, 2002

NCSC Coach of the Year, 1988

Portland's first Top-20 ranking, 1988

CLIVE MICHAEL CHARLES

Women's Programme – University of Portland
2002 College Cup Champions

10 NCAA play-off berths, 1992–98, 2000–02

NCAA Final Four, 1994, 1995, 1996, 1998, 2000–02

Six WCC titles, 1992, 1994, 1995, 1996, 1997, 2000

Two NCSC Championships, 1990, 1991

Soccer Buzz National Coach of the Year, 2002

Far West Region Coach of the Year, 1992, 1993, 1995

WCC Coach of the Year, 1993, 1994, 1995

NCSC Coach of the Year, 1990

Portland's first Top-20 ranking, 1990

Under Coach Charles's leadership, 28 University of Portland athletes
have attained All-America status. In the history of collegiate soccer,
he is only the second coach to have two teams, in the same year,
competing in the NCAA semi-finals.

NATIONAL
Head Coach, US Men's Olympic Team, 2000 (named in 1996)

Assistant Coach, US Men's National Team, 1995–98

Head Coach, US U-20 Women's National Team, 1993–96

OTHER
ESPN television analyst, 1994 World Cup

THE BLACK HAMMERS

Oregonian Banquet of Champions: Merit Award, 1992; Slats Gill Coach of the Year Award, 1995, 2002

CLIVE CHARLES'S – CAREER RECORD

NASL REGULAR SEASON PLAY-OFFS	GP	G	A	GP	G	A
1971 Montreal Olympics	21	0	1	-	-	-
1972 Montreal Olympics	7	0	0	-	-	-
1978 Portland Timbers	25	0	2	5	0	0
1979 Portland Timbers	29	0	5	-	-	-
1980 Portland Timbers	9	0	4	-	-	-
1981 Portland Timbers	4	0	1	-	-	-
Total	95	0	13	5	0	0

Men's Record:
213–92–31 (17 years)
Women's Record:
226–52–13 (14 years)
Combined:
439–144–44 (31 seasons)

UNIVERSITY OF PORTLAND – MEN

YEAR	W	L	D	POSITION	NCAA
1986	8	8	3	5th *	-
1987	13	7	1	3rd *	-
1988	21	1	0	1st	semi-finals
1989	18	2	4	1st	second round
1990	12	6	1	1st	first round
1991	13	7	0	3rd	second round
1992	13	5	0	1st	first round
1993	9	3	6	4th	first round
1994	10	7	2	4th	-
1995	16	3	3	3rd	semi-finals
1996	11	7	1	2nd	-
1997	11	7	1	3rd	-
1998	10	5	3	4th	-
1999	12	5	2	3rd	first round

CLIVE MICHAEL CHARLES

Year	W	L	D	Position	NCAA
2000	10	7	2	5th	–
2001	13	6	1	2nd	third round
2002	13	6	1	1st	second round
Totals	213	92	31		

*In 1986 and 1987, the West Coast Conference held a tournament to decide the conference champion. Round robin, regular season play began in 1988.

UNIVERSITY OF PORTLAND – WOMEN					
YEAR	W	L	T	POSITION	NCAA
1989	10	6	0	3rd*	–
1990	11	3	1	1st	–
1991	13	2	2	1st	–
1992	18	2	0	1st	first round
1993	16	4	1	2nd	regional final
1994	16	6	0	1st	semi-finals
1995	20	1	2	1st	final
1996	19	1	2	1st	semi-finals
1997	14	5	0	1st	first round
1998	19	3	2	2nd	semi-finals
1999	12	7	1	2nd	–
2000	18	4	0	1st	semi-finals
2001	20	4	0	2nd	semi-finals
2002	20	4	2	3rd	National Champions
Totals	226	52	13		

Combined (Men and Women)

W	L	D		
439	144	44	20	NCAA berths

*The Pilots' women's programme competed in the Northwest Collegiate Soccer Conference during Charles's 1989, '90 and '91 seasons. Portland joined the West Coast Conference in 1992.

DALE CONRAD BANTON
HAMMERS DEBUT: 20/8/79

'The hardest thing to get across to white people is what it's like to face prejudice like that.'

Following Clive Charles's last game for West Ham, it was just five days short of six years before another black player appeared in the Hammers first team. It was the start of the Hammers second season outside the top flight that had seemed the club's rightful place since 1958–59. The spell was broken by the 24-year-old Dale Banton in West Ham's second game of the 1979–80 season at Upton Park.

Dale was a midfielder with potential. He had come into a side on the rise. The Hammers were to get themselves into the last eight of the League Cup and win the FA Cup for the third time in their history, defeating First Division Arsenal in the final. However, John Lyall had amongst his middle-of-the-park options the promising Alan Dickens, Alan Devonshire, Pat Holland, Trevor Brooking, Geoff Pike, Billy Bonds and the exciting young prospect Paul Allen. As such, the former Middlesex Schools star Banton was limited to just three starts and three appearances as a substitute before reluctantly leaving the Boleyn Ground at the end of the 1981–82 term.

Dale Banton didn't play a single first-team game for West Ham during 1980–81, playing no part in what was something of a glory season for West Ham, taking European giants Liverpool to a replay in the League Cup final and winning the Second Division Championship. However, Banton went on to have a distinguished professional career including membership of 1984–85 York City FA

Cup giant-killing team. In all, he appeared 311 times in League football over his 10 years in the professional game scoring 100 goals.

I met with Dale in a quiet pub/guesthouse on the outskirts of York where he used to stay when he began to play for York City.

I was born in Kensington on 15 May 1961. I started playing for a local side, North Greenford. I also played alongside Alan Devonshire, at Southall. A scout saw me, came round the house and I introduced him to my parents then he took me down to see a game at West Ham, the Under-18s were playing in the Youth Cup and within a week of that I was involved. I signed on associated schoolboy forms when I was 15.

I followed West Ham from when I was little. I never moved to the district. I stayed in Wembley and commuted.

I have one son. Louis [born 1995]. He doesn't support anybody. I've never pushed him towards a team. He's left-footed [laughs]. I was always right, I could use both but I was predominantly right-footed and all my family was right-footed.

I'm divorced now.

When my mum first came to England from Jamaica she was a teacher. Then from there she moved to IBM, in computers. She was in the sales side of the company. I'm in sales. My dad was an engineer. He was Jamaican too but we lived in Wembley for many years. They met in Jamaica. I have one brother, Cary. He worked for British Airways as a projects manager for many years. He was 'head-hunted' and he works for a company that subcontracts to British Airways. He was a reasonable footballer, but he wasn't dedicated. He just did it for fun.

I represented the county in cricket. I had a choice at 16, start at West Ham or go to Middlesex. I also ran for the county. I enjoyed the academic side of school as well; I took 10 O levels, I got eight.

I played for Middlesex as a schoolboy and had six games for West Ham. My debut was the 0–1 defeat against Chelsea at Upton Park. I can tell you who came off, Stuart Pearson; this was West Ham's FA Cup season. It was probably one of the most successful times for the club. I was unlucky with injuries at critical times ... also at that time the crowd sang a song: 'John Lyall's dads army.' I suppose it was Paul

Allen who made the breakthrough for young players being pushed through. At my time you were young at 23. Those were the two main reasons I didn't get so many games. If you ask me now do I think I had the ability, I'd say, 'Yeah.' With the time I had there I should have played maybe 30, 40 games.

I started at York 1984–85. I made 138 League appearances and scored 49 goals. I went on to play for Walsall and Grimsby, then in August 1989 Aldershot. Brian Talbot led a team in there but we never got on. I was always sub and only got on for 10 or 15 minutes at a time. That was it. But at the end of the '82–83 season I got five goals in one match! That was a bit of a highlight. What really finished me was me knees. I lost that yard of pace that you need as a striker. I came back to York, started looking around for jobs. Then I had a phone call from Terry Curran who was manager at Goole Town, he said, 'Look, come along, Dale, help with the coaching.' I started coaching and playing. I got back the enthusiasm I'd lost; as players do when you get to a certain age, they tend to abuse you in football. They forget about you and the contribution you've made.

The team did quite well for six, seven months then it had a downward spiral and he resigned. I applied for the job and became player-manager. I had about seven, eight months there. I eventually got sacked but it wasn't to do with my record. I'll tell you my record as manager, we played 14, won nine, drew two, lost three … got the tick-tack! I don't know why, there were people there who were telling someone who had been in the game and played under nine managers how to run a team when they didn't know. My first job as manager was to tell everyone that they had to take a pay cut! I called it a day then.

When I came out of football, I think it was '91, I worked for a sales company up here [in York] selling Kirby's, the hoover things. I was with them three, four months and then one of my friends who used to play with me at York City, he used to work for this company, he said, 'Dale, if you can sell them Kirby's, you can sell these machines.' He gave me his boss's number. I rang him. He gave me an interview and it's just gone from there. I started in '92 so I've been a few years with the company now. Once you can sell one thing, you can sell anything. I can't see myself coming out of this area at this moment in time.

DALE CONRAD BANTON

I was York's record signing – I had a great big afro hairdo. That record stood from '84 to about '95 I think. I still play for York City in the odd charity game. They come maybe once a year or once every 18 months. I won't play Sunday stuff, just for charity.

I changed from playing midfield at West Ham. Paul Brush took me aside just before I left and said, 'Go to a team that can get the ball down the channel or into your feet. You're sharp and nippy, you'll score goals.' That's what I did. When I left West Ham, I was then considered as a forward. I had pace, could play with both feet. I wasn't so much a dribbler, I could play one- and two-touch football, I could run into space, I could keep the ball if need be, I think I was more all round. Unlike Paul Allen, I wouldn't tackle, he would tackle and give you the ball, and he was good on one touch and things like that. If you ask the managers I played under, I think they'd say, 'He always had a good touch and his pace was one of his strengths.'

Because I was travelling it was hard to get involved in the social life, go to Frank Lampard's pub and things like that, but as an apprentice you wouldn't. I went to the Christmas dos and so on. When I became a pro I had the odd night out. The year above was Nicky Morgan and Bill Lansdowne; my year was Paul Allen and so on, it was a good crew and the year below me had a great side.

I thought I would go back into management for two or three years but it's too cut throat. I get asked if I miss it all the time; the first year, yeah, but not now. I get the banter I got in the dressing room now with the sales lads, they make up for that. I rarely go and see a game. I see the odd game. Maybe one or two a year at York, that's about it.

Billy Bonds had the biggest influence on me ... his enthusiasm, his desire, stood out more than anything else. He'd hold the team together. If someone was on an off-day he'd grab hold of them and say, 'Come on!'

The reserve team was good. They could give the first team a hell of a game. You'd have the 22 and then there'd be another eight players that could get in someone else's team. I remember the team we put out against Tottenham when they had Ricky Villa and Ardiles, we drew 1–1 at White Hart Lane and our team read like a first team, with the odd young player. Their team read like a first team too.

THE BLACK HAMMERS

The most difficult thing was trying to establish yourself. You had a lot of East End boys. At 18, I bought a year-old Ford Capri. Then I pulled into the car park; Trevor Brooking was only driving an Audi 80. It was on a par. This was an England international and yet an 18-year-old black kid from West London had driven up ... maybe I was me own worst enemy at times. I don't really know. But that was me; that was my personality.

As far as West Ham goes, the players stay with me. You see Trevor on TV all the time. That automatically brings back memories about the games and places you played in. He was up here some years ago doing a sportsmen's dinner. I said, hello ... he was talking about times at West Ham. He remembers me as a good table-tennis player. On 'Talk Sport' I hear 'Stretch' Alvin [Martin]. He first had a mustard Datsun. He'd cram six lads in to drive them back, to get back a little bit early instead of waiting for the van.

West Ham were a family club. From the tea lady up. The crowd was right on top of yer. Going back to the Chelsea game, the atmosphere was incredible. I think there was 36,000 in. To make yer debut in a game like that, it just gave you a nice feeling, because I supported them anyway. Me friends and me family were proud that their son had broken through and played for a club of that standing.

They said I had done enough and that, yes, I deserved a contract when I was 21. It came right the way down towards the end of the season and at the end of the season a list goes up; John Lyall's office at 9, 9.30, 10 o'clock. I wasn't in the first batch nor was Ray Houghton. I thought, 'This is strange, but I was promised so I've got no worries.' A week later another list went up and Ray was in before me and said, 'You ain't gonna believe this, he's released me.' I was next in. So I went in, sat down, and he says, 'Dale, I don't think I can teach you much more.' I remember his words, 'I think you now need to go and play in a first team ... I cannot guarantee you first-team football.' I said, 'I need first-team football ... I can take an easy option on you and give you another two years, but I think you'll do better if you go. I've had a couple of enquiries.'

Obviously, the word spreads. Alan Devonshire and Parksy, all them saying, 'I can't believe he's releasing you' and all that. My mum was devastated. The few that were left went on to do quite well.

DALE CONRAD BANTON

John Lyall was honest. Being a good coach, he could see things that you couldn't actually see. He had said that I was better off going elsewhere and he was proved right. He was fair; I can say he was the best coach I ever played for. I suppose his words were wise. I could have stagnated. I went to Aldershot after West Ham and got 47 goals in 106 appearances. I don't regret my career. I think I ended up with well over 300 games and scored a lot of goals.

Sometimes, when I watched Match of the Day *and they'd focus on the dug-out, some of the old faces were still there. I was at the club six years. I remember being featured in the local paper,* Knocking on the Door. *You go and speak to the people in York, they say, 'I've been watching this game for 50, 60 years and nowadays they get paid a fortune and they can't lace your boots.' All over the country they say the same things.*

There must be racism. Too many people talk about it, too many things happen in this world for it not to be there. I've not had it directly, but I'm sure I've had it indirectly. But in this job, in this sort of area, in the North, people do recognise my name, which helps me a lot.

I didn't realise there had been so many black players at West Ham, that I was the fifth to turn out for the first team, and that I was the first to play for nearly six years. I'll tell people that. That ain't a bad record to have, is it? It was '78–79; at that time you obviously got a little bit of stick. I remember coming up North to play at Barnsley in the League Cup, my hair was out here [he spread his hands to show the parameters of his former 'Afro']. *Because of the logistics of where West Ham was, the population was bound to get an influx of black people, whereas other parts of the country didn't.*

They stamped that out — that needed to be changed. The hardest thing to get across to white people is what it's like to face prejudice like that. How it feels to hear 'You black bastard'. That's hard to put across to white people.

GEORGE PARRIS

'You would think that they'd never seen a black person before.'

I met George at a school for children with hearing difficulties near Brighton. He told me,

We do 'out-of-school activities' here, all different sports. We organise trips with them, to get them off site. Mixing with the community so they can assimilate better.

I was born in Barking [11 September 1964]. I played in 290 games with West Ham. I was an apprentice in July 1981, and signed full pro the following year. I went to Seven Kings High. I played for Redbridge, Essex, London and England Boys; I got eight Boys caps, before I went to Upton Park. At district matches you used to have a lot of scouts coming to watch, the majority of our district side and county side were at clubs anyway. When I was 14 I got asked to come and train at West Ham two nights a week on a Tuesday and Thursday. One or two other clubs were interested but I didn't go there, I trained at West Ham. When I started at West Ham, I lived in Ilford and moved later to Hornchurch.

My mum was a social worker; my dad worked for Ford's. I've got two brothers, one was a very good player, a little bit older than meself and one sister.

As a young player John Lyall was a big influence on me. I joined the club when John Lyall was in charge. If you had any problems of any nature you could go to him. He'd sit down and discuss things. On the football side he was very knowledgeable. He used to come in and,

48

if you had any problems with whatever, he'd come in with yer in the afternoon and do work with yer, which is great when you were in the youth team. He'd stay ages with yer in the gym if need be. Because he was my first manager there will always be that affection. Billy Bonds and Lou Macari were good managers in their own right, but John was the best manager I had.

The first game for West Ham was against Liverpool in '84–85. We got beat 3–0 at home [20 May 1985]. It was Keith MacPherson's debut as well. We struggled to get a team out if I remember rightly. It was the last game of the season and we had a bit of a scratch side, but Liverpool were a good side. I think I hit the post or had a shot headed off the line. I got 17 goals for the club, starting with one against WBA in a 4–0 win. Alan Devonshire passed the ball to Tony Cottee, Neil Orr gave it to me. I think it was a strike outside the box. As I recall I was only playing because Frank [Lampard] was away on England duty, playing against Scotland I think.

I got the 100th West Ham goal against WBA, it came from a cross from Kevin Keen [who was man of the match that day]. *That helped West Ham to their best ever League position in '86. That year we had a good squad. Maybe the League wasn't as tough that year. We had good teams after that but we never seemed to produce the goods. At the end of that season it would have been ideal to go out and buy two or three players but I don't think we did.*

I broke a leg in the home game v Luton in January '88, but came back v Everton a few months later and was man of the match. I wasn't that unlucky with injuries compared to some people. I had a bit of a heart scare, but that got sorted out.

I was part of the promotion team in '91. I think I got eight goals. I was runner-up in Hammer of the Year to Ludo [Ludek Miklosko] that season. The FA Cup semi-final v Forest left me feeling cheated by it all really. You don't get that many opportunities, do you, to get to Wembley. To get it thrown away like that ... even when you see it now you still can't believe that Gale was sent off. We didn't win as much as we should have done with the teams that we had. We got promoted but like getting through to the semi-final, we deserved to be in the final but it didn't happen.

I had a lot of injuries during 1991–92. Knee ligament damage and the heart thing. Towards the end of my career at West Ham, I had a long loan to Brentford. I also went to Bristol City, then Liam Brady took me to Brighton in September '95. I had a spell with Southend in August '97 for about five weeks. Alvin Martin was in charge there at the time. I then played for a team called St Leonard's Standcroft, purely to keep meself fit, hoping that I'd get back with another club. Then after five or six weeks nothing was happening and I realised that I wasn't going to get back in. So, I ended up playing the '97–98 season with them.

Billy Bonds was the most outstanding player I played with. Everyone remembers him for charging about and winning tackles, but he was a very skilful player as well. I don't think people gave him the credit he was due.

I was something of a utility player, I played left- and right-back. But, when Julian Dicks came to West Ham in 1988, I went into midfield. I was seen as a strong tackler. I had a good shot. I could run, I worked hard, I was strong. Me main attribute was me tackling. I like to think I was more skilful than people gave me credit for. It would have been nice if people could actually watch you train on a regular basis. I'm sure they'd see, not just meself but also other people differently, see that I had some skill. I hated playing left-back. I preferred midfield. But I think I played most of me games at full-back. Sometimes you felt like you weren't in the game. That season that we finished third stays with me. To get so close …!

West Ham were a very friendly club. A family club. You could go and talk to someone about whatever and they'd be fine. Alan Dickens, Tony Cottee, before he left, Steve Potts, most of us were good mates, even the older ones, we used to go out together. It was March '93 when I went to Birmingham for £100,000. Terry Cooper was in charge. Billy called me in and said that Terry had been on the phone. He said he didn't want me to go but that it was in my interest to go and talk to Terry. He said if what they were offering was not what I wanted then I could stay at West Ham.

Birmingham was a little bit different to West Ham. It was all right when Terry and Trevor [Cherry] were there, but as soon as they left it was a different ball game. After Barry Fry came in the October I didn't really get in the side. It's strange, football wise, for whatever reason, he didn't rate me, but apart from that he was fine. You could go and chat to him for hours on end about different things. He was good as gold, but he just didn't fancy me as a player. The side got relegated.

I've always played a bit of cricket. We used to play quite regularly. Once or twice a year we used to have West Ham games, charity matches. In one match I got five sixes in one over. I still try to keep me eye in. I've played for Brighton University.

The players called me Smokey after Smokey Robinson. I still don't know why they called me that, I was definitely not a singer [laughs], that's a certainty. The team spirit was brilliant.

As a black player I never see myself as breaking any ground in that respect. You just go out and play. You don't think about yer colour. Some people may but it wasn't an issue for meself. Looking back, I suppose it must have had some significance, especially at West Ham. You can always remember sometimes when opposing players came the fans gave black players stick but they gave everyone stick, then again they were appreciative. I remember a few times they gave Cyril Regis stick, but come the end of the game they'd be applauding him, this, that and the other. They were always fair in that respect. Now it's commonplace to see black players. I never come across any racism at West Ham, not at our place. When you used to go up North it used to be quite a laugh really [smiling]. You would think that they'd never seen a black person before. When you used to go and play it was quite funny really. People used to get a bit excited about it. Throw coins and food and all sorts. You just laugh at them.

The fans called me 'Chicken George', after the character from the TV series Roots, *and blue nose. I like to think that the fans liked me. I was compared to Billy Bonds, which was nice, but all you do is just try yer best, don't yer.*

On 11 April 1995, George came back to Upton Park for his testimonial game (against Ipswich). George represented West Ham in the Masters seven-a-side tournament held in London's Docklands in July 2001, along with other ex-Hammers including Ian Wright and Liam Brady; the side became Southern Masters.

Since the end of his playing days, Parris has been constantly involved in coaching, mostly in schools but he has also worked with the University of Sussex and trained adults looking to take up coaching. Since August 2005 he has been the director of the Village Camps, England, Soccer Programme. He lives in Rottingdean, Brighton, with his wife Sharon, who he met 'at a do at West Ham' and married in 1991, two children, Elliot, born in 1992, and Harriat, who is two years younger, and a cat.

He is coaching a couple of teams at the present but would eventually like to coach a professional team either at home or abroad. Having overcome a number of challenging problems, George is using his experience (alongside Tony Adams and former Hammer Neil Ruddock) with 'Sporting Chance', an organisation that helps top sports people combat alcoholism and other addictions.

DAVID OSWALD 'BOBBY' BARNES

'What is really going to hurt a player is when he has nowhere to go in the game when he's finished playing.'

It was mid-September of the 1980–81 season when a young black winger came into West Ham's first-team squad. David Barnes, who was born on Monday, 17 December 1962, made the perfect start to his League career in a Second Division game at Upton Park. The 17-year-old from Kingston, Surrey, the only black player in the Hammers XI that day, scored the opening goal in an exciting 3–2 victory over Watford.

I scored against Watford and Trevor [Brooking] got the winner with a header in the last minute. You couldn't ask for more at 17. That's what you dream of doing when you're a kid. I was a West Ham fan when I was a kid. I was and am a local lad and you know your mates, local boys too, are watching you and wanting you to do well. That's not so much the case now. Unfortunately now there are not many players who play for their local club.

I'd played in pre-season games but it's not the same. I hadn't even signed a pro contract at the time, although I did sign two days later. There were over 24,000 at Upton Park that day, but 40,000 had watched my senior debut at the Bernabeu against Real Madrid's nursery team Castilla. It was the first round, first leg tie of the European Cup Winners' Cup. That was three days before the Watford game. I came on as sub in the Bernabeu, replacing Nicky Morgan. There was about half-an-hour to play. We lost, 3–1, but it was a great experience, like a dream, playing in Europe for West Ham. West Ham had always been my first love and Trevor Brooking was at his best when I was a kid. There was only one sub in those days, generally a forward at home and a defender away. I remember I borrowed Pat Holland's boots. David Cross was great. He looked after me when I first game into the team. We were flying out for the game and I said to him, 'This is my European debut.' He said, 'Mine too … and I'm 30!'

The fans called me 'Bobby Digger Barnes', a play on the name of a character from the popular American soap of the time Dallas. The nickname stuck nationwide; John Barnes and Peter Barnes were also called 'Digger'.

I must have done OK in Spain as I was in for the next game with Watford. I was just hoping to be on the bench, but I started the game. We didn't have a good start to the season and that game sort of kick-started the promotion campaign. The Second Division race was no-contest. It was fantastic that season for me, being at the club with the likes of Trevor Brooking; Alan Devonshire, at his very best there was no one better than Dev; Alvin Martin, he was top quality, one of the first 'cultured' centre-halves; Billy Bonds — total commitment; Ray Stewart, Tonka, you'd always bet on him to score from a penalty anywhere and at any time. And there was Paul Goddard and Stuart Pearson.

But I got only seven more games that season and only three the next. I got on just the once as sub in 1982–83. But in 1983–84 I played 17 times. I didn't have a lot of patience. The next season it got up to 24.

I had the ability to take on and beat opponents. I played in the Youth Cup-winning team of 1981 and was very much a product of West Ham's youth policy. Paul Allen, Tony Cottee, Alan Dickens and Ray Houghton were all around. It was a good time to be a young player at Upton Park. I was 17 and John Lyall took me as a non-playing member of the squad to the FA Cup at Wembley in 1980. I'd been away with England Youth before the semi-final and John said I should come and join the first-team players. I got to Villa Park for the first game against Everton. Frank's [Lampard] goal in the replay started a big celebration on the way back to London. I was just an apprentice but John made me feel part of the squad for the final. I got the suit and everything.

DAVID OSWALD 'BOBBY' BARNES

But part of my motivation was my familiarity with the club; being brought up in the area, I had a deep-seated loyalty to West Ham. My mum, who worked in the National Westminster Bank, used to take me to look through the gates at Upton Park and I went to Tom Hood School, Bobby Moore's old school, so from an early age I had decided that I wanted to play for West Ham.

We lived in Leytonstone. I was the middle child of seven; four sisters and two brothers. I was the only one who didn't go to university. All my brothers and sisters are professionals or have their own businesses. One sister is a barrister. Dad, who was a supervisor of schools, had wanted me to go to university; the plan was to study law, but I became an apprentice at West Ham. Other clubs came in for me – Millwall and Palace wanted me. Eddie Bailey, a great coach and scout at West Ham and Spurs, got a bit agitated because as far as he was concerned I was West Ham through and through so in the end he said, 'You're signing for West Ham. That's it!' Eddie was good with me. He gave me lifts to training and home again. He was my mentor as a kid and later on as well. Whenever I saw him he'd tell me off, but he was the one who got me to go to West Ham and he was right because it was the right club for me and that decision is one I've never had cause to regret.

I had been with the club since I was 13. John Lyall would watch the youth team. I knew him when I was 14. He was as likely to be at a youth training session watching the kids as he would a first-team training session. He understood the benefits of bringing young players through the system. As a manager he was secure in the knowledge that he would still be in charge five years down the line. That being the case, those 14- and 15-year-olds would be in his first team in a few years. Unfortunately, clubs now don't operate that way; Premiership managers are unlikely to have much involvement with youth training.

I first came to prominence in schools football with Waltham Forest, Essex and London. I gained seven England Youth caps. As a kid I looked up to players like Trevor Brooking, Charlie George, Cruyff and Platini. Brooking and Devonshire were good players, but there was Billy Bonds and David Cross was a marvellous bloke; he gave 100 per cent in every game. Stuart Pearson was my hero when he played Man U.

THE BLACK HAMMERS

Finance has always been a problem to West Ham. The club has never been in a position to buy really big. We also lacked consistency.

I got an extended run in the first team during an injury crisis at Upton Park in 1983–4 and got a regular spot on the wing in 1984–85. However, the following season I lost my place, getting in just one appearance, replacing Alan Devonshire in a 1–0 League win at Portman Road. That was to be West Ham's best ever League season; the club finished in third place in the First Division. Jimmy Neighbour came along, I think John wanted a bit more experience, and he did well for a season. Francois Van der Elst and Steve Whitton were brought in and then, in 1985, Mark Ward arrived from Oldham Athletic and became a fixture for the 1985–86 team. I was disappointed as my chances were limited. I had the ability but didn't apply it. I often say to kids now, 'It's great to get in the first team but that's only a start. Actually staying there is the key.' I didn't fulfil my potential and it was down to me.

I just got games as substitute that season. I wanted first-team football. I had enjoyed being on loan to Scunthorpe United in '85–86, and I think this led me to feel that I needed to take a step back to take a step forward. I played 54 games for West Ham before leaving in March 1986. I scored four goals. I was transferred to Aldershot for £15,000 in November of the same year.

I spent around a year with the Shots before moving to Swindon for £50,000 plus exchange for Steve Berry on 14 October 1987. I scored in six consecutive games at Swindon. I had a bit of a love/hate relationship with Lou Macari. He based everything on fitness and worried about the physical side of things. He didn't go down too well at Upton Park. But then there were Frank McAvennie, Alvin Martin and Alan Devonshire there who were accustomed to doing things the 'West Ham way'. Lou was the direct opposite to how I experienced Harry Redknapp at Bournemouth.

But I was with Swindon when they got promoted. I scored 13 goals in 50 games there. I was sent off in the New Year's Day game with West Bromwich Albion, and after that I wasn't getting a first-team place for the rest of the season. I started the following season in the first team, but in March 1989 Harry [Redknapp] took me to

DAVID OSWALD 'BOBBY' BARNES

Bournemouth for £110,000. Bournemouth didn't work out for me. After only 14 games, in October I went to Northampton for 98 League games scoring 37 goals. In February '92 I joined Peterborough. The following season I found myself in the Scottish Premiership with Partick Thistle. I was 32. I thought my legs were slowing a bit. I was training with John Lyall at Ipswich Mondays, Tuesdays and Wednesdays and went up to Scotland, flying from Stansted, on Thursday for the Saturday games and back again straight after matches. John was a great coach and a good man. A very thoughtful manager and one of the most honourable men I have ever known. You'd never meet a more honest manager. Most of all you didn't want to let him down. He made you feel he had put his confidence in you and you wanted to justify that. John was completely devoted to West Ham. He told you how much your wages were and if you had a game whether you were playing or not. He threw one or two teacups, yes, but in the main that was not John's way. He wasn't a man who shouted and screamed. He had a quiet authority. Looking back it was like the club was his responsibility totally. He was quite unusual in that he organised almost every aspect of things at the club from the smallest thing to the biggest things. When first-team training was finished he'd be back out with the kids. That was the strength of the club. There's not a bad word to say about John. He was a father figure. He always stressed to young players that they were in a privileged position to play professional football and if he didn't think that was getting through he would take them around a hospital or a hostel to show them what the world, reality was really like.

Players would take notice of John; he had integrity, a calm authority. You didn't argue with him, you respected him, even if I didn't agree with him, and sometimes we didn't. He was one of the main reasons why West Ham had such a good atmosphere and that there was good feeling amongst the players. John looked after players. He might have played me a bit more though! [laughs]

I had one game as a sub at Torquay then went to Rangers in Hong Kong for a couple of seasons – we won the FA Cup there.

I never saw myself as a 'leading the way' as a black player. We were a bit of a cosseted dressing room. We'd joke about the race thing, like,

THE BLACK HAMMERS

'You'll get it today!' But there were a lot of players coming through at the time, John Barnes, Luther Blissett and so on. At Newcastle or Leeds, 15 or 20 years ago, you'd get some stick if they knew a black player was playing. The blokes used to send me out first for a laugh and you got 30–40,000 people booing you. We went to Leeds once, we had been playing quite well but I was getting a lot of stick. At half-time Tony Gale said to me, 'You've been playing well first half, so I want you to lead us out for the second.' So, like an idiot, I lead out the team. There was a chorus of boos. I turned around to find that the rest of the blokes hadn't followed me [laughs].

It did get a bit silly at times, throwing bananas and that, but it all got blown out of proportion, including questions in the House of Commons. In the 80s, when I was playing, the game was going through a tough time. There was racism and hooligans. I remember playing at Newcastle United and they threw loads of bananas on the pitch. But St James' was one of the worst places as was Elland Road. It got politically hijacked really and I didn't want any of that. Of course, the biggest problem has always been black players becoming managers or getting on the board. You don't even see former white players on the board. The crowd you could cope with and most of that has gone, at least in England. But what is really going to hurt a player is when he has nowhere to go in the game when he's finished playing. There is still no career structure for former players who are black; I mean, there isn't for any player really, but there is less opportunities still for black players. But in recent years we have made headway. It's important to get everyone on board. Players of the 70s and 80s did break through. West Ham have worked hard in terms of race issues. I'm proud of the fact that my old club has made positive steps. You don't get the chanting any more, there is still the odd incident, but at Upton Park crowd-related racism is a thing of the past.

West Ham was and always will be my lasting football love. We were well supported by the fans. I grew up in the area. There were people I went to school with on the terraces. The Chicken Run could be hard to please, they let you know when you weren't doing well, but, on Cup nights under the lights, Upton Park had a great atmosphere. We didn't get turned over too often on those occasions. I wouldn't have swapped

DAVID OSWALD 'BOBBY' BARNES

West Ham's supporters. You wore the shirt and that was it; that's who you were for them. I left West Ham 20 years ago but the supporters remember you. You are West Ham for life. They remember me even though I had that great big hair and now I haven't got any! Hammers fans are incredibly loyal, through good times and bad. Look at the attendances. For relatively unattractive Championship games 34,000 turned up! All the myths about West Ham ever having racist supporters is built around other myths about East London. Around the docks people were more used to seeing people from all over the world so it was never going to be so pronounced as it would be say in some northern towns. And the likes of John Charles had paved the way. Local lad done good John was, as far as anybody in and around the club were concerned. Of course there were remarks, but none of that really got in the way. Most criticism from fans at Upton Park was directed at the opposition or was out of disappointment that the team could have done better. There were white players who came in for a lot more stick than black players, but then West Ham never really had any black players that lacked ability. When you run through the list they were all more than useful. But then that maybe provoked opposing fans to have a go more. Most of any stick emanated from the way you played. I didn't get any racism from the West Ham fans, although some gave opposition players a bit of stick. For me that was strange. They were there supporting me to play for their team, but a black player on the other side got it. Maybe I was just seen as one of them – and I was, of course. I grew up in Leytonstone; I married Teresa at St Thomas of Canterbury Church, Woodford, and still live in Wanstead

West Ham had a family atmosphere. The dressing room was fairly constant; players seemed to move about less than they did at other clubs and now. The social life at the club was good. We went out or went away together as a team. The celebrations in the early 80s were probably the key to the success of West Ham as a team. It created a bond as we often went out as a group, even the more experienced players like David Cross, Phil Parkes and Alan Devonshire – they maybe had more of a right to do that, but I'd go as well. Probably that wasn't a good idea. There'd be parties, have a drink after training. Again, that wouldn't happen now at the top of the game. There were no cliques in the dressing room and that was probably one of the best things about being part of West Ham at the time. No one acted like a big star. We would mix together. Now the press put a stop to that. If the cameras had been on us there would have been one or two stories [laughs]. We enjoyed ourselves. It was good to be part of something. We were all friends. I never really recaptured that spirit.

At 16, my ability attracted a lot of interest. There weren't many left-footers around, just like now. But I was a good example of a lad who thought he had it all by getting into the first team at 17; an object lesson to younger players [laughs]. One day Eddie Bailey sat me down and told me that I had to stop messing about and make up my mind. I was given the opportunity to play for Crystal Palace, but there was only one club I wanted to be involved with. I 'socialised' a bit too much and as a result didn't achieve as much as I should have, given the promise I had. It went to my head. I started doing things I shouldn't and didn't concentrate on training. I look back and think, 'I'd have done a lot more if I'd just had a bit more focus.' I wish I hadn't started at West Ham. I thought I had arrived, but I got too involved in the distractions. I only understood this when I went to smaller clubs. If I had my time again I think I would have had more appreciation. One of my most lasting memories was coming on as sub at Norwich and scoring the winner, six days from the end of the season; it meant we stayed up and they went down − it was a small justification for my time at the club.

I was a skilful player. I could take on and beat opponents. I think I could play a bit [laughs].

I went into the finance world after I finished playing in 1995. Worked for Friends Provident after I got a diploma in business studies. I was a senior investment consultant. I'd get to go out to Hong Kong a fair bit and that was nice because I knew the place well.

Since 2000 Bobby has been involved with the PFA at executive level. It is work he enjoys immensely. Talking about his job, he said,

I'm not jealous of the financial rewards players get now. My age group were probably not given what we were worth, as we drew the crowds, more than now really. The vast majority of players never get to be big earners. They spend their playing lives in lower divisions. Those guys have families. They have all the insecurity every time a contract expires. The PFA is a union, and we have to look after those guys.

The money has transformed the game for the better. The Premier League is now very attractive to sponsors; it's 'trendy'. That's got to be better than 20 years ago when football supporters were treated almost like criminals and Margaret Thatcher was trying to introduce ID cards.

His role has also involved him acting as a Reading Champion by 'Reading The Game' and helping the PFA promote the RTG campaign to increase literacy through football. He commented,

I was an avid reader as a child. I would lose myself in books. I loved being read stories. Teresa and I have two children, Chris [born in 1985] and Karli [who is two years younger]; when they were young they loved being read to. I grew up on the Just William, Billy Bunter *and* Jennings *books. I generally read three books at a time with them scattered around the house. I like books focusing on the countries I regularly visit such as France and Hong Kong. Reading is a wonderful source of information or escape. I cannot imagine a long journey without reading. Everyone should make time to read.*

Bobby had a distinguished career. With Aldershot, he won promotion in 1987, and played well for Swindon, Bournemouth, Northampton and Peterborough United, for whom he appeared in the Division Two play-off-winning side at Wembley. He still keeps fit running round the greener parts of East London. He has worked alongside and supported initiatives like the West Ham Learning Zone and a Black Players Career Forum, looking to address the shortage of black coaches and managers within football, given that 20 per cent of footballers within the game are now black. He recently said,

The thing you miss most when you retire from the game is the banter amongst the players, but I work alongside ex-players like Paul Allen and Peter Smith so we've got our own mini dressing room in the office.

THE BLACK HAMMERS

Bobby also attended the TUC Congress in Brighton and was instrumental in the decision to allow unions the facility to expel members of the BNP from their own union. But he made it clear that it was important that the PFA looked after all its members equally – whatever their colour, race or religion.

Bobby is also a trustee of 'Kick It Out', an organisation that works to tackle racism in football. He is one of those players that make me proud to be a West Ham supporter – he was at the 2006 Cup final with a group of lifelong West Ham fans and was pleased

> ... to be at a game as a normal supporter rather than wearing a tie in the executive box. I missed the last two play-off finals because of work commitments so hopefully it will be third time lucky for me and the Hammers can win the Cup. We've waited a long time to get there!

As such, 'Digger' remains true to his football roots:

> For me, it was a great achievement to wear the colours of the club I supported as a kid; I was very proud to wear the shirt. As I run round Wanstead I still get people shouting 'up the 'Ammers' at me. I'll always be West Ham through and through. I was lucky to play with some of the greatest players to ever turn out at Upton Park.

EVERARD LARONDE

'Everyone wanted the best for everyone else ... I walked along with the crowd to get to the game.'

I met Everard in a meeting room at Canary Wharf.

Everard was born on 24 January 1963 in Forest Gate, just a few hundred yards from West Ham's Boleyn Ground. He skippered the Youth Cup/Championship double-winning side of 1981. He made his League debut against Coventry in April 1982. LaRonde joined Harry Redknapp at Bournemouth before returning to the local junior game.

I was playing for my school, St Bonaventures, some good players came from there, then I played for Newham Boys. I was picked up by Dave Wally, the scout. He came down to a couple of the games at Terrence McMillan Stadium. And obviously, being district captain, it started from there really. I was approached by Arsenal at the time. I played for Poplar Boys. I started off as a goalkeeper. They wanted my services as a keeper. It's quite funny. A three-foot goalkeeper [while not 'vertically challenged' Everard is not tall], *you don't see many of them* [laughs].

Me mum was a district nurse and me dad worked at the docks and then Ford's. I'm single, fortunately. No one'll have me [laughs]. *I've got four brothers. Tony, Michael, Peter and Keith. I got Everard. That's the luck of the draw* [smiles]. *Tony was at West Ham with me.*

As a youth player we had so many goals; we wanted to win everything. It wasn't just me, it was the whole squad; we all felt the same so it made life a little bit easier. We didn't care who came in the

63

side, you'd encourage them, whether they were younger or older. Our goals were the same, so, no, I didn't see myself as anything special at the time. I don't know really. I was very pleased with the FA Youth Cup and I ended up captain. But I think it takes 11 captains to win a trophy like that.

I'd finished playing in Bournemouth, after a couple of dozen games. I played eight games with Peterborough on loan. I had an operation at Barkingside, took me cartilage out. They said, 'Have you ever thought of doing something other than football? You've got arthritis in both yer knees. Unless you want to be pushed around in a wheelchair … so that was that. I don't need telling twice.

I'd gone out to Saudi Arabia. I did some coaching out there with Peter Osgood. Came back from that and I was playing non-League … Sweden … I went out there with arthritis on me knees (I'd also had stomach and hernia problems) and packed up when I came back. I played at Kalmar and the following season I went to Nybro …

I don't play at all now. Golf is more my game now. I never played golf when I played football. The very first person that introduced me to golf was Harry Redknapp when I was down at Bournemouth with him. I was forced into that as well. We'd beaten Man United in the third round of the FA Cup and we were told that we would have to turn up to play golf the next day. I borrowed his clubs and I remember on the second hole – they were pretty old these clubs – I went to tee off and I'd never teed off before; I made a swing and looked down at the ball and it was still there, then I looked at the club and the head had shot down the fairway [laughs].

That game against United; I was 19 and got the man of the match. I was 'a rock in defence' they said. Manchester United were the defending FA Cup winners and had lost only one League match away all season when they turned up at Dean Court on 7 January 1984. Bournemouth were struggling; fourth from bottom of the Third Division, we'd lost to the bottom club Port Vale the week before. Harry Redknapp was three months into his first job in charge and the captain, John Beck, was out with the flu! We won 2–0; outplayed 'em, we did.

I played seven first-team games for West Ham, the first was a 1–0 defeat at Coventry, an own goal, nice start. It was just one of those things. It was a low cross, hit hard and low, it was Thompson I think. I stuck me toe out to knock it off for a corner and it went in the roof of the net. I think that was my first touch of the ball. It didn't go down very well [laughs]. *Fortunately it didn't ruin me.*

I skippered the '81 Youth Cup-winning team and the Championship side. A record that still stands, I'm quite proud of that one. It was a good win; 2–1 over the two legs. Exciting. I remember it as if it was yesterday. We had an excellent first leg; 2–0 against what I thought was a really good Tottenham side, probably one of the best teams I'd ever played. It was an advantage that we probably never hoped to gain over 'em and obviously we needed it, going down 0–1 at home. We was a good little side. The good thing about that side is that we had great camaraderie. We were all the same age; we were all apprentices, all striving to break through to the first team. I don't think I've seen it at any other football club. We used to get together after we'd cleaned the boots and washed the van, got our chores out the way; we used to head off down to McDonald's and have our team talks. Form our own plan of attack for the evening game. Being local as well, I was just down the road, Chester Road; me mum still lives there, just round the corner from what was the East Ham Memorial Hospital. They used to come round to me mum's, sit round and have sandwiches and stay, especially if we had a home game and it was great. A lot of 'em didn't make it through. Like anything, you need a little bit of luck, but also it's dedication and hard work. Some of those players were a year younger, but then you had the experienced lads, like Bobby Barnes, who had a taste of first-team football; Paul Allen had just made it.

If I look round and thought of the full-backs that were in front of me at the time, Paul Brush, he was two or three years older than me, there's not a lot in it. And you've got Frank Lampard! If you're striving to make the first team, you've got to be better than these guys or at least be able to compete with them, but you've also got to have the opportunity.

Looking back, if I could do it again I'd have hung on at West Ham; without a shadow of a doubt. I remember going on deadline day. I think I signed two minutes before five o'clock. I probably spent three-and-a-half hours in there; there wasn't any agents around in those times. I probably would have benefited from one. You're 18 looking around the room. Where do you go from here? I'm sitting here saying 'yes' to you and 'no' to the club where I've been so many years, the club that has looked after me. You haven't got anyone in there to help you. You've got people who want yer, like Bournemouth, the director and manager sitting there, saying, 'It'll be good for yer', but you've got no one saying, 'Well, you could play out yer contract, things ain't terrible.' I didn't have that and ultimately said yes and went. I could have stayed, but there you go. I don't know what the feedback on my leaving was, it was done so quick. I was at the training ground on the Thursday morning and by the afternoon I was in the director's room discussing a move. I'd signed the deal Thursday evening.

The difficulty with having so many good players around is that players didn't come through. When you look at West Ham's youth team, their youth policy, they've got a great youth policy, but how many of those players actually make the first team? Going back again, if you look at our youth side, just one or two of those players came through. That isn't many for a team that won the FA Youth Cup. Yet, if you look at the other sides, yer Man Uniteds, you see six and seven coming in. They all play at a young age and I think that was West Ham's biggest downfall then, under John Lyall, that he kept the likes of Frank Lampard and Trevor [Brooking] going into their mid- to late thirties whereas other teams were pushing youngsters at 17/18. I don't know if he'd agree with me [smiles].

I went to Bournemouth in '82 on loan. They tried to buy me. I spoke to John Lyall. I don't know what the fee was but West Ham were asking way too much money. I went back to Bournemouth with a hernia. Again, a disastrous injury that went all wrong. I ended up with gangrene, eight months out of the game and that was virtually the end of my contract. They took so long to diagnose the problem, of course, I've got a hole there and in the meantime it's gone all septic. I had to see a specialist. He tells me I had to leave it another couple of weeks to have another check. I went in a month later and found out I had gangrene.

To be honest, Harry [Redknapp] was absolutely miserable to work with. He was difficult. Don Megson was the manager when I first went to Bournemouth. Harry used to come in and swear blind he wasn't going to take the team over and that he wasn't managerial material. The next week he took it. He was awful, absolutely awful. He just flew into a rage. He didn't know how to manage people or deal with people. Whether he's any good now I don't know. Back then he wasn't.

I played at York City with Dale Banton on loan from Bournemouth. I might have stayed there, but, again, it was to do with money. Dale had rung me up, I'd met him in the West End, so I went down to York with Viv Busby. I spent two months there. After that I went to Saudi and then Sweden.

When I came back from Sweden I had the operation. I had a long time on me own to think about what I was going to do next. Fortunately, I'd gone to college when I was an apprentice at West Ham. I enjoyed college so I decided to go back. I went back to college full-time as a service engineer. Come out and started here, working for Canary Wharf Management. I'm very happy. I do all their access control and CCTV for the whole wharf. I've got 72 acres here to look after; I'm the special systems technician and it's like running a small city.

I see Trevor [Brooking] walking through occasionally. I've never stopped him, because he's been going one way and I've been going the other. He used to go up to the Telegraph. One day I'll stop him in his tracks and we'll have a little chat. I'll invite him over for a cuppa [smiles].

The majority of the lads at the club were very helpful. The likes of Billy Bonds, Trevor [Brooking] were always very encouraging. Frank [Lampard] always wanted yer to stay behind and do a bit extra. Alvin Martin was very encouraging. After taking his place on the field at Coventry, at the training ground he'd pull you over and have a little word, tell you about the things you were doing wrong and straighten you out without making a big scene. On the West Ham training ground under Harry it was all screaming. They were all doing this wrong and that wrong. Alvin was the most calming influence and, being in the back four as he was, he just talked along the line. It was a confidence builder I suppose. My favourite, once I got there, was really John Lyall. He was the most encouraging and anything you wasn't very good at he was quite prepared to stay behind with yer and work at the game or just encourage yer to sort of do it yerself really. He was an excellent man, a very nice person. A very genuine guy. I mean, he said things to yer and he meant 'em. He just didn't say things for fun.

West Ham were a very friendly club. I don't think anyone can deny that. There was such a good team spirit there, with the coaches, everyone wanted to win, but everyone wanted the best for everyone else. It was always enjoyable to go training. Used to get up and look forward to it and the games, and just generally meeting up with the lads. As I say, there weren't too many of us that were that local, just finding out what people were up to.

You hear a lot of things from fans that make yer laugh. I remember being a spectator and watching Clyde Best and someone threw a banana on and he picked it up and ate it. He came back to the club once. He was in a great big Jaguar [laughs]. My first game after leaving West Ham was against Millwall, not the easiest of games – the bananas did rain then. Not the best introduction to Third Division football. I didn't come across a lot of that sort of thing at West Ham. Even if it had been about, I probably wouldn't have noticed it, being an East End boy. I never had a chip on my shoulder. Probably 90 per cent of my friends were white anyway, still are [laughs]. It didn't bother me. Most of the so-called West Ham hooligans were people I knew anyway. I didn't socialise with them, but you know a face in a crowd. Some people had problems; I don't know whether it's a case of just handling something like that. I didn't see myself as a trailblazer or anything like that at the time.

You couldn't go out at somewhere like Upton Park unless you had the fans' support and that was something that they always gave me. I don't know whether that was because I was local. I never drove a car, I still don't now; I do drive but I don't feel the need. Having my boots over my shoulder and walking down Green Street was just the norm. Even for the first team. I didn't get dropped off, I walked. So I walked along with the crowd to get to the game. They were always great! Without a doubt, very special … very special.

KEITH ANTHONY MACPHERSON

HAMMERS DEBUT: 20/5/85

'We mixed well together ... I wish I had longer at West Ham.'

I'm a South Londoner, born in Greenwich on 11 September 1963.
Played for Blackheath and Inner London as a schoolboy. I got a
phone call from a scout one evening and he asked me if I'd fancy coming
down to West Ham. I was 12, 13. I was playing Sunday-league
football at the time as well. I had some enjoyable years there.

I followed Liverpool as a lad but I didn't really support a club. I still
look for their results now, but I didn't go to their games. I went to a
couple of Charlton games. There was a couple of players I liked at
Millwall. Millwall was notorious for agro. There was no way my
parents were going to let me go down there [laughs]. They were
interested in me when I was at Reading, when Billy [Bonds] was in
charge at the New Den, but I signed another two years at Reading.

I first recognised I had some talent when I was playing for Inner
London and Blackheath. Representing yer county and yer district,
obviously you were getting highly praised by the school and you were
getting time off and all that. I went away with the county to Canada.
The possibilities of getting into the pro game and doing well, that was
probably the ambition, but you never think it might happen. My
parents were stringent in making sure that my studies went on and I'm
glad. At the time we went down to West Ham, I went with my mum
and dad, they wanted to sign me on schoolboy forms. My dad wasn't
too sure about it. He wanted me to stay on and do my A levels. My
mum was saying, 'It's up to you. Whatever you do, I'll back yer.' My
dad came round to the idea.

THE BLACK HAMMERS

My mum's name's Mavis, she works in a local-authority nursing home. She worked at that for years doing night work four nights a week. My father worked for the council, he did various jobs, mainly in care, he died in '93. His name was Leslie. They were Jamaican. They settled in Brockley. They married over here. I've got one brother, Melvin, he's a heating engineer, and one sister, Francine, she's a sales manager, a team leader with a newspaper. My brother's older and my sister's younger. I'm married to Jenny, we've been married since '98. We met in Brighton about '89.

I played number 7 for the side that won the FA Youth Cup in '81, v Spurs. Only the second time West Ham had won that trophy. Bobby Barnes, Tony Cottee, Alan Dickens, Everard LaRonde were all around then. I remember us beating Spurs in the final. It was a big crowd at Upton Park and we also did well in the Southern Junior Floodlit Cup and South-East Counties League. It was great just going in to train every day and we all got on. Tony [Cottee] and me got on good. Clive, his dad, had an insurance business. I insure my car through him.

September '81, I signed pro, it was on my 18th birthday. It was a proud moment. But so was getting to be an apprentice with the club – YTS came later of course. My mum was particularly pleased. She had given me a lot of encouragement in football. Dad was more concerned about my education. My parents weren't big supporters of football. They came over once or twice. My mum didn't mind it and my dad was quite proud that I was playing for West Ham. It was a great time to be at West Ham. I got around £150 a week after turning pro, according to what happened. I'd spend all my money just enjoying myself.

I was at the club for six years. It was one of their most successful periods. They won the Cup in 1980, same time as I joined West Ham. I got just the one full first-team game. I think I was sub against Notts County. It was when West Ham got back into the First Division too. John Lyall was fair. If you had problems, he sorted them.

I was good at most sports at school. I was lucky enough to be good at most things and enjoy them. The one sport I didn't want to play was rugby. Because of my pace they wanted me to play, but I always tried to get out of that. They said, 'Can we have you on the wing?' I knew it was a bit rough and tumble and I didn't fancy it. I played district for

KEITH ANTHONY MACPHERSON

basketball and cricket. I was gonna do A levels or go to college or something. West Ham always encouraged the youngsters to carry on with yer studies. I used to go on a Thursday full day. At the time I always wanted to be a draughtsman or something like that, you know, architect. I went to Vauxhall College, I think I did three years there. I got some qualification for that. West Ham were allowing me to go to a building site, just to get a bit of experience. Surveying and bits like that. They encouraged a lot of kids. I say to the kids nowadays, especially at that age, 15, 16, 'Don't always think yer gonna make it. Some players do drop out very early.' I got four or five O levels. I wouldn't say I was the brightest, but I did OK [laughs].

When I was at West Ham my idol was Bonzo [Billy Bonds]. He come to Reading as a coach before he went to Millwall. Him coming there made me up. There was loads of players I respected. They had such a great team. I've always looked at West Ham as a family club. It was close knit. They looked after young players and also the older ones who did well. At the time when John Lyall was there, it was an ageing side, but they did so well for him.

I started as a right-winger with Blackheath and converted to a defender, played full-back at youth level, then into the middle. There were lots of good, good players there then; Dev [Alan Devonshire], Alvin Martin, David Cross, Trevor Brooking, Pat Holland, Paul Goddard, Billy Bonds, Frank Lampard and Geoff Pike were around. They did well so John Lyall kept them in. I realised that opportunities were limited at the time. It was difficult for young players to get into the side. At the time there was me and George [Parris]. I think Incey [Paul Ince] was a couple of years behind us. I was lucky, with George and a few other young lads at the time, to get into the reserve team at such a young age. We played a lot of reserve games. Nowadays if you're good enough you're old enough, they put you straight in. John Lyall probably thought I wasn't ready. Tony Cottee, Paul Allen, Bobby [Barnes] and Alan Dickens came in and they did all right. But only a few of the young lads made it through and adjusted to the first team, like TC [Tony Cottee], he matured early.

John Lyall gave me and George our opportunity against Liverpool.

71

THE BLACK HAMMERS

League Champions they were. It's getting on for 30 years ago now but I can remember it like it was yesterday. I think that game was on a Monday. I remember training with the first team in the morning and John Lyall called us both in the office, I think maybe it was separately. He said, 'After training you're probably going to be playing tonight. Get home and see if yer can get some sleep.' I didn't sleep at all [laughs]. Billy Bonds was injured and I played alongside Alvin Martin and there was a big crowd. The game didn't matter much and I didn't do as well as I might have done, it was a good experience though. The game seemed to flash by. After that they took me on the tour of Japan, which was another fantastic experience. We got beat 3–0 at Upton Park. It was the last game of the '84–85 season. I think we just avoided relegation against Ipswich on the Friday.

John Lyall signed me. He was a good manager. I looked up to him. He was a good communicator, a very good coach. I look back and look at his methods and think, 'That was quite enjoyable.' At such a young age, I probably didn't appreciate it; he had some great ideas, he had a way of relaying them to other coaches. He also put over what he wanted the young pros to do. At the same time he looked to help the youth team to mature ... that was a good thing. Ron Greenwood and everyone else were in the same mould.

West Ham had very good support at home. When you had a night game you always fancied West Ham to win. On a Tuesday night you'd usually get over 20,000. I never experienced any racism towards me at West Ham. Not at all. I've experienced it at other clubs and maybe from away fans. But I've never had it from my own fans.

I went on loan to Cambridge United in September '85, I played 11 games, scored a goal. Then I went to Northampton in January '86 for £10,000. It wasn't like West Ham was saying, 'We don't want yer.' It was just that Northampton wanted me and at the time I just decided that that was the next step for me really. I had 224 games for them. Nine goals. Got a Fourth Division Championship medal in 1986–87. I enjoyed it. They wanted to keep me. It was a way of playing first-team football, that's what probably lured me. Northampton is about an hour-and-a-half's drive from London. I stayed in digs sometimes, but I went back and forth quite a bit on a Thursday, Friday.

KEITH ANTHONY MACPHERSON

When Bobby [Barnes] came to Northampton, we used to meet up and take it in turns driving.

In August 1990 I moved on to Reading. Nine years, around 300 outings; Second Division title '93–94; just missed out on getting into the Premiership with them; with Reading, lost at Wembley in the First Division play-off final against Bolton Wanderers in '95. Player-manager was Jimmy Quinn. He'd been at West Ham of course.

I just missed out on a testimonial. I won't go into that [laughs]. Ian Wright and Shaka [Hislop] got me a couple of shirts from West Ham though. They had a benefit for me Reading. I still keep in touch with Shaka. He's a really nice lad. We used to travel together when he was at Reading. Very down to earth. I used to travel with Dale Gordon as well when I was a young lad.

I went to Brighton in '99. I went on loan at first, with a view to sign. I'd been there two, three months and Micky Adams took over. He decided he wanted to keep me and I signed a year's contract ... after that ... I decided to go to Slough in the Ryman League; from July 2000 to 2002 I was with them.

I kept to my studies over the years. Doing non-League gave me that opportunity. When I was at Reading I did my UEFA 'B'. I started doing my coaching badges at Slough. I've done a bit of radio work at Reading matches, but who can say what will happen and we'll have to wait and see. I'll maybe go into coaching. It's great, but sometimes you need that little bit of luck to get the opportunity. Fifteen years ago if someone had said to me do you fancy management, I'd have said, 'Not really.' But I'm older now, nine or 10 years ago I started to see what a coach and a manager sees and you start to think how they think. When you're playing you get other lads now who look up to you and ask you for advice and then you try to give them advice, you're helping them and you're developing their skills. So, who knows? I miss football and would like to get back in some way.

Getting into management or coaching is a matter of luck sometimes. Sometimes it's who you know, but if you have got the qualifications it helps. Someone just needs to give you that opportunity and you need to grasp it and develop it from there ... sometimes your reputation as a player can help.

THE BLACK HAMMERS

When I left West Ham I was offered a year. The money wasn't great, perhaps when you're young it shouldn't be. John Lyall said to me, 'Cambridge want to take you on loan.' So I went there on loan and I quite enjoyed it, playing first-team football. You were playing in front of a decent crowd, not compared to West Ham, but a good-sized crowd. Even though the level was a bit lower, I quite enjoyed it.

I wish I had longer at West Ham. Maybe if I'd have had another two years, just to have developed a bit more, maybe learn a bit more, but I wouldn't change anything at all because I've had some great experiences. But you get frustrated. The coaches, the manager possibly thought I didn't have the talent at that time. You get a bit concerned when you're in the reserves so much. I didn't see much changing. It was a let-down to leave West Ham for a lower-League club, but I reckoned I had to take a step back to go forward, push on with my career. At least starting off with West Ham gave me a good start. Loads of players went through West Ham and carried on playing after.

I've had a good career, to be fair. I've been very fortunate and still to be playing now. I can't complain. I enjoyed meself at West Ham. I always lived at home. Billy Bonds used to give me a lift sometimes. When we used to do the kit and the boots we used to go down to the old Wimpy in Green Street. We'd meet in there and have a Wimpy or we'd go back to Ev's [Everard LaRonde] house. I had a great time. We had a good youth team. A good crop of lads. We mixed well together, we'd go out together. Ilford Palais, Room at the Top ... we had a good team spirit. We had no problem with the pros. That's what's maybe missing nowadays, I don't know, maybe old pros don't help youngsters as much. When I was at West Ham you could ask older pros to show you where you might be going wrong; they helped yer. West Ham was my biggest club. You miss that atmosphere. When you're coming into a first-team game, you knew it was going to be a big crowd and you're playing maybe Tottenham or Liverpool, even though you weren't involved yerself.

Leaving West Ham, it was hard. It was difficult, especially as a young lad, it was your first club. A big pro club and you always wanna do well there. I was thinking, 'Will things be the same?' But you get over that. In the end I played more than 500 Football League appearances, so it weren't really a wrong decision. What I learned at West Ham had been useful right the way through my career. I'm proud that I was with West Ham and whatever I've done started there; the good coaching I had there from Tony Carr and Mick McGiven. Mick was in charge of the reserve team. I got on very well with Mick. He helped me as a defender. I got a lot from him. Ronnie Boyce also gave me lots of good advice. The coaches at West Ham were great generally. It was an enjoyable time for me. I got good advice from them and John [Lyall]. I was lucky with injuries and I played for 20 years. We were coached well at Chadwell Heath and I did OK with that behind me.

I had half-a-dozen great years at West Ham, made some good friends. I always look for their result.

After leaving football Keith lived in Purley, Surrey. Late in 2002 he was player–coach at Slough Town while working for Inkfish Call Centres Limited in Redhill. Early in 2003 he was still employed in Redhill but as a customer service officer for BUPA International.

PAUL EMERSON CARLYLE INCE

'I did what my agent told me to do, then took all the crap for it.'

Paul Ince was born in Ilford, one of the border boroughs between East London and West Essex, on 21 October 1967 and grew up with his aunt in Dagenham. He was spotted by then West Ham coach John Lyall when he was 12, and signed for the Hammers as a trainee at 14. Lyall became something of a father figure to Paul early on, supporting him through troubled times at school. Paul was recruited to the Upton Park YTS in July 1984. He made rapid progress, turning pro a year later. Lyall never doubted the young man's ability, and after keeping a watchful eye on him gave Paul his first-team debut in a Full Members' Cup encounter with Chelsea at the Boleyn Ground (25 November 1986). Ince's League debut came five days later and was covered live on TV, coming on as a substitute for Alan Dickens in a 4–0 defeat at St James' Park. The following season Paul started to establish himself as a regular in the midfield, demonstrating pace, stamina, uncompromising tackling and good passing ability. He also possessed a powerful shot. His all-round aptitude was rewarded with England Under-21 honours that confirmed the potential he had shown as a Youth international.

After missing the opening game of the 1987–88 season (a defeat by QPR), Ince was recalled to the side in the role of sweeper. He could also fill in at full-back, although his best position was as a hard-running midfielder who liked the ball at his feet. Yet it was only in his third, and last, season at Upton Park that he retained a regular first-team place.

PAUL EMERSON CARLYLE INCE

In November 1988, Paul, playing in a struggling Hammers team, shot to national recognition with two stunning goals in a unexpected 4–1 win over Champions Liverpool in the League (Littlewoods) Cup. It was the Liverpool Reds' biggest Cup defeat since 1939.

Ince continued to score goals as the Irons reached the last four. However, the Boleyn Boys lost to Luton Town in the semi-finals and, despite frequent displays of individual brilliance from Paul, West Ham were relegated at the end of the season. He played just once in the Second Division the following season before a notorious £1 million transfer to Manchester United.

The desire for fame and glory grew in Ince with the departure in July 1989 of his long-time mentor John Lyall. At the same time, new manager Lou Macari was looking to cash in on Paul's undisputed talent. The move to Old Trafford was controversial because Ince had been photographed wearing a Manchester United shirt long before the deal was completed. The picture appeared in the *Daily Express* and some West Ham fans, reacting out of disappointment at the seeming duplicity of a player they regarded as 'one of their own', were provoked to bitter acrimony. The situation was made worse because of a three-month delay in the finalisation of the transfer when Paul failed his initial medical examination. An old hernia injury showed up on X-rays and Alex Ferguson would give no more than £800,000 up front for the young Hammer's signature with the balance payable in instalments. In a unique pay-as-you-play deal, West Ham collected £5,000 for each first-team appearance Paul made, up to a total of £1.5 million. United certainly got good value for a player who first showed promise for Essex Schoolboys.

Sadly, a section of Hammers' supporters have never forgiven Ince; while this has as at times been portrayed by the media as representative of the racism of West Ham fans, it has been lost that this animosity has probably prevented Ince from spending at least some time at Upton Park before retiring, instead of being obliged to play out his career in a mediocre Wolves side. It is even more lamentable given that Paul did not intend any offence. He recalled that he spoke to Alex Ferguson when he thought the deal was close to being done. He then went on holiday, and his agent at the time, Ambrose Mendy, told him that it wasn't worth his returning to pose for a photograph wearing a United shirt after the deal was completed. This being the case, Mendy advised that Paul should go through with the photo-shoot before he took his break. Lawrence Luster of the *Daily Star*, the man who took the picture, placed it in the newspaper's library. However, the *Star*'s sister paper the *Daily Express*, searching for a picture of Ince playing for West Ham, found the one of him in the United shirt and published it. Paul returned from holiday to discover that West Ham fans were up in arms. Looking back he commented,

> *It wasn't really my fault. I was only a kid, I did what my agent told me to do, then took all the crap for it.*

After 81 games and eight goals for West Ham, Ince made his Manchester United debut in a 5–1 win over Millwall and (despite wearing the number 2 shirt all season) became a strong presence in the Reds' midfield alongside England's captain Bryan Robson, the long-serving skipper of the United side, and Neil Webb, another new recruit to the Old Trafford cause. In his first campaign with the Manchester Reds, they won the FA Cup, beating Crystal Palace 1–0 in a replay at Wembley following a 3–3 draw.

As Robson's career wound down, Ince became the fulcrum of the United midfield, with snapping tackles, raking passes and some terrifically hit shots, though he was not a prolific goalscorer. He won his second winners' medal when Ferguson's furies defeated Barcelona in the final of the European Cup Winners' Cup in Rotterdam in 1991 and received his third a year later when his team overcame Nottingham Forest in the 1992 League Cup final.

Ince made his debut for the full England team in September of that year in a friendly match against Spain in Santander. England lost 1–0 but Ince proved a success.

Paul helped Manchester United win the inaugural 1992–93 Premiership, their first League title for 26 years. Ince completed his domestic medal set just three years after arriving at Old Trafford. He made history during England's summer tour of the USA when, in a game against the host nation, he became England's first black captain. Unfortunately England lost 2–0.

Manchester United continued to dominate the domestic game and Ince was the midfield general in the side which won the Premiership and FA Cup double in 1994. Paul was the United Player of the Year.

A year later, Ince endured the chants of '*JUDAS*' when Manchester United travelled to Upton Park on the last day of the season, needing a win to reclaim their Premiership crown, but the main media talking point surrounded the torrent of abuse he received from large sections of the crowd. The Irons got the draw and gave the title to Blackburn Rovers.

Ince was again in the United side for the FA Cup final won by Everton. The double winners of the previous season became the double losers. This capped something of a calamitous season for Paul. It was the term that Manchester United's temperamental French striker Eric Cantona received a prison sentence (later commuted to a community service order on appeal) following his attack on a Crystal Palace supporter who had chanted abuse at him following his sending off for a foul. Ince was deemed to have got involved in the aftermath and was charged with common assault. He was acquitted after a trial.

Paul's abilities as a player were, at this stage, at their peak but Ferguson sold him in the summer of 1995 to Inter Milan for £8 million. Stories had emerged that Ince had been insisting he was called the 'Guv'nor' by the other players (Paul later said it was a phase which went over the top). After selling Ince, Ferguson labelled the cockney who had helped make United a dominant force in English and European football a 'big-time Charlie'. Ince had played 278 games for United, scoring 28 goals. He was later to regret that his time at Old Trafford had ended on a sour note.

Ince almost quit Italy soon after arriving following racist abuse from Cremonese supporters. But he continued at the San Siro for two years. I saw him play several times for Inter and the whole team moved around him; he was central both in terms of the play and the very spirit of the side. Although he became an even better player technically during his time on the continent and declared his love for Inter Milan, the team's home fans and the Italian lifestyle, he won nothing in his 54 Serie A games; he scored nine goals for Inter.

When Euro 96 got under way, Ince was in the England team as the midfield ball winner and got the label of 'Gazza's minder'. He was given the job of creating room for Paul Gascoigne's natural ball skills. Paul was to name Gascoigne as the best player he'd ever played with, saying he had everything and that he was 'amazing'. In the semi-final against Germany, Ince was consigned to play at right-back to cover for the suspended Gary Neville. He and England played well but could only manage a 1–1 draw and lost the penalty shoot-out. Paul was criticised for not taking a penalty (the crucial missed kick from Gareth Southgate was England's sixth) and for spending the whole shoot-out sitting down in the centre circle with his back to goal.

Glenn Hoddle took over the England job and Ince played in the five crucial qualifiers for the 1998 World Cup in France. During the first of these games against Moldova in Chisinau, a famous photograph of Ince was taken as he tried to climb a wall at the stadium, only for Gascoigne to pull his tracksuit trousers down, revealing Ince's bare buttocks in front of a mass of cameras.

Paul was a central part of England's bid to make the 1998 World Cup finals and it came down to a need to avoid losing against Italy in Rome. Matching the courage and determination that Terry Butcher had shown against Sweden seven years earlier, by the end of the game Ince's white England shirt was dyed red with his own blood, following a deep cut to his head. The game ended goalless and England qualified.

By now, Ince was once more playing his football in England, having left Internazionale so that his son Thomas, who was almost five, could attend an English school. Paul joined Liverpool for a fee in excess of £4 million. It was a move which surprised many because of the long history of rivalry between Manchester United and Liverpool; few players had ever plied their trade with both clubs during their careers. But he was appointed captain, and wasted no time making himself indispensable to the team.

PAUL EMERSON CARLYLE INCE

Ince kept his England place for the World Cup, winning his 40th cap in the opening group game against Tunisia in Marseille. England got through the group but were sent home after the second round following defeat by Argentina, again after a penalty shoot-out. This time Paul did take a penalty but saw it saved.

Paul's second season with Liverpool was once more devoid of honours but he achieved a personal high point when he scored a late equaliser against Manchester United at Anfield and celebrated with some ferocity in front of the Kop. However, in the summer of 1999, Liverpool coach Gerard Houllier told Ince he was surplus to requirements and, after 95 League and Cup appearances and 17 goals, Paul joined Middlesbrough for £1 million. Although past his peak, he played in all England's games in the 2000 European Championships in Holland and Belgium. Immediately after the tournament Paul retired from international football. He had won 53 caps; he had scored just two goals for his country, both against San Marino.

Ince was a tower of strength in Middlesbrough's midfield, making exactly 100 League appearances for the Teessiders and 13 Cup appearances – he netted nine times for the men from Riverside. After three seasons Paul was given a free transfer in 2002. He joined Wolverhampton Wanderers, playing outside the top flight of English football (excluding his time in Italy) for the first time since his one brief appearance for West Ham in 1989. Before Wolves showed interest he didn't have a club and thought that might be the end of his career. He signed a one-year contract but he couldn't prevent his former club West Ham inflicting a grievous 3–1 defeat in the fourth round of the 2003–04 FA Cup at Molineux, but Paul was in the Wolves team which instantly won promotion to the Premiership in his first season with the club, although they were relegated straight back again in 2004.

In January 2005, Paul, as skipper of the Wolves side, got the third goal in a 4–2 Championship win over the Hammers.

Expected to retire in 2005, Ince played out the season but the arrival as manager of his former England coach Glenn Hoddle midway through the campaign prompted a change of heart. In June of that year, he signed a new one-year contract with Wolves and continued to play for the club.

Paul Ince was one of the most talented young players ever produced by West Ham. In 2003, he was placed 95th in a BBC poll to name 100 Great Black Britons, showing him to be a respected and popular figure in British culture.

JUSTINUS SONI FASHANU

HAMMERS DEBUT: 22/11/89

'If you've got life too easy, you don't learn how to be strong.'

Born 19 February 1961, Justin was the son of a Nigerian lawyer. His mother was a nurse from Guyana. He and his brother John, who played for the Premiership Wimbledon side of the late 90s, were fostered by an English couple, an engineer and music teacher. In 1981, Justin was the first million-pound black football player when he moved from Norwich to Brian Clough's Nottingham Forest. He was later the first professional footballer to come out as Gay, displaying a courage that drew many admirers. The *News of the World* blasted the front-page headline 'I'M GAY', close to the end of his playing career; he was paid £80,000 for the story.

When I was three years old, I went to Dr Barnardo's. My dad left my mother and with five children to support she just couldn't cope. I was six when me and my brother John were fostered by Alf and Betty Jackson and we were brought up in Attleborough, Norfolk. I went to school there. I took to football because I was a fast runner. I wasn't particularly skilful, but I could run with the ball and hold on to it. I never did anything that was too hard for me. I always needed an immediate pay-off for what I did.

I was the only black kid in all the school and schoolteachers were all white. Everybody bar the PE teacher hated me playing football, even my foster parents; academic achievement came first. Their natural children had done well and qualified academically. Tennis was the only sport they got involved with. But John and me were into sport. When

83

THE BLACK HAMMERS

I was punished I'd be stopped from playing football. But the PE teacher seemed to have some belief in me and I got on with him.

I don't think all that did me any harm. It made me more independent. Of course I wanted my mum and dad to come and watch me play like other people; I had no one to guide me in that respect. But by the time I was 13 or so I'd learned to be guided only by people who I thought knew something about the game. I had learned to be careful. I was always suspicious that people were trying to con me. I don't really know why I felt like that.

I literally sold myself to Norwich. As a teenager I was always down the training ground. When I was 14, they gave me an apprenticeship. I was convinced I had a future in the game. I was still at school and the local papers gave me a lot of coverage, saying that I would go right to the top. I suppose that affected me. But my first love was boxing. I was a double ABA junior finalist. At around 16 I didn't know if I wanted to box or play football. I wanted to be a professional boxer but I decided to stick with football for a year and go on to box. I carried on boxing, going down a London gym but things happen so fast in football. By 17 I was playing first-team football. I made my debut in 1979. I went on to play for England Youth and the Under-21s. I got Match of the Day's goal of the season in 1980. So by then it didn't make sense to jack it.

I got on well with supporters in Norwich but outside Norwich I got some stick. But I'd turn on players at times if they had a go at me. A lot of footballers are pretty cowardly and I suppose they used to think twice before they said anything to me and that helped me. It had to be like that or I'd have been slaughtered. So, you can use these kind of experiences. They can be good for you. If you've taken it, it has made you stronger. It's no good to have it easy all the time. When trouble comes along, you don't know how to cope. If I was to get a bad injury that stopped me playing I'd be sick, but it wouldn't be devastating for me. I can always earn a living. There's more to life than football and more to me. I don't like to owe anyone anything. I like to be in charge of myself. Confidence in your own ability is so important. For me being black is a good thing. Because of that fact I've had to survive some tough times. That's been good for me. It's made me stand up for and look after myself. There's a lot of people making black people out to be victims, incapable of looking after themselves, saying that white people have to look after them. Black people need to be careful of listening to all that. It can make them very reliant on other people's definition of them.

Perhaps I was a bit sheltered in Norfolk but I never saw my colour as a disadvantage. I never thought about it making any difference. The first time I thought anything of it was when I was involved in a trial. A scout said, 'I'm interested in the coloured lad.' That was the first time I realised that I might be thought of as anything other than my name. In my early days with Norwich I took some stick from other players, but, at the end of the day, colour doesn't matter. If you've got a strong character, that kind of personality that wants to make it, you will. It might be difficult and there'll be hard times, but you'll make it. I know it can be bloody hard, but you've got to bounce back and do the business. There are black people who use being black as an excuse, but that don't make them stronger. At the end of the day, it's the strongest that survive. Maybe that's a good thing.

When you're black, living in a small place that is mostly white and you've got a bit of style, then that's an advantage. It was the same for Garth Crooks. If you can be just a little bit clever, stand out, but not too much, it can help you. People in the know like originality. If you look good and are polite to people, show them you're not stupid, you get on well. You have to have a little bit of something about you, something special. I'm not a crawler, but I haven't gone steaming in unless I've had to. I've tried not to give people the opportunity to dislike me.

I've been told that I lack stamina, that I've got no bottle, but that kind of thing has made me stronger. Hundreds of years of suffering has made black people stronger, tougher. If you've got life too easy, you don't learn how to be strong. If you experience problems, you learn to come back.

My career went on the rocks following a serious knee injury and when people started to know about my sexuality. It was in Nottingham that I first became active on the Gay scene. When I was with Norwich I was in a heterosexual relationship but I got into Nottingham's Gay scene. When word got to Brian Clough, I was suspended. It was then *that I found out just how narrow-minded professional football is. It's a business. You put your head over the barricades and you get it shot off. I still turned up for training, but Brian Clough had the police escort me from the premises. After a loan spell with Southampton in 1982 I went to Notts County. Howard Wilkinson was very understanding, but the knee worsened.*

After a time at Brighton I went to the United States, then Canada and played for Edmonton. I hoped to continue playing there, running a Gay bar at the same time. But that didn't work out and I came back to England in 1989. I had a short spell at Manchester City before coming to West Ham. Although I wasn't at Upton Park long, everyone was decent to me, the crowd, the players and the coaching staff. I made my debut coming on as a substitute in the last quarter of an hour against Wimbledon in the Littlewoods Cup at Upton Park [22 November 1989], and started matches against Blackburn and at home against Stoke. Everyone at West Ham was good. I'd like to have done better for them and stayed a while.

Justin had set up businesses in Glasgow and went to Los Angeles but without success. After short periods with Orient and Newcastle, he spent a couple of seasons with Torquay, making 41 appearances and scoring 15 goals. After moving to Scotland, he spent a brief time with Airdrie before joining Hearts. After 11 outings the Edinburgh club sacked him in 1994. He'd made 298 appearances in British League football and scored 84 goals.

Justin moved to the USA. Having become a born–again Christian, he managed to find work in Ellicot City coaching the Maryland Mania Club, a new professional team. In 1998, Justin was (apparently maliciously and wrongly) accused of sexually assaulting a 17-year-old male. He was fired from his job before details of the scandal were disclosed. He went back to London where, on 2 May, he hanged himself from the rafters of a lock-up garage under a bridge in Shoreditch, East London. He had mistakenly believed he was wanted by US police on sex charges. He left a suicide note saying he would not get a fair trial.

At the inquest into the death of Justin Fashanu the Coroner for

JUSTINUS SONI FASHANU

Poplar, Dr Stephen Ming Chan, said, 'This was a very tragic end for a man who had become a fallen hero, but in the eyes of many, was a man who succeeded in life against tremendous odds ... He appeared to have triumphed over his disruptive upbringing and in the face of prejudice against his colour and particularly against his sexual preference. Sadly, in the end, he felt overwhelmed by these pressures.'

Friends and family told the inquest that Fashanu had seemed happy and confident on the day of his death. A doctor said the player had not been under the influence of drink or drugs. His brother John spoke to the press after the inquest. He said, 'We are glad it's all over. We are just very happy that Justin can now rest in peace.'

Justin had certainly tried to fit in, but he had never compromised. This perhaps is the reason why the list of clubs he served is so long and diverse:

1978–81: Norwich City
1981–82: Nottingham Forest
1982: Southampton, on loan
1982–85: Notts County
1985: Brighton and Hove Albion
1989: Manchester City
1989: West Ham United
1990: Leyton Orient
1991–93: Torquay United
1993: Airdrieonians
1993: Heart of Midlothian

In his short time (one month on loan) at Upton Park during 1989, under the management of Lou Macari, he played two Division Two games and a League Cup tie, but that both club and fans treated him with respect is a testament to West Ham and its supporters.

Justin Fashanu was a trailblazer as Britain's first million-pound black footballer, and the first (and only) professional player in Britain to come out as Gay. Despite all the rejection he endured, he had a remarkable, praiseworthy capacity for forgiveness. Talking of the hurt inflicted on him by others, and acknowledging his own errors of judgement, Fashanu wrote in 1994:

I don't think you ever forget those mistakes, or the mistakes that other people make that wound you, but it is important to forgive.

LEROY DE GRAFT ROSENIOR

HAMMERS DEBUT: 19/3/88

'With your back to the wall, you can only go forward, and you can only go forward by being strong and focused.'

I first met with Leroy while he was working for Bristol City. A powerful and influential striker, particularly strong in the air, Leroy was born in Balham, London, on 24 August 1964. He began his career with Fulham in 1982, making his League debut for the Cottagers at Leicester City (4 December 1982). He played 54 League games, scoring 15 goals, before moving to Queens Park Rangers for £50,000 in the summer of 1985. He made 38 League (scoring eight goals) and nine Cup appearances (twice hitting the net), before returning to Craven Cottage in 1987 for another 30 matches in Division Three, scoring 20 goals. A transfer fee of £275,000 took Rosenior to Upton Park, where he made his debut on 19 March 1988. The following season 'Rosie', as he was christened by Hammers fans, became West Ham's top scorer with 15 goals. He left the Boleyn Ground in 1992 having found the net 19 times in 65 first-team games, but he created many more goals than he scored.

An England Schoolboy, Youth and Under-21 player before he came to Upton Park, Leroy has been praised for speaking openly about the racism that he experienced as a player and a manager. He has said that there is a 'glass ceiling' holding back qualified black coaches from getting the top jobs.

I went to the Fulham training on the Friday, got a phone call to say that John Lyall was interested. West Ham offered me a deal. I went straight over to Chadwell Heath. I think it took me about 20 minutes to agree the deal. When I saw John I just wanted to play for West Ham because I thought they played great football and I could learn a lot. I didn't even talk money.

I liked John. He was brilliant. John Lyall was the one who influenced me the most in wanting to go on and coach. He was the calmest of people. He was the one manager I learned the most from. All the time I was at West Ham he never told me to do anything. He'd always just make suggestions and let you find out for yourself. He was a very, very clever man. He was way ahead of his time in terms of football – how to play the game and how to get the best out of players. We all respected him. I can't remember him raising his voice more than once or twice. He always wanted to get his point across. What I find today is that you'll say things to players and you'll say, 'Do you understand?' and they'll say, 'Yeah', but they don't. But John always made it very clear. He'd never tell you, he'd just make an analogy. 'What if you did this … or that?' It got you to learn very quick.

The silliest thing West Ham did was to sack John Lyall. I was devastated. It was hard to believe. I don't think anyone was really sure why he was sacked and I don't even now. West Ham just went downhill after he'd gone. He was the best manager I played under. He had a fantastic manner and all the players liked him, as well as the wives and all our kids. He was able to treat you with respect as well as be a father figure. You had to go through the gym to get to the player's bar and the kids would be there, warming up with the players before games. There was a relaxed atmosphere because John wanted us to go and play football in a relaxed way. He was one of the best teachers I've seen; no, the best. He'd put you in situations and you'd learn things without knowing. He influenced me as a coach … given what he did for the club, rather than sack him he should have been made life president, although he might not have wanted that.

John was the biggest influence on the way I manage. I didn't realise how good he was when I was playing. I suppose we took him for granted. But everything he said and did made sense; players need to be told things in a way they can understand and see work on the pitch. The way he got his teams to play was amazing and he got the best out of his players.

LEROY DE GRAFT ROSENIOR

I was playing at Upton Park the day after I was signed ... we were up against Watford in a relegation battle.

The Hammers had won just one in 10 games and were 15th in the League before the game with Graham Taylor's Watford. The Hornets were also in need of points.

I was in the dressing room, I met the lads; I only knew Tony Gale, I'd played with him at Fulham. I played and after an hour scored the winner on my debut.

We stayed up that year ... The next season I played up front. We had a fairly successful season, even though we were fighting against relegation. We got to the quarter-final of the Cup. I got the winner at Highbury, in the replay of the third round. Liam Brady got the ball on Tony Adams's head. I took a chance and let it drop before nodding it back towards the other corner. It took ages to go in. I celebrated by running towards the Arsenal supporters! I hadn't meant to. I kind of got lost in the moment. It felt great to beat 'em on their own ground. Arsenal had never been my favourite team [laughs]. The FA Cup's about staying strong and we did.

We got to the semi-final of the League Cup. I remember going down the Mile End Road and getting caught in traffic before the semi-final. I had to jump off and a bloke on a motorbike gave me a lift into the ground. I picked up the injury in the run-up to the semi against Luton and it was niggling most of the time. I had a cartilage operation. I was desperate to play and the club was desperate for me to play. So I was back within a week after the operation. I played against Luton but we lost 3–0 at home. After that game I went back into hospital and had another cartilage operation. At that time we were again battling against relegation, so what used to happen was that I'd train on a Friday and play on a Saturday and my knee would blow up and I'd have to try and get it down. The doctor said it wouldn't be a problem; just it would maybe need cleaning out at the end of the season. But I kept on scoring, we had to keep winning.

I was the club's top scorer [15] in my first full season. For about 10 games I kept on going out and my knee just kept on swelling up. The knee was drained. I was in agony at times. I was having painkilling injections, but I kept playing, but I was limping at points and wearing loads of strapping. But I was scoring goals, we were winning, and we really thought we could stay up. I was prepared to do that because the doctor said that it wasn't doing it any harm. We went to the last game at Liverpool. We needed to win to stay up. It was 1–0, then I equalised with a header. It was 1–1. We ended up losing that game 4–1. It was during that game that the knee finally went for good. I heard it crack.

I went into hospital a few days after that and they opened my knee up. I thought it would be just for a clean-out and get ready for next season. The anaesthetist came in to see me and told me, 'You can't play football any more because you've got a hole the size of a 50p piece in your knee.' So, I was a bit devastated by that because people had told me that my knee was fine and that I'd be able to play on. I couldn't accept a payout as neither the club nor me was insured. I was upset, but determined to get back. I was only 25 and so of course I wanted to play again.

It took me more than 18 months to get back. But I wasn't the same. I was bitter for a time. Coming back too early after injury wouldn't happen now. I think I was fortunate to play and get goals at the top level. Players are privileged and sometimes that slips their minds.

I had three-and-a-half years on my contract and that's why I decided to give it a go and try and get fit. Although I played a few more games, I wasn't as mobile. I had to learn to run differently. In September 1990 I went on loan to Fulham and then Charlton [November 1991] and I went to Metz in France for a week. I could have gone there but I didn't fancy it. The last time I played in a West Ham shirt was when I came on as sub at Nottingham Forest [28 September 1991]. I left the club after four years.

In March 1992 I went to Bristol City as player/coach. I think I scored eight in 42 League games during 1992–93. We finished 15th in the old First Division. I got a hat-trick in a 4–1 win over Brentford on the last day of the season! They were the last goals I'd score in the Football League, but I made a couple of starts in 1993–94 and came on as sub four times. I had wanted to coach and I got my opportunity in 1993. Russell Osman became the manager and I got a job as reserve team manager ... played for them at centre-half now and then for a couple of years. I worked with the kids, learning all the time.

LEROY DE GRAFT ROSENIOR

I was made redundant from Bristol City so I went and played for a mate at Fleet Town for a few months. Then I got the manager's job at Gloucester City. We got to the semi-final of the FA Trophy, it was great. I left because of the money.

I was asked to come to Bristol City, I was sort of headhunted, to take on the job as the academy assistant director. I did the 17s down to the eight-year-olds. I still wanted to manage.

You went through barriers when you was a player, this is another barrier. There's a lot of talented black people out there. I think I'm quite good at the job I do. I think that being black and being quite young is difficult as well. It's an experienced man's game. Yeah, I wanted to be a manager at the right time. I did jobs to get the experience, to get it on the CV. It's difficult. It was always gonna be harder for me than it is for the players coming out of the Premier League. I've had my full coaching badge for around 15 years and I've got a lot of experience behind me. I think you get opportunities if you work hard enough.

My dad was an electrician. My mum worked in the post office. They were both from Sierra Leone. They came over in the 50s. I've got four elder sisters. I was spoiled rotten [smiles]. *I played once for Sierra Leone in a 1994 African Cup of Nations qualifier against Guinea. The game was one of my best experiences in football. Knee trouble restricted my appearances. Playing in that game against Guinea was a fantastic experience. I got a tremendous welcome from my people even though the match ended goalless.*

I'm separated. I've got two boys. Liam was with the academy at Bristol City. He spent some time with West Ham with Glenn Roeder. I think they were interested in him but couldn't agree a fee with Bristol City. He went back to Ashton Gate.[1] Daron, he plays rugby for Bristol Under-19s.

At school I was into cricket in a big way. I was a wicket keeper. I played for London Schools. When I finished school I didn't really want to go to work so I thought I'd do some A levels, if I'm honest that's the reason why [smiles]. *Up to then I used to play football for fun. Then*

---

[1] Liam spent some time on loan with Torquay and is now a regular first-team player with Fulham.

93

THE BLACK HAMMERS

I started playing for London Schools, England Under-18s. I was playing for London Schools against Fulham up at Bisham Abbey sports ground. A Chelsea guy left his card with a friend. The Fulham scout waited for me after the game and said, 'Would you like to come up and have a trial with us?' I thought it was a bit arrogant of the Chelsea guy to just leave his card, wanted me to ring him, so I went to Fulham. Malcolm Macdonald was the manager there. After a month I signed pro forms.

I'd been a Man United supporter [laughs] but keep that quiet, because my family were always Man United; Lou Macari, Gordon Hill, Jimmy Greenoff. I used to like watching Jimmy Greenoff, Martin Buchan, that team. The players who were most influential for me I suppose were Laurie Cunningham, Cyril Regis and Brendon Batson. They were some of the first black players to make it big.

At West Ham Liam Brady had an impact on me. He came in at I suppose the end of his career, but he was just pure class and in that respect the best player I played with at Upton Park. The one I liked best was Mark Ward. He was a great crosser of a ball and could put it just where I wanted it.

I gave effort and I expected everyone to give the same effort. You should come off of the pitch in pain through the amount of effort you put in. That is the only way I felt satisfied; that I'd done what I had to do. I was strong and I was quick but I think I was quite intelligent and had a nice touch as well.

But the team we had … Alan Devonshire and Alvin Martin; Julian Dicks joined at the same time as me, he should have been an England player; Paul Ince was just a young lad; Ray Stewart; Phil Parkes, he'd have a little tot of whisky or rum immediately before a game. Tony Gale was a much underrated player. It was just a team of footballers. I was close to Paul Hilton, Georgie Parris and Stuart Robson.

In November '88, I think it was in the Zenith Data Cup, against West Brom, I scored four. One was a real cracker. But it's the Chelsea game that stands out in my mind. We needed to win to stay up. It was the last home game of the season. They needed to win to stay up. I got two goals then I got sent off because Steve Clarke kicked me off the ball and I grabbed him round the throat. But we ended up winning and we stayed up and Chelsea went down. He deserved it! [laughs] *It ruined things a bit, but I got the biggest cheer I can remember when the crowd saw that I'd been sent off. I was feeling that I had let everyone down, but the supporters were just great, they were always great to me. West Ham is the best place to ever play football.*

In the 1988–89 season, I got the injury and we were relegated. Lou Macari came in around that time. He'd done well at Swindon. I'm not sure he had much of an idea about the culture at West Ham. He had his own ideas of course. He thought the players should be fitter without the ball, but at the time West Ham had players who were sharp with the ball. He tried to change the attitude but didn't work. To be fair, he had other problems that probably distracted him. He wasn't helped of course when Paul [Ince] put on that United shirt [smiles]. *I think most people were disappointed about that. It certainly wasn't the cleverest thing to do. I think he regrets what happened, and he was young at the time and probably he should have been advised better by those handling the situation.*

Although we got relegated and I'd got a very bad knee ... the thing that stands out in my mind that year is that we went to Hillsborough, with about three games to go. It was the first game after the disaster. After all these years I just remember the fences being covered with flowers. What I went through with injury stood me in good stead as a manager, managing people. But it also made me a better person.

I lived in South London while I was with West Ham. That's where I was brought up, so I always lived there. I was brought up, just down the road from Brixton. The friends I had then are those I've still got now. But when I went to West Ham I was West Ham through and through and the way they treated me was tremendous. You pull the shirt on and that is it. I played with West Ham with my heart and I think people appreciated that.

I've never been the type to be like a superstar. Turn up in stretch limousines. When they used to have the parties down at the Apollo [a steak-house in Stratford, East London], *I used to get the bus. Frank* [McAvennie] *used to turn up with the likes of Page 3 girl Jenny Blythe and the rest of the Page 3 girls.*

It never occurred to me that I was something of a pioneer [laughs].

THE BLACK HAMMERS

If you're a black footballer, you know they're going on about all this stuff about racism in football, and people calling you names and stuff like that, but if you're comfortable with yourself it doesn't bother you. Whether they call you 'black bastard', or call you this or that, it doesn't really matter. I think it's if you're uncomfortable with yourself and they call you a 'black' this, and you react to that, then I start to worry. When people say they're going to take you to court and stuff like that, it means that in themselves they're insecure, in what they are. Now, I've always been secure in what I am. I am black, and so if I ran out on the pitch I think the first thing that people notice about me is that I am black, big and black. And so I mean, if they didn't see that, they'd be lacking in intelligence really. I always say I played with Sam [Lee], and Sam used to get more stick than me, you know, 'He's short, he's round, he bounces off the ground', and it was just something that supporters did. So, no, it didn't matter to me that I was — it still doesn't matter to me that I am — black. I am proud to be what I am. I'm black, and I've got a cockney accent, and my name's Leroy. You know, a lot of people say I haven't got a lot going for me, but you use what you've got to your advantage. What it did do for me was it made me stand out from people. You have to get things in perspective.

But, although it is not as bad as it was, there are still problems. I've been prevented from going into boardrooms because people didn't believe I was the manager. Is that racism or ignorance? I've been told I'm the top black manager in English football. That's shocking, given all the great black footballers there have been, and the good black coaches that are around. The likes of Cyril Regis, Luther Blissett and Viv Anderson are not even involved in the playing side of the game and that is ridiculous. So, if I can make a success in management, it shows black footballers can coach and perhaps that will mean others might be given the opportunity to prove themselves. But I don't see myself as representing black people; I say that young coaches should be given a chance.

What I've been through has made me the person I am. Value who you are and a lot of what you thought were problems are in fact not problems at all; they are other people's problems.

If you're on the other side and you was black, you'd get it horrendously. You'd get the old monkey stuff; I've been to Portsmouth and had bananas thrown at me and things like that. I've ate them. We were told by the FA to do that, to defuse the situation. 'It will defuse the situation.' Right! OK! I was hungry at times as well [laughs]. I'd say, 'Give me more!'

It's bound to happen with other supporters. But that's something other supporters do, but they do it to all players. They don't just say, 'Right he's black, we're going to have a go at him today,' do they? They say, 'Right, he's playing for Sheffield Wednesday, you've got a Sheffield Wednesday shirt on, we'll go and have a go at him. What can we pick on? Oh, he's black. Oh, he's fat,' that's what football's about. But it's a motivator. When we went away it always used to motivate you. Oh, yeah! I loved all that [laughs]. I loved interacting with the crowd, during the games and stuff.

West Ham are my favourite club. I actually love the club. It's just a shame that behind the scenes I wasn't treated how I would expect to be treated. I go to West Ham and I see the coaching staff, Tony Carr. We just used to pass and move the ball about. They talk about how Man United move the ball, but we used to do that anyway all the time. It was just great. You just looked forward to playing at Upton Park. It was just fun, every day was fun.

West Ham has got a culture that not a lot of other clubs have got. It's about the way the game should be played, about the way people should be treated. It is a family club West Ham. West Ham is very close to real life and the crowd were so close to the pitch. I can understand how players go there and want to try.

John Lyall was always big on loyalty and finishing what you have started and I have stayed true to that as well in everything I have done from the time I left West Ham. I learned many things there that will stay with me for the rest of my life. It was a special time in my life and a unique place. Unless you have played for West Ham you can't grasp how special it is.

I got on well with the fans; the best fans in the country! People have said it was a racist club, but it's got nothing to do with racism. If you're one of their own, if you give 100 per cent, that's all they care about. So, if you went out and were prepared to give it your best shot, they'd support yer. Even if you had a nightmare. They didn't care as long as you tried.

In the 1991 FA Cup semi-final, when Tony Gale got sent off at Nottingham Forest, I wasn't involved, but I just went and joined in, it's that sort of club. 'Billy Bonds claret and blue army!' From the first minute to the last minute and they didn't stop, not even at half-time. For two hours they just sang right through. I never ever heard the likes of that. You know, you usually have a little break, but they didn't stop. They just kept going and going and that just typified them [West Ham lost 4–0].

I was called 'Sydney' after Sydney Poitier. I'm quite pleased because he's really handsome [laughs]. I played at Wembley for QPR in 1986, but at Upton Park, especially at evening games, we had some great matches and the atmosphere the fans created was electric. The way we played as well and the players we had, playing was a pleasure – you'd look forward it. My abiding memory of West Ham was just the supporters … all they were interested in was you playing well and them being entertained. That's why people like Di Canio go down well at West Ham. The culture at West Ham will never change. They wanted to win as well, but they want to see a good game of football first and foremost. That's a culture that they've got and they should be proud of it. We were down near the relegation zone but the fans didn't mind because they would rather us lose 4–3 than us be halfway up the table and have a 0–0 draw. I think if I'd have stayed fit I might have stayed at West Ham a long time. But I didn't stay fit, but that's life. One day I'd like to be back involved with them. I'd love to manage West Ham. It is a fantastic club. The West Ham result is the first I look for.

I think the supporters at West Ham knew I cared and I think they valued what I did because of that. I used to love scoring a goal at Upton Park because they appreciated it. I've got a picture at home and it shows me scoring a goal, and I look at it and it's got about a thousand people in the background and you can see their faces. And I loved scoring a goal, 'cause I loved it when they used to shout my name. They used to go, 'Leeeroy! Leeeroy!' and it used to ring out. It was like church bells!

Of course, Billy Bonds is a West Ham legend. He was still amazing at 41. Billy could have been a professional in any sport. He was awesomely fit and a real athlete. He got the club back where it should have been before John Lyall was sacked. I got on well with Bill when we played together. But I think I was a bit of a nuisance to him when he was manager. It's hard trying to get back after injury. I wanted to play but Billy saw I wasn't fit. He decided to let me go. I was young and made my mind up that he didn't know what he was doing. But now I can say he was right. I have total respect for Bill. We always stop for a chat when we meet. He deserves my apologies for some of the grief I gave him.

When Tony Pulis left Bristol City Leroy took over the management of the club alongside Tony Fawthrop and David Burnside; they won 'Manager of the Month' award in February 2000. He later became the first-team coach under ex-Barnsley and Sheffield Wednesday boss Danny Wilson. In December 2001 Leroy took charge of Merthyr Tydfil, but within a few months he accepted the massive challenge of attempting to revive the hopes of struggling Torquay United in the lowest reaches of Division Three. At the time he was one of only three black managers in the English game (Keith Curie was in charge of Mansfield Town and Keith Alexander was with Lincoln City). He had applied for the job previously, along with a number of other posts, and, although having gained experience at every level in the lower reaches of the game, Rosenior had found it hard to get employment. He recalled,

After I stopped playing, I wanted to be the first black football manager. I applied for jobs and people said I didn't have the experience, but I'd coached at Bristol City, managed a non-League club and in Division Two of the Football League.

But Leroy not only as good as saved the Gulls from being condemned to the realm of non-League football, in May 2004 he also led them to promotion to the newly named League One, just two years after almost slipping out of the Football League completely.

Rosenior left the Plainmoor hot seat in the wake of United's 3–1 home defeat by Rochdale in which the Gulls slumped back into the bottom two of League Two in January 2006.

Leroy had taken the side out of Division Three in 2004, making a little bit of history for Torquay; although the club had been in the division before, it was always the old Division Two, and, because of the restructuring of the Football League in 2004, it was the first time Torquay had ever been able to claim: 'We're in League One.' But the sale of star forward David Graham to Wigan for £215,000 showed the club's lack of ambition and in the new environment Leroy was obliged to continue the battle against the odds. The Gulls were relegated on goal difference at the end of the 2004–05 term. Rosenior had been fighting against the odds for three-and-a-half years. In the end the club were just not equipped to move on and so he moved on without them

Leroy worked for radio as an analyst and commentator and was linked with managing Sierra Leone. He commented,

> *I want to help get Sierra Leone back on its football feet after several years of political turmoil ... But I want to be asked and there's got to be a right situation to move the team forward ... Playing for Sierra Leone was an occasion I will never forget, and that is why I want to manage the team and take them to the World Cup.*

It looked like Rosenior might become only the fourth West Ham player to manage an international side but on 14 June 2006 Leroy took over as manager of Brentford, replacing another former Hammer, Martin Allen, who had resigned after two relatively successful but frustrating years with the club.

MATTHEW JAMES RUSH

HAMMERS DEBUT: 6/10/90

'I can't stand people that let life pass them by, always complaining and moaning ... there's always an excuse ... "Well, this is why this is happening to me." Well, no! The reason it's happening to you is because of you!'

I met with Matthew in Wapping. Known as a good–looking player in his heyday at West Ham, he is still a handsome man, fit and with a wry sense of humour that is enhanced by a mischievous glint in his eye and a way of answering questions with an intelligent wit and a playful smile.

I was born on 6 August 1971 in Dalston, Hackney. I moved to Silwood after about six months of being on this planet and at around the age of five to Deptford.

I captained Deptford Green School teams at football, cricket, basketball, athletics and even chess before the football scouts started knocking at my door during the mid-80s. There were the usual scouts doing the rounds and I looked at all the clubs – Arsenal, Spurs, Palace etc, but West Ham had the best atmosphere and environment. They had the training facilities, there was a genuine feeling. They made me feel more welcome than the others did.

After graduating through the schoolboy ranks at 16, I joined the club's YTS in July 1988. I signed professional in March 1990. At the time, turning professional was the best day of my life and a great day for my family. I signed a two-year contract for about £300 a week. Not great by today's standards but much better than YTS money, which was around £31 a week.

When I was growing up, from embryo right through to joining West

101

Ham, I never had any football influence at all, apart from playing for school and county level. No male role models, apart from my wayward brothers. I was one of the studious types. I'd come home, do my homework. I had every intention of going on and doing my A levels, and a degree and work like all my other friends did. I had a childhood dream of aviation, but no intention of playing football at all.

I was at West Ham with my twin brother Marcus; to the amusement of the coaches, we were always bickering and arguing. We'd turn up to training separately even though we probably got the same trains, we wouldn't walk together. We were both offered apprenticeships, but he didn't want to take it up. He was more involved in fashion. I have two older brothers, John who was born three years before me and [posh voice, with laugh] *Tim who was two when I was born. Timmy is the member of the family we don't like to talk about* [smiles]. *Brother John is involved with fashion like Marcus. He's been headhunted by various companies. He does marketing. Diesel tried to get hold of him. He's doing quite well. John was a good footballer, but he had a bad injury. I think he was at Palace and Southampton. He had a series of injuries and never quite made the grade. I never saw myself following Marcus and John* [laughs] *but I like shopping, that's about as close as it goes.*

My mum's from Ireland, 'a Paddy off the farm', that's why I played for Eire. My dad's Trinidadian. I got married to Caroline, my partner of 10 years, in June 1999. We've got Lana now, she was born in February 1997. We thought it would be nice if both parents had the same name [smiles]. *Lana's not interested in football* [smiling] *and she's especially not going to be interested in footballers* [laughs].

I went to school at Deptford Park, Deptford Green, and then a sixth-form consortium in Deptford. I was one of those kids that was good at everything, from chess to cricket. I did it all. Swimming, diving, long-distance running, sprinting. I was one of those horrible kids at school that was in all the top classes and captain of all the sports teams. I was West Ham's fastest sprinter [smiles] *but not any more, after 10 operations!* [Matthew went into the technical details of his surgical career. His knowledge and understanding was impressively thorough, losing me almost immediately.] *It was all focused on the right knee and included three reconstructions.*

MATTHEW JAMES RUSH

I had a pretty good school set-up. Deptford Green was a relatively new school. My school years were nothing but good in all different aspects, academic and sporting.

The youth academy director at West Ham was [as he still is] Tony Carr. Tony was strict, but good. At the time I had the odd complaint but, looking back, he helped me a lot and refused to give up on me. 'Rushie,' he'd say, 'if I pack up trying that's when you should begin to get worried!' He never stopped going on at me. When you're young you think, 'Leave off!' but later you say, 'He done the right thing to keep on at me.' I probably needed a kick up the arse because I was (and still am) well laidback.

Tony Gale used to give me a lift in from Rotherhithe Tunnel [smiles]. I was a late driver. Leroy [Rosenior] too later on. Leroy didn't endear himself to the crowd. I think he had a bit too much arrogance about him. Maybe his time at West Ham would have been better if he hadn't have been quite so arrogant.

My first appearance for West Ham came on 6 October 1990. I came on as a substitute in a Second Division game at Upton Park. West Ham crushed Hull 7−1. It was a memorable day. Bill [Bonds] had confidence in me and I understood that and it carried over into a match; with the old self-esteem boosted, you can go out and enjoy the game. I think it was 4−1 when I came on so it was a comfortable game for me to come into the side.

West Ham had a good team at the time; Frank McAvennie, the joker of the group but he was also ready to help young players a lot. Alvin Martin was fantastic with young players. His understanding of the game was boundless and he'd pass that on. He was team captain and took the responsibility seriously. Tony Gale was good for me too. Him and Alvin were about the same age. They were both class players, and couldn't help but boost young players psychologically. Fozzie [Colin Foster] was good at the back. You could be sure he'd win the ball in the air, leaving you to pick it up. Pottsy [Steve Potts] was 'Mr Reliable' in defence. John Moncur had a lot of ability; at times faultless distribution. Dicksey [Julian Dicks], on the left; he was a right-winger's dream − he'd have the ball and everyone would wonder what he was going to do. I'd be 50 yards from him and say to myself, 'I'd better make some space for myself.' I knew he'd ping it across field and it would be dead on my right foot. That would give me loads of time and space to run into. No one was better than Dicks in terms of distribution with his left foot.

I scored five goals for West Ham altogether. The first two came by way of headers from right-wing corners. The official records say Ian Bishop took them but I'm sure I was on the end of Julian Dicks's left-foot missiles. A good day for me and the team was 11 April 1992. We beat Norwich 4–0 at Upton Park. Alvin Martin was given the man of the match champagne, but he passed it on to me, feeling that I had done a magnificent job and that this should be acknowledged. I got on well with Alvin.

My last goal for West Ham came on 29 October 1994, the only Hammers goal in a 3–1 defeat at White Hart Lane. The reason I remember that one is because it was scored with my left foot, a rarity! It was just before half-time and put us level. I think it was a half-volley in the box. But most games just gel into one. I can't remember one from the other for the most part.

I was capable of losing my temper. I was sent off in the last 10 minutes of a reserve game with Swindon in April 1993 and was involved in a highly publicised training-ground punch-up with Alvin Martin. That started, unpredictably, when I tackled Alvin. Apart from leaving West Ham, one of the most disappointing things that ever happened to me at the club was that run-in with Alvin because he'd helped me a lot as a kid. Always encouraging and worked with me to improve me as a player. The press had a bit of a field day of course.

Although he wasn't an idol or anything (not big on idols), I had total respect for him. He had a great footballing brain; that was obvious in all the games he was involved in. Shortly after that, I left the club. He apologised to me personally and publicly and I really appreciated that. He's a big man in more ways than one.

I think that it's a shame if people fail to exploit the situation they're in, the place they find themselves. If you're given loads of time and money and notoriety, a small amount of fame, you should take advantage of it. I used to take groups of 12 people into the best nightclubs for free. I was treated really well. Having fun is all that life's about. If you're not having fun you should just give up. Most footballers don't earn millions of pounds. What they do earn they spend. I used to spend money at a phenomenal rate when I was playing. It was 12 years of mayhem — I was a social freak!

I played a couple of games in the Anglo-Italian Cup. In my first game in that competition, we went over to Italy and it was absolutely pouring down, torrential rain! And we played the game! You couldn't run with the ball because it was like playing in a shallow swimming pool. The next game against the Italians, at Upton Park, I was sent off. I got past the full-back, it was me and the goalkeeper, and he pulled me back. I snapped. I hit him, kicked him to the ground. The Italians came running after me. There's me standing there like some crazed imbecile, 'Come on then!' And then I complained because I got sent off. In retrospect I think what an idiot I was.

I had 52 games with West Ham; in the League I had 29 start appearances as a sub. Before leaving I went on loan to Cambridge in March 1993; I had 10 games with them. I also had a spell at Swansea at the start of 1994, 13 matches. That was a good loan period. That's when I renewed my contract at West Ham for three years.

In August 1995 I moved to Norwich of all places, for £330,000. I was Martin O'Neill's first signing. Norwich — inbred capital of the world! It was a tremendous wrench. I didn't realise how far away it was. I went back once to visit some friends, but it's still murder. It was just three days after I got there that my knee got injured. I was 16 months out of the game. Martin O'Neill left Carrow Road … Goodbye! [laughs]

I made just three substitute appearances for Norwich before being farmed out on loan to Third Division Northampton in October '96. I got four goals in 15 games and they wanted me to stay but couldn't raise the cash, then I moved to Oldham in March 1997 for £165,000, the manager there was Neil Warnock. He'd tried to sign me when he was with Notts County.

Oldham I hated anyway, but my wife's family all live up in Manchester and I was about to start a family, that was probably the reason I went. I'm a city guy. Manchester's OK, it's like a poor second to London and, my God, did the social life kick off in Manchester. I was there at the time of the city's regeneration. Bars, restaurants and hotels were opening. I was a football player and because I was injured for so long it was partying.

I played 30 games and scored three for Oldham before I retired from League football in September 1998. I got a cruciate ligament injury at Carlisle and the specialist advised me to stop. But I played in the Rymans League for Dulwich Hamlet from the summer of 1999 and in November 1999 moved on to Dagenham and Redbridge in the same league, but the state of my knee caused me to 're-retire' [smiles]. About a week after that I went to university, I studied sports science; got a BSc (Hons) in Applied Sports Science (Sports Development) from the University of East London in 2001. I had a great time at university but looked forward to using my skills in education.

I couldn't see myself as a manager of senior players, juggling the various personalities. Football players are adults in terms of the amount of years they've been alive, but that's it. Big-headed, arrogant, twisted and you've got to pander to them all the time. You can't upset them because they may have a bad game. You've got a squad of players with so many different types of personality to cater for. The stress and politics are not for me. I like straight talking so I don't want anything more than youth-team coaching.

On 8 May 2002, Matthew signed for Droylsden in the Unibond League. He was teaching PE at Gorton's Wright Robinson Sports College, South Manchester (as part of teacher training). The knee was fine and he kept fit and trained four days a week. He just wanted a kickabout and Droylsden was local. The Unibond is below Conference standard and Rush felt the same as ever and he was still at his playing weight. He decided to see how it went. It was a chance to get involved in dressing-room banter again, something he missed.

He enjoyed living in the North. His wife has a good job in PR, while their daughter settled at school. He moved to Maple Hall School in Stockport in the summer of 2002 and in November of that year Matthew joined Droylsden's Unibond League rivals Ashton United.

MATTHEW JAMES RUSH

I think I'm one of the few West Ham professionals to have played under four managers at Upton Park. John Lyall was always fair. But he was something of an institution at West Ham by the time I started.

The club was having problems following relegation from the old First Division in 1989. It was a bit of a shock when John Lyall got sacked in the summer. Lou Macari's appointment was a bit – what's the best way to put it? – 'contentious', but he didn't cause me any problems. John was great for West Ham. He was well respected and everybody was friendly with him but some thought he was a bit set in his ways and it was probably the case that he'd served his time and it was time for him to go.

The older players knew more about Lou, but as a young pro you say to yourself, 'Right! I got to get my head down and show this man what you can do.'

I got on really well with Lou and I think he liked the fact there was a physical side to the way I played. He was very straight talking; good or bad he'd let you know what he was thinking. That's what some people didn't like, although, me, I prefer to know where I stand. I don't really do the cloak and dagger stuff. John Lyall's man-management was probably better than Lou's because of the time he'd been at the club, but Lou was good. He rubbed some people up the wrong way, maybe because he had no previous links with the club.

Lou wasn't at the club long enough for me to build a strong relationship with him but I haven't anything bad to say about him. It was a shame he had to go.

I always respected Billy Bonds. He was youth-team manager when I first came to West Ham. I'd to stay behind and work with him after training, throwing medicine balls at each other, abdominal work, extra running, stuff like that. He was good for me, as my youth-team manager and when I was in the first team. He had faith in me and that gave me confidence in myself. If Billy had stayed, I would probably have never wanted to leave. I was happy at West Ham.

Billy Bonds's blood was claret and blue. No one would argue with that. I know he'd have happily seen his days out at West Ham. But he was offered the golden handshake and turned it down. With Bill there had to be a reason for that. Harry was his assistant. Bill was an

THE BLACK HAMMERS

inspiration to the players, and there was no one better to get them fit, strong and get their head right. Bill's finest quality was his honesty and there isn't a bad thing to say about him. Everyone has their opinions but pedigree and record was and is respected. For me he was brilliant and what happened to him was a real pity.

For Bill the politics was a problem. He wouldn't set out to just please the media or the board, or the players. He talked straight and you can't be that way with everyone, more's the pity; being honest didn't really fit in with the way things were. That was probably his undoing, but the way he was dealt with was pretty bad.

Before Bill left I had no desire to leave West Ham but when Harry took over I told Caroline I had an idea about his feelings about me, although I got my longest run of first-team football with Harry in 1994–95. I think I made 26 appearances before being sent back to the reserves. I think that had a lot to do with Harry wanting to put me in the shop window. He certainly didn't want me around on a permanent basis.

I'd just signed a new three-year contract under Bill. But when Harry took over I knew it wasn't going to be good for me. Perhaps I might have put on a front and pretended to be the sort of personality he wanted around. That might have got me in his good books. I could have taking up gambling, golf and drinking, but my personality probably worked against me.

Like everyone else, I was pleased with getting promotion in 1990–91 season, but this was followed by the supporters' protests over the bond scheme and relegation, and Harry Redknapp came along as assistant manager from Bournemouth in 1992. Harry Redknapp! Some people like him, others don't. What can I say? I left when Harry took over. I spent the entire 1992–93 promotion season on the sidelines. I didn't understand it. Harry was instrumental in keeping me out of the team, no doubt about it. I don't think I was his type of player and I'm not sure he warmed to my personality. I had a tendency to speak my mind a bit. At that point in my career I wanted to be more involved. But it wasn't happening. There were excuses; they were using a particular formation and so on. I had to accept this, still not being a senior player, so I kept on slogging away playing reserve-team football. I did get frustrated but I didn't show it in front of Harry. But I did OK in the reserves and got into the first team in time to help the club stay in the Premiership towards the end of 1993–94.

I had a rapport with Bill, I trusted him. Maybe it was the trust factor more than anything else with Harry. It was a real wrench when I left West Ham. The crowd were always cheering me on. The Chicken Run would sing 'You'll never catch the Rushie'. I was a bit of a crowd favourite down at the Chicken Run.

Harry didn't let me know Norwich were interested and what they were willing to pay. He just said stuff like, 'It would be a great move for you.' When it's put in that way, you know it's time to move.

It was a big disappointment. I'd been with West Ham since I was 13. But I don't want to blame people. I could say Harry hindered my progress, but, if I wasn't the kind of player he fancied, then that's the way it was.

Harry has called me 'an enigma'. Comments of that kind don't make you feel you're going to be in the team. It was hard to leave but I felt if I'd stayed I'd have been sat in the reserves.

I thought Bish [Ian Bishop] was a very good player. He was the playmaker. A lot of people knocked him. He had a bit of a down period when he promised not to drink [laughs]. That was his downfall. When he started drinking again he got back on form. I did like playing with Bish. Trevor Morley, in terms of playing with somebody, with him up front and me on the right wing, it was good. He wasn't particularly big, but he used his body well, held the ball up and he was a great feeder as well. You could play the ball up to him, move about a bit, then all of a sudden make a run and he'd still have the ball, ready to react to you. I liked playing with him.

Bish and Trevor were a laugh. I was about the only one at the club who didn't drink. Ian used me as a breathalyser. It was like when miners used canaries to detect fumes, he'd breathe on me to see if I fell over. Before training on the mornings he'd come up to me reeking of booze and say, 'Can you smell anything, Rushie?' I'd reply, 'Yes, Bish … don't go anywhere near the manager this morning 'cause you stink of alcohol!'

THE BLACK HAMMERS

The West Ham 'social scene' then was always 'lively', but for me, getting pissed with the boys never appealed. The social side was a bit problematic and some of the younger players got pulled along, wanting to be involved with the senior players. But I had a lot of interests outside football. I went to a few social things but I didn't drink or play golf, never have done, so that sort of killed the social side a bit, although there was part of me that didn't want to play up to the role of the stereotypical football player.

I respect people who do well in life; people that achieve things for themselves. I can't stand people that let life pass them by, always complaining and moaning. It just kills me, it really does. And there's always an excuse. They always throw in, 'Well, this is why this is happening to me.' Well no! The reason it's happening to you is because of you! I like people that have succeeded, that get on with things, rather than be miserable. Any of my friends will tell you, even though I was out for such long periods of time with career-threatening injuries, I was never miserable. Not with my friends and people around me. Otherwise they wouldn't be friends with me. I'd be on my own. I would have probably have been at my earning peak just a few years ago. I was in the Republic of Ireland 'B' squad at the time of my first major injury. I was an attractive, promising player at West Ham. Jack Charlton played me in his European Championship Under-21 side on two occasions in 1991–92.

Matthew laughed when talking about how Mike Small had compared him with the great Brazilian player Jairzinho.

No one quite knew where Mike Small came from. Mental capacity or what planet he was on. He was a funny bloke though. I'd like to agree with him, but I'd never seen Jairzinho play. I didn't know what other players were like. I'd say 'yeah, yeah' and pretend I knew what he was on about. I could've said, 'Who's he?' But that was my first response at the time.

I was a strong, fast right-winger. I wasn't a flair player. I had a fair touch, and fair control of the ball, but I wasn't a player as say Bishop was. I had good strength and amazing speed. I was quite direct, with the occasional wayward crossing; players and managers would cringe at

my crosses. But that came on with experience. Now my crossing is
superb, even with a crooked knee [laughs].

My first game against Hull stays with me. I went up for a header and
knocked somebody out [laughs]. That immediately endeared me to the
crowd. When we were winning and I was playing well, every game was
an amazing experience. I've been to a lot of games around the country,
but, if you're on the opposing side, West Ham has got to be one of the
most intimidating places to come to. And when we were winning, it's one
of the most fantastic places. But I would say that. People at other clubs
say the same thing about their home grounds. The worse thing that has
happened over the last few years is the seating. You don't get those
powerful surges of people. I was really well looked after at West Ham.

Politics and football. Hmmm! Any business set up in this country,
there's institutional racism, but West Ham didn't flaunt it; they didn't
stick it in your face. If that's an organisation's viewpoint, that's the
viewpoint. You just have to look at the Football League and look at the
managerial positions held by black players. John Barnes was up in
Scotland [laughs] – there's about five black people living up there!
There's Mark Bright, he's working as a TV pundit. There aren't many,
but, in any form of industry in this country that has a white heritage,
there will be institutional racism. It's changing slightly. There's also the
education aspect of it. Traditionally, when the blacks came over here,
they came to run the infrastructure, so there wasn't an educational
background there. That's slowly changing as education changes. Maybe
in football managerial places will be taken by black players. A football
player with education [laughs]. Education and football ... hmmm,
doesn't really mix.

When I was a youth-team player, George [Parris] handled things.
Because of George my life was made a hell of a lot easier. He endeared
himself to the crowd, 'Bruno' as he was referred to. He became a
favourite with the supporters. Then I came into the team after George
and he'd won the fans over for black players. I never had any problems
at all. I never had any racial taunts. When I was a kid, playing on the
fields, I had loads of them, but it went straight over my head. Never
bothered me in the slightest. Just used to wind me up to beat their side.
But at West Ham they never attacked me. I didn't see myself as

breaking any barriers, I'm not that way inclined. I used to play football. I had no political standpoint.

Going back to West Ham, I didn't like the feeling. It was like going home and being an outsider at the same time. It wasn't a very comfortable feeling. Especially when I was still quite young and knew that if I hadn't been injured I'd still be playing. It was too frustrating really. I steer clear of any football club. I don't go to see any games.

The old stereotype about West Ham being a family club is true. I'd been there from the age of 13. It was a huge episode in my life. I was living in Wapping, I had been for a few years. I was happy in my house, I was happy with my club. My biggest regret about my time at West Ham is that I left.

Football was the best way in the world to earn a living; I loved every minute. But there is so much more. I've always thought the more experience you can cram into your time on this earth, the better person you will become. Football was a path which led me to everything else. I'm glad I had my time in the game.

Matthew has since left Ashton and now lives in Cheadle, near Stockport. He was a natural sportsman and is a gifted person physically, intellectually and, I think, after spending some time with him, spiritually. As a footballer he amassed a tremendous amount of experience in his 11-year stay at Upton Park. He has always expressed himself eloquently in an honest and forthright way and has never been afraid to state his case and speak his mind but he never reached his true potential as a footballer. Looking at his biography, the resignation of Lou Macari in February 1990, following allegations over illegal betting activities at Swindon Town, may have been the real turning point for Matthew. Under the tutelage of a former international player of Macari's standing, who knows the heights Rush could have reached. There may have been no move to Norwich, no knee injury and perhaps a means to have been part of the 1998 World Cup in France with the Republic of Ireland.

CHRISTOPHER WILLIAM GERARD HUGHTON

HAMMERS DEBUT: 3/11/90

'How far we've come in a relatively short period of time.'

The first black man to play for Tottenham Hotspurs was Walter Tull who scored two goals in 10 League appearances between 1909 and 1911. Chris Hughton, in 1979, was the next black Spur. Chris was to wear the cockerel over his heart in 297 League games (scoring a dozen goals). As a Hotspur, he'd won UEFA Cup, FA Cup and League Cup winners' medals and been awarded 50 caps for the Republic of Ireland, including appearing in every game at the European Championships in 1988 – Ireland's first ever major Championship finals. This said, Hughton was not a North London nor a Dublin boy. He was born just a few hundred yards down the road from Upton Park in Forest Gate on Thursday, 11 December 1958, to an English father and Limerick-born mother. Hughton grew up in the Stratford area of London and joined White Hart Lane straight from school.

After progressing through the ranks with Spurs, the young Hughton made his first-team debut on 1 September 1979 in a 2–1 White Hart Lane defeat of Manchester City. Two months later, Alan Kelly, then caretaker manager of the Republic of Ireland, called Chris into the Irish team that beat the USA 3–2 at Dalymount Park. Chris played at right-back that day, but played most of his games for the Republic at left-back. He would have probably played many more games for his ancestral homeland had Jim Beglin and Stephen Staunton not emerged while Hughton was at his peak.

Chris came back to his childhood roots to cover for Julian Dicks

113

in the Hammers defence in November 1990, and was a determined, reliable part of the Irons side that won promotion from Division Two in the 1990–91 term.

Hughton first turned out for the Irons on Saturday, 3 November 1990 at Notts County. West Ham won 0–1. This was the start of a two-month loan after which Billy Bonds made the move permanent, with Chris finally breaking his links with the Lads from the Lane in December 1990 by way of a free transfer. He was ever-present thereafter for the rest of the season, including the now legendary game v Nottingham Forest in the last four of the FA Cup, a debacle that strangely transformed into one of the seminal matches in West Ham's history.

An eloquent and intelligent professional, Hughton steeled the Hammers defence at a crucial point and while at Upton Park won three more international caps, in 1991 v Chile and in 1992 twice facing Turkey. However, when his erstwhile teammate Mitchell Thomas came to the Boleyn in August 1992, Chris became surplus to requirements. He had one more appearance in claret and blue as a substitute, kind of poetically, during a Boleyn Ground encounter with Notts County.

Hughton was still hungry enough to crave a first-team place after 40 appearances as part of the Docklands' finest and he joined Brentford for the last 13 matches of the 1992–93 season.

The repetition of a knee injury halfway through 1993–94 obliged the now veteran defender to opt for retirement. Hughton was appointed assistant manager of the Republic of Ireland side in February 1993. But during the summer of that year, Argentinean Osvaldo Ardiles, who had just become Spurs' manager, asked his former teammate to coach at White Hart Lane. Chris returned to work with the Tottenham Under-21 team.

Hughton was appointed manager of the Spurs reserves side in July 1994 and then first-team coach. He became assistant manager in 2001 and in this role has worked under men seen as some of the most talented coaches in the game including George Graham, Gerry Francis, Christian Gross, Glenn Hoddle, Jacques Santini. Briefly, in between Gross's and Graham's reigns as manager, he was caretaker boss helping to bring some stability after a bad start to the 1998–99 season. At the time of writing he is the sidekick of Fred Elliot looky-likey Martin Jol. Holding a UEFA Pro Licence and with a reputation as a top coach, Chris remains involved with the Eire team.

Chris has had his problems with racism. He asserted,

> There certainly were racist problems in England, which I'd have to say the authorities and the different anti-racist groups involved in the game have done a very, very good job of eradicating. For example, there was an incident with England in Spain, which caused a big, big problem. People in England were enraged by it, which shows how far we've come in a relatively short period of time. But there certainly was a regularity in the late 70s and the early 80s in getting racial abuse from opposing supporters and opposing players. That was something that unfortunately we almost got used to.

Although Hughton has reached the heights of English and international football, his most memorable moments, while being associated with the game, have not been on the pitch:

> There were two moments that clearly stand out for me. I was part of the Republic of Ireland team that played in the World Cup in Italy, which was a wonderful experience, and we were fortunate enough to have an audience with the Pope. As a Catholic, that certainly was a very, very pleasing moment for me, and also for my family and particularly my mother. The other experience was when Nelson Mandela came over to England for the Nelson Mandela concert and I was fortunate to be invited to the House of Commons to meet him.

For all this, it seems Chris's day-to-day fulfilment is working with people and on the game:

> I've had spells where I've perhaps been the third assistant and not spent so much time actually working with players … but the favourite part is being on the training pitch every day, working with players and seeing their development. To me, that's the ultimate.

SIMON NATHAN CLARKE

HAMMERS DEBUT: 12/1/91

'The racist thing is a bit of a fallacy ... as soon as you pull on that shirt, it doesn't matter if you're white or black.'

S imon Nathan Clarke was born in Chelmsford, Essex, on 23 September 1971. I met him in a pub on the Redbridge exit of the A406. He played three first-team games for West Ham in his seven years with the club. A slim, tall striker, he played over a hundred games for the Hammers youth team and the reserves. He made his senior debut coming on as a substitute in the final minute of the 12 January 1991 Division Two game at Vicarage Road. West Ham won the game 1–0. He later played for all of the second 45 minutes at Maine Road on 18 April 1992. His last first-team appearance came in the 72nd minute at the Den on 25 November 1992.

I went straight to West Ham from school when I was 16. I knew I had an apprenticeship waiting for me. I done the two-year apprenticeship, then was there three years as a pro. I had been for a trial, they asked me to come training and it took off from there when I was about 15. I was with Charlton before I went to West Ham, but West Ham had better facilities at Chadwell Heath. Charlton still didn't have their own ground; the set-up at West Ham was more professional.

I got two brothers, Floyd [born 1963], Jeff, he's a year younger and my sister is Tanya [born 1968]. She works in a bank up in the City, Floyd works for an employment agency, recruiting people. Jeff works for an insurance company. Mum and Dad were born in Jamaica; Dad's an engineer and Mum's a housewife.

116

SIMON NATHAN CLARKE

My first game for West Ham was against Watford. I come on in the last minute for Jimmy Quinn [laughs]. I ran the ball into the corner. The last game I played in the first team was in November '92. I went on loan to Kettering in December and I picked up a serious back injury. I woke up one morning before we were supposed to play a reserve game against QPR and I could hardly move. I got to the game and came on as sub for the last 15 minutes, set up the winning goal, I think Alex Bunbury was the scorer. The next morning I just couldn't move. I went to see John Green, the physio. I said, 'There's something up.' He goes, 'It's just sciatica.' I had numbness in my foot; my left foot is my powerful one and I just couldn't kick the ball from one end of the gym at Chadwell Heath to the other. This just carried on. The first team get preferential treatment, I was just a reserve player on the fringe of the first team, so I took John Green's word for it: 'It'll get better.' It's gone from January till my contract had nearly run out in June and I'm still not fit. I said, 'John, what's going on? I'm getting worried.' I had no chance of playing or anything. He told me I could go and see a top consultant. Then Bill [then West Ham manager Billy Bonds] told me that he wasn't going to renew my contract, which I thought was a bit hard, 'cause I hadn't really played. But I was a bit naive at the time. I should have told them to give me another year to get better, but I panicked and let them force me to play one of the reserve games in June; they were really short of numbers but I sort of limped me way through it. I had to have cortisone injections to get me back playing again.

I don't think I left West Ham because I weren't good enough, but I hadn't played from January to June. I was thinking to meself, 'I'm never going to be playing again here.' After I'd done that loan period with Kettering, the manager phoned me up in the summer and asked me if I was available and asked me to come over there. That was May '93. I've gone up there on a Friday and signed a contract at Kettering and on the Monday Alan Ball's phoned me up from Exeter asking me if I wanted to come over there. I was sick. I said, 'I've already signed for Kettering.' He said he'd keep an eye out for me, but that was that.

I was a bit upset that West Ham didn't give me the time I needed to get over me injury. I wasn't faking or nothing. In the end it was diagnosed as a bulging disc. That's me only sore point at West Ham.

THE BLACK HAMMERS

I split up with my wife around 2000. I've got children, Edson Ray (after Pele), he's the middle one (born 1995), Paisley (a year older), my youngest is Courtney (born 1998). Both me girls have got good left pegs, the boy's right-footed. Me youngest one's mad about football. Hopefully, when she's a bit older, I can get her over to the States or something [laughs].

I was getting good reports at Kettering, I went back to West Ham and was supposed to go on loan to Colchester, but because me loan period hadn't finished Dean Martin went there instead. Harry [Harry Redknapp, then assistant manager at West Ham] *said, 'You don't want to be going to Colchester, I can get you a better club than that, a higher-up club.' So I came back from loan from Kettering. I'm injured, so I signed for them and done two years over there, then me contract run out, but the travelling was getting too much. I signed for Hendon, 1 August 1996.*

I played over 70 reserve games for West Ham. I played 33 in 1991, more than anyone else that year. I got on really well, I ran me heart out in the reserve side, me and Matthew Rush. We turned over some teams. I really enjoyed it.

I've always been a quiet person, but in the end I was saying, 'Bill, I want a chance.' They probably thought I was getting a bit cocky, but I wasn't. I was thinking, 'How many more times can I play in the reserves?' I wasn't getting big for my boots but looking back now I wish I'd have said nothing 'cause I was only 21 at the time. I could have waited and my chance might've come. But I was getting a bit eager. I might have been raw but I was worth giving a chance. I was confident and I just wanted that chance, but it didn't come along. You can't prove much when you come on as substitute. You need to be thrown in at the deep end even in a Full Members Cup or something like that. I'm a bit gutted that I didn't really get a chance. I can't say if I was good enough or not good enough, I never got the opportunity to prove meself.

I went to Raynsford School in Chelmsford. I played all sports, cricket, basketball. I was 100-metre, 200-metre champion at school. They tried to get me to play in the rugby team but I was a bit too clever for that [laughs]. *I played for Chelmsford Schools.*

I played from when I was about three with me older brothers and I

*used to run rings round their mates. That's when I knew I could play
football. My brothers played for good Sunday sides, Floyd played for
Chelmsford City, he was just on the brink. We all used to go over the
park and play together. Ronnie Boyce was a major influence on me.
When I was about 15, over Chadwell Heath, Ronnie Boyce pushed
me along, just to get the apprenticeship really. From that November till
the end of the season, that's May, you had to prove yourself. That's what
would determine if you were going to get an apprenticeship. There was
me, Matthew Rush and three others that got apprenticeships that year.
And there were loads, people who had been over there from when they
were six or seven years old, lads on the YTS, and to see them coming
out of the office crying, I thought I'd jumped the boat! I'd only been
there four months! Those lads had been there all their lives, West Ham
through and through. I felt for them. The first nine that were called in
were told they weren't good enough and they left us to last.*

I used to get on well with Matthew Rush, Pottsy [Steve Potts] *and
George Parris. I saw Matthew Rush when he was playing for
Dagenham and Redbridge. I was marking him. He's a bit elusive,
South London boy* [laughs].

*Liam Brady and Alan Devonshire were the best players in my time
at Upton Park. Playing in the reserves with them! And Alvin Martin
of course. He was a different class. Mike Small was a nice bloke. So
laidback* [laughs] *maybe too laidback. A lot of the players were laid back
over there! All nice blokes. George* [Parris], *Kevin Keen, Steve Potts,
Eddie Bailey, the old chief scout, Ronnie Boyce. You got treated right.*

*Things are changing in management, especially at non-League level.
There's a lot of black players going into coaching, some into
management. People have got more of an open mind nowadays. In the
professional ranks a few of the players are getting their chance. I think
the opportunity is there. I'd like to go into management. I was the
longest-serving player at Hendon. Played more than 400 games for
'em.*

*I was a grafter. I used to work really hard. They improved my touch
at West Ham, and helped me as far as holding the ball up. Back then
I was an out-and-out centre-forward. Sometimes they tried to make me
play on the wing if they had too many forwards but I was a very*

versatile player. I see myself as an all-round footballer. I even played in goal a couple of times in the reserves [laughs]. I should have stayed behind and trained a bit more. The money side of things now, you regret it. Like Ronnie Boyce used to say, 'do that extra hour', he used to tell you about what Bobby Moore used to do, but you sort of think, 'Oh no!' You think it's going to last for ever.

I haven't been back once to Upton Park. It would be very emotional I think. I'd like to go back but the players who were there when I was there have long gone. Pottsy hung on the longest. I used to get on well with Julian [Dicks].

The fans always liked me; I used to get good reports, even players like Julian Dicks and Tony Parkes used to say that I should be given a chance. Alvin used to say it, as did all the players, Pottsy, Kevin Keen. If the fans know someone is willing to work hard at their game, they'll give 'em the time of day, more so than someone who's got all the ability but won't graft. Other players will appreciate a worker more too.

I never came across any racism at Upton Park. I got some stick when I was warming up at Millwall for one of the games on the box [laughs]. I was getting the Zulu chants and that, but you learn to shut yourself away from that. It was never anything major. I think you get it more in non-League football now. I've had it a few times. Altrincham, Gravesend. 'Cause there's less of a crowd you can hear everything they say. Probably in a bigger crowd you'd just wash it off. I didn't really experience that kind of thing at West Ham; never experienced it from the West Ham supporters. I always had full backing from West Ham fans. The racist thing is a bit of a fallacy.

I didn't see myself as a pioneer. Bill signed a few black players, Mitchell Thomas, Mike Small. There was Rushy, Leroy there. John Lyall brought in Leroy. By the end of my time at Upton Park there were about six or seven black pros there and there were some people coming through the youth team as well. I don't think racism was a problem at West Ham when I was there. Not at all. The way the Paul Ince thing was handled was a bit bad. All that in the Daily Express. *I was gutted at the time because I was pleased for him. To think he'd come up through the ranks and everything. He was with Ambrose Mendy at the time; it was wrong for him to be wearing the Man U shirt before he'd even signed but I don't think he'd done that intentionally. He probably would have wanted things to have been signed and sealed before that picture was made public. But he had the bit about HP and it didn't go through as smoothly as he might have liked. Good luck to him! Look at what he's done! I'm just gutted that he can't come back to West Ham as a hero, as an approval of West Ham.*

John Lyall signed me. It was Billy Bonds's first year as the youth-team manager. He was good as gold with me. I was one of his favourites. Then Lou Macari came in. I got on well with Lou Macari, but obviously he had all his problems. Then Billy Bonds got the job. He kept putting me in all the first-team squads, he really looked after me. Bill's the one who give me the chance in the first team. I got on well with Bill. Then Harry come and it changed a little bit for me. Difference of opinions. Everyone knew that one day Harry was going to end up being manager. I didn't like the way it happened in the end. I think Bill should still be at the club now. Harry was supposed to be his mate as well. I think Harry had different views on players. Things started to change a bit. They used to have a five-a-side in the gym on a Friday. Every Friday, that was from when John Lyall was there. Soon as Harry came in, that was it. No more five-a-sides in the gym on a Friday! He changed everything. He changed all the eating habits. We used to have a fry-up on a Friday, all the traditional things that John Lyall had installed all changed and you thought, 'Harry's going to be the main man sooner or later.' John Lyall was a very nice bloke. Him and Ronnie Boyce really helped me along. Ronnie Boyce was the one who made me make pro. He was a grafter and he instilled that in me. I owe a lot to them to get that far.

Anyone who pulls on a claret and blue shirt will get respect from West Ham fans and you appreciate them. Of course, there's certain players who you think, 'I could do better than them', but, in the main, as soon as you pull on that shirt it doesn't matter if you're white or black. The Chicken Run sticks in my mind [laughs]. I don't think you can beat it with all them heads popping up in the Chicken Run. Once they were chucking a policeman's helmet around [laughs] and they slung it out on the pitch. From the player's pen, just watching the

THE BLACK HAMMERS

Chicken Run! [Simon shook his head and smiled.] *The way they used to get involved with the game. The support in that Chicken Run! It was a different class!*

At Hendon's 2002 end-of-season dinner and awards ceremony, long-serving defender Simon Clarke picked up the two main awards: the Chair's personal award that celebrated Clarke reaching 350 appearances, including 10 in various FA Cup runs; Simon also received the Hendon FC Supporters Association Player of the Year award.

But, after breaking a leg in a pre-season friendly, Simon had found life difficult at New Lodge, but he fought his way back to fitness.

After nearly six years with the Greens, Clarke joined Dr Martens Premier League side Chelmsford City in June 2002 and, having switched to central defence, won an Essex Senior Cup winners' medal with the Clarets in March 2003. He was the club's player of the year 2004–05. He moved on to Maldon Town in the Ryman Premier League for the following season. He spent a spell with Boston United but returned to complete the term with the Town.

Simon Clarke has become a distinguished player in non-League football, much respected by officials, fellow players and fans.

FRANZ ALEXANDER CARR

'Football, watching or playing, is about enjoyment; I had and I've given a lot of that ...'

Born in Preston, Lancashire, on 24 September 1966, Franz started his career with Blackburn Rovers in July 1984 and moved to Nottingham Forest in August 1985, before making his debut on 25 September 1985 against Bolton Wanderers. While with Forest he gained Full Members Cup (1989) and League Cup (1990) winners' medals.

Franz started just one League game for the Hammers, on 13 March 1991, v Oxford United, while on loan from Forest (he'd had a dozen outings on loan to Sheffield Wednesday at the end of 1989). He made two more appearances as a sub that term. Working under Clough, Carr was once rated as the most promising youngster in England. He played 131 games for Forest scoring 17 goals. He won England Youth honours and represented the Under-21s on nine occasions.

Carr had a string of clubs after his time with Forest and a lot of money was paid for his services. Brian Clough forked out £100,000 for him; on 13 June 1991 Newcastle United paid £250,000 for his contract; Sheffield United splashed out £120,000 for his signature on 12 January 1993; a year later he went to Leicester for the same fee and on 10 February 1995 Aston Villa paid £250,000 for the three games the right-winger played under their colours. In total he made just 59 appearances for these clubs, finding the net eight times.

Possessing stunning pace and good ball control, Carr could, at times, beat the best defenders with seeming ease. These abilities meant that he excited and entertained crowds wherever he went. Chris Waddle once said of Carr, 'He preferred to come up against players with a bit of skill and he always did well against me.'

But Carr's finishing crosses were often inaccurate. It was not unusual for him to destroy defenders only to fail to provide the final ball. However, a winger who can't cross is like a keeper who is unable to save, a defender who tackles poorly or a forward who can't shoot.

From Villa Park, Carr went to Reggiana in Italy. After returning to England in 1996–97 for a trial with Everton, five games with Bolton and four with WBA, he joined Pittsburgh Riverhounds in the USA during 2000 and also played in South Carolina for Charleston. After being linked to Lancashire non-League side Darwen, Franz is now a players' agent based in Nottingham, but living in Golden Valley, Derbyshire.

MICHAEL ANTHONY SMALL

'The biggest fight I've ever had is being black, more so again in the football world.'

Mike Small was born in Selly Oak, Birmingham, on 2 March 1962. He was brought up in Balsall Heath and still has a trace of Brummie in his accent.

I met with Mike at his place of work near Liverpool Street Station.

I have two sisters, they still live in Birmingham. One's a mother, the other is a nurse. I was never a supporter, I never went to St Andrews as a boy, didn't do any of that.

You can never remember the first time you pick up a football, or the first time you play, but we had a back yard. At the back of around 10 houses, there was a little driveway, a little community place. There was a lad, Tony his name was, his house had a fence and where we lived had one, you couldn't dribble or anything, all you could do was shoot at each other's fences and we'd try to save each other's shots. From there we progressed to the park. I found that, having the park so near, I was playing with boys who were much bigger than myself and enjoying watching games. Then, all of a sudden, I got interested in it on the TV. I knew the football clubs more than the names of footballers. Once I got to school kids found out that I could play football. You get into games in the school yard, it just went on from there. I started playing organised games at seven in teams with boys of 11, going to secondary school.

As I progressed through primary school to the third and fourth year,

125

I got invited to play for the district, South Birmingham. I could run the sprint hurdles, I could always run. I always liked sports.

Mum worked in the Chrysler factory. Mum was from St Ann's in Jamaica. My dad was born in St Kitts, he was an arc welder. My dad, he's passed away now, was the biggest influence in my life. He was against confrontation. He calmed my mother down, who was very quick tempered. I respect him for that.

I went to loads of interviews for jobs outside of football when I left school ... I did a couple of jobs, although when I saw what the pay was like I went back to school, just to see if I could get a bit further.

I went to Australia for the England Under-20s World Cup in 1981. I played in all the games. We finished fourth. We lost 1–0 to Romania in the third-place play-off. West Germany beat Qatar 4–0 in the final.

Small started his League career with Luton, making three appearances as a substitute in 1981–82.

My first senior club was Knowle. I only stayed there two weeks before I went to Bromsgrove. Frank O'Hare, he was the manager of Bromsgrove Rovers who thought he saw a footballer in me, he knew I could do it ... this Luton scout came round and he said, 'Do you want to come to Luton?' David Pleat was there. He says, 'Very interested, like to have you back.' I didn't hear anything for a whole season. Then I went back down there and it started from there.

After a year with the Hatters, Small had a loan spell at Peterborough – he made four appearances for Posh, two as a substitute. Following this, Mike moved on to Holland and Belgium.

When I came back there was two blokes sitting there and he said, 'Do you fancy going to Holland?' I didn't know what club it was but I'd been to Holland for tournaments, so I went. I wasn't afraid of going. That was the best move I ever made in football. I was with Twente, Vitesse and Go-Ahead Eagles in Holland. Hanklin Carter was like a big brother to me when I went abroad. He was the manager of Rotterdam. It wasn't common for a British player to go abroad at that time.

At the time I went, it was a great set-up. Everyone trained in the afternoons so in the mornings it was my opportunity to get individual training. When I look at how things have turned out! Raimond van der Gouw and I would meet in the mornings on the way in. He was there, he followed me to Vitesse. He was Ferguson's first summer signing to United in '96. Played for Holland. He was also at Go-Ahead with me. He was a good goalkeeper. I used to enjoy having him there in the morning. I found out that I might have been strong athletically, but I was wanting in terms of real ball control and doing a lot with the ball. That's what you learn over there. There've got a vast love for skill more than just aggression and passion. They can all do something with a ball. They can all control it. Football is just programmed over here. Over there, you give a ball to a Dutch guy, he'll take that ball off the training pitch and it's there with him when he changes and that is something! So I enjoyed that. It was a good experience.

Louis Pillow, he was the manager of Standard Liege. He took me from Go-Ahead.

Following this, Mike played for PAOK in Greece.

Then I went off to Greece for a while. Greece is very much a mini Italy in a way. They try and get people through the turnstiles. They sign players just because they're big names, or supposedly big names. The chairman has to be seen as somebody. One chairman knew nothing about football. He bought the club. Things didn't go too well, then he got on to another chairman and I didn't like the way things were going on. He wanted to speak to me, telling me to do all this. I said, 'No.' I stood up for myself. So I says, 'Look, I wasn't born in this country. I don't need football here.' That's how I got back to England and Brighton.

But it was great going to all these places, through ambition really, and nobody to hold me back.

In his one season with Brighton, Mike scored 21 goals (including a single against the Hammers at Upton Park) and helped take the Seagulls to the play-offs.

Small signed for West Ham from Brighton and Hove Albion for £400,000 just before the opening of the 1991–92 season.

When he got to Upton Park, he began to show his potential almost straight away. On 17 August 1991 he made his debut against one of his former clubs, Luton Town, starting an impressive run of 13 goals in 20 games that included the winner in a tight match with Arsenal.

Billy Bonds bought me, and I appreciate the fact that he wanted me at Upton Park. I had a lot of respect for him and his reputation as a player, even though we didn't see eye to eye in the last couple of years I was with the club. I wanted to do my best for myself and West Ham and the first year was brilliant.

I came to West Ham about the same time as Kenny Brown and Mitchell Thomas. My first game was against Luton. My debut goal came in the next game at Bramble Lane in a 1–1 draw. I was friendly with Mitchell. We were at Luton together and he was vastly experienced. But it was a big achievement for me to be back in England playing in the First Division.

In the 1991–92 season I got 18 goals. A game's a game. Yer get yer derbies. When I scored that goal against Arsenal! Years down the line you realise that that one goal that won the match against Arsenal meant a lot to a lot of people. I didn't realise how much at the time. It was a shot, but I only saw it after it had gone past David Seaman. Then the crowd reacted. The emotions were high. It was a great goal. It's the only part of that game I can remember. Everything happens so quick. You're so focused. You want to win every game. When you don't speak to supporters, you go into that game and it's very, very tense.

Mike could look awkward in terms of style, but, despite what some people saw as his problems with the offside rule, he was one of the few consolations for many West Ham fans during the relegation season of 1991–92 – his first term at the Boleyn Ground.

Although Mike's 18 goals were a more than good tally for his first season in the top flight of English football, his progress was abruptly curtailed in the New Year.

A cartilage operation put a stop to my purple patch at the club. I was back after just 15 days. If I had my time again, I don't think I'd do that for anybody. It was just that I wanted to play. I'd never been injured in that way. When John Green, the physio, was talking to the specialist I didn't want to have the operation. I believed, once broken, always broken. I played, didn't have no more problems. Then I found I just lost form. We'd played about 20 games then and the whole situation was swarming on us. Maybe I got found out. The goals were few and far between. I got sent off against Barnsley after colliding with Trevor Morley. But I reckon there were other things missed there. I got a bad back injury as well.

What upset me was that some of the coaching staff thought I was putting it on. That was quite hurtful. The coaching staff weren't exactly honest.

Billy Bonds doubted my desire for the game. He'd listened to people, but I never lost respect for him, even though we had arguments. Billy got carried away with some of the coaching staff's view of things. I would never cheat on Billy. I never cheated on anybody. In the end I had to look to see what I'd done and see where I was gonna go and it was a case of I wasn't going knocking my football club.

I only really played for two seasons in the League. West Ham and Brighton. I scored 21 goals. I got called up for England 'B'. With better coaching, I think I would have recovered better. I found out from a very good friend abroad that the management at West Ham reckoned I'd gone soft or become comfortable, that's quite hurtful. Even when I was training at West Ham and turning up, I was made out to be a bad person. I've never been a bad person. I was getting calls when I was playing for West Ham from somebody from Woking to come down. In the end I thought, 'Well, if this is the way it's gonna go ...' Everybody who said they wanted me weren't exactly convincing that they wanted me. There was only one person who really wanted to find out what the problem was and that was Martin O'Neill. He was at Wycombe at the time, he'd given me a call. I respect him for that.

THE BLACK HAMMERS

There was one thing I noticed, Harry Redknapp said to me, 'Have you got no mates?' That was a killing factor. I didn't have any mates in the game in a position to say, 'Come out and do this.' I know for a fact every morning I got up I might have felt like I didn't want to train, but I achieved a standard every day, 'cause I got picked. In my playing career I got picked the majority of the time.

After my injury, I went on loan to Wolves and Charlton. When I went to Wolves, that was an escape route for me; it didn't really feel quite right. I always thought I was going three-quarter pace. I never really had a change of gear. I'd always had the thrill of running past people. When I couldn't take someone on over 15 yards I knew there was a problem. Your power and strength all comes from yer back.

When I went to Charlton, that was just to get away from the indignity of training with the youth team and being surplus. That was all Harry's doing. He looked to get rid of people in that way. I just stood up for meself and said, 'Look, I come in every day and do what I gotta do.' I wasn't fighting with my mouth. I'd met better people, who had treated me better. You treat some people with the contempt they deserve. After Charlton, I went back to West Ham and that was it. I just went off to Sweden to see if I could get football in the summer.

Alvin Martin, just on frustration, was very difficult in training. If I played against him in a game, I'd think I'd really have to nobble him to get a chance. In terms of having the ability and playing I had a lot of respect for Ian Bishop. I've seen him doing so many things on the training ground. Dale Gordon used to have a saying, 'You couldn't get a beach ball off me in a telephone box', and I think that's Ian Bishop. Potential wise, I likened Matthew Rush to Jairzinho. It shows you how much he knew about football, he didn't know who Jairzinho was ... [laughs]; know the shame? I thought he could have been good. I appreciate Trevor Morley because I'd learned to be a European centre-forward, but playing and watching Trevor! He was shorter than me, but he made the most of what he had. I likened him to Alan Ball. I respect him. Like Billy Jennings, who was very short, but he had absolutely brilliant timing. Trevor Morley was a good centre-forward. If anybody was going to model himself on someone to learn the game, to play in the English League, Trevor Morley would have been the one. Other than that, the only time I've ever forgot I was playing was when I played against Maradona against Napoli. It was brilliant just to watch him doing what he could do.

I got on well with most of the lads. I had a good laugh. Galey [Tony Gale] was there, Bishop, Morley, we were all about the same age. It was a club with a lot of egos, but not crushing egos, we all got on together. Mitchell Thomas, he's the godfather of me daughter. He's the only one who rings up. I don't see him too much. But everybody I see I know for a fact that I'll get a smile 'cause I did have some good times with them.

If I look at all the clubs that I wanted to play for as a 29-year-old, if you've got ambition, West Ham would be one of them. I knew London and the West Ham area very well. It was a good experience. For around 10 years I'd been playing football European style and I thought at West Ham I'd be a bit of surprise, being a big lad who had a bit of control and who could play. If I had to describe myself as a player, I'd say I was awesome [smiles]. The football that was being played elsewhere didn't really appeal to me. But we got relegated and I think after playing so many years abroad it had taken two seasons to get back into things. I had a very testing time. The physical side was on another level and the type of game was different. These were things I hadn't been used to.

The best moment I ever had was when Man United came down and Paul Ince was there. They had to beat us to win the League. Knowing that I was part of that team who beat them with Kenny Brown's goal that night – that was something! Ferguson reckoned we put in a hell of an effort to beat them, but it was the crowd that did it. It meant a lot to them to beat Man United. I would have liked to have stayed up with West Ham that year, but we didn't. But stopping United winning the League was a good moment. What do I remember about being at West Ham? ... The goals!

I got on well with the fans, but I was never going to be their idol. I wasn't Julian Dicks. If I were to put my money on supporters, I would say that West Ham fans are the best fans in London. The core support always comes back and they're still there when things are not going so good. I'll always say they are number one; no matter what the team does, you can guarantee the West Ham fans will be there. That's one of the best things you can ask for in supporters, and I've known quite a few. The fans were OK with me. Because of the way the fans were situated round the ground you could hear one or two funny things, and it is quite funny at times. I enjoyed it. I'll always remember the Chicken Run. You could play in front of 100,000 people, you've got the pitch, the running track and then the crowd. But at Upton Park you'd have the pitch, the sand and then you've got them! There were times when you could look people straight in the eye, and if he says, 'Come on, Mike,' you can say, 'I'm trying ...' You can have that sort of contact, which is quite good and you felt the atmosphere.

As far as West Ham's reputation as a racist club is concerned, I can say that I didn't think twice about going to Upton Park. When I was at Luton one day I was playing in the reserves against Chelsea. As soon as I got out of the dug-out the Chelsea fans started to go 'Zieg heil, zieg heil'. I never forgot that and you don't really pay attention to what's progressed; has it progressed in a club like Chelsea? So, when they came in for me, I didn't really fancy it. When I was at Brighton there were chants against me and that helped me make up my mind to go to West Ham. I remember how Clyde Best had played for them and they'd always been a side that played football. That's why I said I'd go there. One or two people, getting involved in the passion of the game, will use the colour. I can imagine a lot of people feeling abused by that sort of thing, but it's just for 90 minutes. You can look at it and see one side and say, 'Fair enough, for 90 minutes. They can express themselves and if they do it without the colour I can take it.' But when I was out there people saw me and they'd say, 'Yeah. Mike!' The only time up North that I got problems was at Middlesbrough or Sunderland, where they were against me, but it just got me going. You put on a show and the next time it comes around it all changes.

But I'm not stupid. John Barnes was a great player. The wealth of ability he's got. It's all about skill. Of all the players that have finished in the last 10 years, no one had more skill than him. When he was finishing, he let it be known what he'd like to do but nobody came straight to him to ask him to manage. When someone like David Platt can go and get two or three jobs because of where he's been and his personality! What's going on? Kenny Dalglish had to take John

Barnes to Celtic to give him that position. Leroy's [Rosenior] right about the institutional racism in football. But given the chance I'd like to pass on my experience to others, maybe not to grown men, but, if I can deal with kids and people who want to train and find out what it's like in Europe, I know what's what, but I've never tried to be a manager of a professional football club because I don't think I'd be given the time to do anything.

In this country there has to be a role model who is white. The only person I feel sorry for as a goalscorer is Ian Wright. Ian Wright was the best thing, scoring goals for Arsenal at the time, the way he scored goals! He weren't predictable. He scored good finishing goals. All of a sudden he's gone into the national team. The pressure of scoring goals at international level is high. It was a natural progression where he needed someone to say, 'Look, I support yer,' not just the manager, although that would be good. I ask people if Wembley would see seven or eight black players taking the field for England and the national icon being black. Would people go there seeing themselves as being represented? Everybody says yes, yes, yes, because at club level … I'm saying 'no'! At a national level there's more to it than that. If you have a look at anyone who's remotely good, they will get a big company behind them. Ian Wright was just as good as Alan Shearer but he never once got a really big company behind him. It stinks, but you can see it. Alan Shearer scored goals against Luxembourg, which you wouldn't get a bet against him doing, because he's bound to. I'm just one voice here and I'm just saying … I just let it go because I know what I've got to do. The biggest fight I've ever had is being black, more so again in the football world.

In the end I did something that I never thought I would do. I went into this publishing, even though I was a director and had my name involved with a company. I decided to find out how publishing worked and try to get involved. At the time, which a lot of people didn't know, while I was at West Ham, I was involved in a basketball magazine; that's where I'm at today. I've been in publishing from the early 90s. I've always had my eye on something else; to break away and do something for myself. We've worked with the football boards for Bucharest, Udinesse and Benfica, helping sell the advertising.

THE BLACK HAMMERS

I knew I was going to need a steady career and the way football was going on I wasn't too convinced that a black face would populate the managerial role of football. My life had been football and the obvious next stage would be to become a manager. I thought I'd be in football at best for about 20 years. Then you think, 'There's no more fight left in me.' You just relax and hope that the fighting bit will come back and you start up again. When people have got money they like to circulate it in their own environment, they won't put their trust in somebody coming into their environment. I've learned a lot.

I'm not married. I have two kids, Jarrard (born 1991) and Camilla (who is four years older). Camilla was a bit good. She had ideas about playing abroad. Jarrard now is very much into football. He watches the game when he can but I think he's exposed to a lot of other sports.

I just watch football on TV now. I only live at Buckhurst Hill, but I don't go down to Upton Park. I like to see how things are going for them and how they're progressing. There've got a good youth team and I just hope all the players locally get a chance. It would be good if they became the club that gave all the London boys a chance. It's no good advertising that you've got Frank Lampard and Rio Ferdinand for a few years and you just sell them on and have no one to take their place.

MITCHELL ANTHONY THOMAS

HAMMERS DEBUT: 17/8/91

'When West Ham came in for me, I was delighted ... they played good football and had a great tradition.'

When I told Matthew Rush that I had experienced problems contacting Mitchell Thomas he smiled and said, 'That's probably about right. A woman chasing him or something! Mitchell's a character. A very bizarre character. He was confident. Very confident [laughs].'

Mitchell was born in Luton, Bedfordshire, on 2 October 1964. He ran out for his initial first-team game on 4 January 1983, ironically, at Upton Park; Luton lost 3–2. Mitch remembered,

> *I was an 18-year-old playing against some very good players, like Phil Parkes, Paul Allen and they had Francois Van Der Elst on the wing.*

In the main Thomas filled the left-back position for the Hatters, while Tim Breaker played as the Beds Boys right full-back in a side that won much respect for its enterprising football in the mid–80s.

As the summer of 1986 came to an end, David Pleat, who had signed Thomas from school, left Luton bound for White Hart Lane. The Pleatster's first signing when he became manager of Tottenham was Mitchell, for a fee of £275,000. His regular full-back partner at Spurs was Hammer-to-be Chris Hughton.

Tottenham finished third in Mitch's first season with them. He recalled,

> *Spurs are a big club and they played marvellous football, but so did*

135

THE BLACK HAMMERS

Luton and the same applies to West Ham – all three clubs tried to play good football.

Thomas made close to 200 appearances for Spurs and he was the North Londoners' left-back at Wembley when they were defeated 3–2 by Coventry City in extra-time in the 1987 FA Cup final.

However, Mitch was to find himself third-choice left-back, waiting on Pat van den Hauwe and Justin Edinburgh and as such missed the FA Cup final against Nottingham Forest. Billy Bonds gave £500,000 to bring Thomas to Upton Park. He recollected,

> *I was just pleased that another footballing side came in for me. At Spurs I was only playing the odd game here and there or being substitute. You ask any footballer and whether they are at a big club like Spurs, or anywhere else, being in the first team regularly is the biggest part of it all. To be on the bench is not very nice. I honestly believe I did the right thing going to West Ham. They were another big club, they played good football and had a great tradition.*

Although Mitchell spent most of his career at left-back, shortly after signing him, manager Billy Bonds said, 'Mitchell is a very versatile player and will provide good cover right across the back four; he reminds me of George Parris.'

That was OK by Mitch who, looking back, commented,

> *I enjoyed playing in midfield because I liked to get forward as much as possible. I played occasionally in central midfield as well.*

Thomas turned out 38 times and scored three goals for the Hammers. At 6ft 2ins, he was a slim but powerful defender and came to Upton Park with England Youth, Under-21 (three caps) and international 'B' team credentials and covered for well-loved Julian Dicks, making his West Ham debut on 17 August 1991, once more coincidentally against Luton Town. He recalled,

> *Obviously I was a bit overawed by the occasion, but fortunately it went*

well for us on the night. It was interesting to face Luton in my first game for West Ham.

On 26 October, Thomas pleased the Boleyn Ground fans by scoring the winning goal against Tottenham (he also hit the post in that game) and was also on target v Crystal Palace and Oldham Athletic. Following the return of Dicks in January 1992, Mitchell moved into midfield to keep his place in the first team.

When Thomas became a Hammer, he passed up the opportunity to work with David Pleat for a third time. The former White Hart Lane lieutenant was once more head honcho of the Bedfordshire Hatters and wanted to bring the defender back to Kenilworth Road but according to Mitch,

It wasn't necessarily a difficult decision to make. I always think that it's never wise to go back on old territory unless you really have to. So when West Ham came in for me I was delighted.

However, at Upton Park the fans were in revolt against the club's ill-fated bond scheme, and the lamentable performances of the Irons on the field resulted in relegation. Thomas played just three more League games in 1992–93 (covering for the suspended Dicks) and never made the first team again after facing Crewe Alexandra in the League Cup tie at Upton Park on 23 September 1992. Despite the efforts Billy Bonds made to recover some of the cash paid for Thomas, there was scant interest in him. But David Pleat took Mitch on loan before signing him in March 1993 for the bargain-basement price of £50,000.

Thomas had played 130 games for Luton in his first stint with the club and in all made 292 League and Cup appearances for Hatters, scoring six goals. He joined Burnley in July 1999. The Clarets had avoided relegation with two games to spare. Thomas had an outstanding season and went on to have a distinguished career at Turf Moor and became a huge favourite of the Burnley crowd as evidenced on the last game of the 2002–03 season when, with just 25 minutes to go, he was substituted, being replaced with Gareth

Taylor. He left to a standing ovation from the Lancashire fans and also, and significantly, from the bench and subs. It was to be his last appearance for the club and just two days later he was released on a free transfer. Thomas had made 112 appearances in the Lancastrian version of claret and blue.

ALEXANDER BUNBURY

HAMMERS DEBUT: 28/11/92

'I never really look at my colour. I think of myself as a human being first.'

Alex was one of Canada's greatest internationals. He made three appearances in the 1983 CONCACAF (The Confederation of North, Central American and Caribbean Football) Gold Cup (Championship), scoring a goal. Alex was chosen to represent Canada in the 1987 World Under-20 Cup in Chile. He made his international debut on 24 August 1986 v Singapore and scored the first of 16 goals for Canada six days later in a 4–0 win over Indonesia in the Merlion Cup (an international competition conceived and played in Singapore in the 1980s and featuring the likes of Australia, Canada, South Korea and regional neighbours). He was Canada's leading scorer in their bid to qualify for the 1994 World Cup finals that only just failed in the match v Mexico. The North Americans were unlucky in the play-off v Australia. Bunbury missed a penalty in that game. He was Canadian Player of the Year in 1993 and 1995 and played in the Olympic qualifiers in 1997.

Bunbury played many times for Canada alongside West Ham goalkeeper Craig Forrest. In all, Alex made 65 appearances for his adopted country (he got half-a-dozen of those while at Upton Park) making him the nation's fourth leading all-time cap winner, and was the third-highest scorer ever with 17 goals when he retired from international football. He was the first Canadian to score a World Cup hat-trick (v Bermuda – 15/11/92). He told me, in his now rich Canadian/American accent,

THE BLACK HAMMERS

That was one of the highlights of my international career alongside the fantastic games v Mexico; we were in the lead and I had scored the goal, we were so near to qualifying for the World Cup finals.

I was born in Plaisance, Guyana [18 June 1967]. It was then 'British' Guyana, still under the colonial influence. I was the youngest of 13 children. The family moved to Montreal when I was nine. I was into cricket. My hero was Clive Lloyd. The family was looking for a better life, my older brothers had led the way and the rest of my family followed. I started playing ice hockey, that's THE big sport in Montreal. I played to a high level. I hadn't really played soccer, but my brother played well and took me along to his club, St Leonard, when I was about 12. Within 18 months I was playing for the Under-15s. I went to Rosemount High School in Montreal and became a member of the Quebec Selects team in 1980. I was selected for the national Under-16 team in 1982 and the national Under-19 team in 1984. In total I represented Canada in 21 Youth internationals, including the FIFA World Youth Championship in the Soviet Union in 1985. At that time there was no financial promise in soccer in Canada, unlike hockey, so I was playing for the love of the game. My family has always been my foundation. They made sure that education was the number-one objective. Dad passed away in 1993. Years ago, he had been a manufacturing manager in Guyana, but he had a stroke just before we moved to Canada and couldn't work. Mum did a collection of jobs to support the family. Mum and some brothers are still in Canada, Mum's in Montreal. I've got two brothers and two sisters in New York; others are in Baltimore and Toronto.

I've been married to Kristi for nearly 20 years. We met when I was playing for Minnesota Strikers in the indoor league. She had her own beauty salon, but has looked after my business interests since we've been married. She has been my rock. She works for us. We have three children; Kylie, she was born a couple of years after we got married, Teal is a year younger and Logan (born 1994). Teal will destroy anything I've done, he reached Minnesota Under-14 standard and has progressed to represent Canada at Under-15 level in 2005. We all live in Prior Lake.

Billy Bonds brought me to West Ham for £200,000 from Montreal

ALEXANDER BUNBURY

Supra [Canada] *following a trial appearance v Spurs – we won and I scored a couple of goals – in December 1992. The bankruptcy of the Canadian Soccer League meant that I had to look abroad for opportunities. It wasn't financially viable for me to stay in Canada. I'd played for Toronto Blizzard in 1990 and Montreal in '91. My first professional club was Hamilton Steelers. I joined them in 1987 and was with the club for four seasons. I scored 28 goals in 76 games. A lot of enquiries came in from European clubs, but I was probably too young. I'd been to Le Havre in France and met Graham Rix there, he recommended me to Liam Brady at Celtic. I spent some time with Dundee when Simon Stainrod was manager there and with Big Ron Atkinson at Villa. Ron rated me but couldn't make up his mind, so I moved to Wimbledon with Joe Kinnear, but that was when Dad passed away so I had to interrupt things there. It was then that my agent told me that West Ham were interested and within a week I'd signed.*

West Ham was a great learning experience. It was a great thrill to be playing for a big club like West Ham. I guess I was a little 'gun shy' at the time, not at my best physically, but they did a lot of long-distance running. Billy Bonds always put an emphasis on the physical side of the game. I struggled. I'm an instinctive player, quick and skilful. He thought that I wasn't working hard enough. But I was playing well for the reserves. I think I must have scored in 95 per cent of the reserve games I played in. But I was probably the first Canadian to move directly to a club of the West Ham standard. I know Craig Forrest had been at Ipswich, but that was a much more gradual thing. It made me a better person. It moved me on. I believe that everything happens for a reason, but the whole experience was very traumatic for Kristi and me. I really wasn't allowed to show my true talent. I believe that I was as good as any of the forwards at the club at the time.

There were difficulties with the club v country thing. I didn't believe I could turn my back on Canada. I lead the team and was probably one of their better players at that time. There were a lot of people in Canada that I didn't feel able to let down. This was used against me at West Ham. I'm proud of my international career. But the things I've learned, the cultures I've come across because of my international career, have made me a better person. I knew I could play in the Premiership, but I was treated like a second-class person. When I got back, Harry [Redknapp, then assistant manager] *insisted that I trained with the youth team, then the reserves and then the first team. This was frustrating. But even when you got into the first team, it wasn't a good feeling, it was all about filling in the blanks – 'Hold up the ball', 'Don't try to do too much', there was never anything to encourage creativity. Mike Small was a big support at that time. He was like a big brother to me. George Parris was also helpful and Trevor Morley and Ian Bishop did their best to give me tips.*

I was never a cheat. Harry called me a cheat and that hurt. He would tell me that I didn't deserve my wages, that I was lazy. This kind of thing, shouting at me in front of my teammates embarrassed and humiliated me. It just had a negative effect. It might have been a psychological thing that was being tried, but if it was it didn't work with me, but I was never disrespectful and always tried to do my best. I did try hard. I busted my nose and still turned up for training. At that time I just probably needed someone to take the time to stroke me on the back and tell me, 'We're running a business here, but we can work with you. There are problems but together we're gonna sort them out', but there did not seem to be the capacity for this. At that time it was just push, push, push. But I did have talent and that's why Udenio, who was the manager of the Portuguese First Division club FC Maritimo, took me on. He was three times a World Cup winner, twice as captain. I moved to Madeira on loan at first. The £50,000 fee went through in November 1993. Although West Ham said the reason for my move involved work permit problems – they said I had to play in 75 per cent of West Ham's games in a season – this was not the issue. Comparing Udenio with Harry is not really possible; the difference is just too great. There is no comparison.

My first game for West Ham was against Brentford [20 December 1992]. *I made six appearances for West Ham including a game in the Anglo-Italian Cup* [v Pisa].

I think the black players that went before me did much to pave the way. I never really look at my colour. I think of myself as a human being first. My wife is white, but it is strange how it was her who asked me the question about the way black players were treated at West Ham.

ALEXANDER BUNBURY

There did seem to be a pattern at times, maybe it was just a trend. Maybe colour was an issue, I'd like to think not. To be honest, while I was at the club other things took priority, there wasn't much time to think about my colour. People on the management side were helpful to me and there was some support from Billy Bonds, but an attitude did come across at times that just made you wonder a bit, not from the fans, they were always fantastic. It was a constant grind in training, harsh words, never a hand on a shoulder. The fans are the people I will always remember at Upton Park; their support is the thing that stays with me and is my most enduring and fondest memory of my days with West Ham. No matter what, they will come out and support the team, even the reserves, big time. I always got on with the fans at West Ham. They were very supportive even in the reserve games.

I don't think I had much impact on the club, but history will tell, I suppose. I think I have proved Harry was wrong about me. I was Maritimo's top scorer on their all-time list – 59 in 165. I was their player of the year 1996, '97 and '98. I went to the Cup final with them in 1995, the first time ever for Maritimo, after scoring the winner and only goal in the semi-final v Porto [Bobby Robson was in charge of them at the time]. I was Portuguese Foreign Player of the Year in 1994–95. I scored 12 goals that season. I was consistently in the top 10 strikers in the Portuguese League and was Athlete of the Year, Footballer of the Year and Personality of the Year on Madeira in 1998. I played against Leeds in UEFA Cup. I just missed out on being the Portuguese Player of the Year by three or four votes.

When I joined Maritimo they were a mid- to lower-table side. While I was with them they were never out of the top five. In the last two years I was only playing at around 50 per cent due to my ankle problems. Most of the time I was there, offers came in from other clubs. I could have moved to Italy or Benfica or Sporting. But every time an offer came in Maritimo matched it.

I left Portugal at the age of 31 with a year left on my contract. They wanted me to finish my career with them. In all modesty I have to tell you that I was the most popular person on that island; over the six seasons I'd been one of the most well-known foreign goalscorers of the SuperLiga but we had no privacy and after a while that can become a *little tiring. My transfer fee was set at about $4m or $5m, so I went to the president and asked him to cut this in the light of the service I had given to the club and he was good enough to do this to allow me to move to the States. I could have extended my contract. I'd scored around 15 goals for them in the previous season, but it seemed the right time to move on. I had an operation on my ankle when I got back to the US and I hoped that I'd be able to give two or three more seasons in major league soccer. So I joined Kansas City Wizards on a free on 22 June 1999, making my debut in Washington v DC United on 26 June. I joined KCW as they were the nearest club to my wife's home state of Minnesota. Family is the most important thing to me. I left Portugal primarily because I always promised my wife that we would return to her home state. While I was with Kansas, they went from a struggling side to become a Championship-winning team. I played 19 games and managed four goals, but it was clear that I couldn't give of my best and that being the case I thought it was time to try something else. So I retired at the end of the 1999–2000 season along with the former Celtic and Everton player Mo Johnson.*

I now have a business, the 'Alex Bunbury Soccer Elite Programme', working with youngsters, but it's not just about football, we promote good values with the kids and hope the young people can learn something about morality from the game, giving some consideration to community and country. It's more about that than gaining playing standards. We try to get them to consider each other, help each other out and think about how to do the right thing. It's a way for me to put something back into the game and society.

I've also co-founded 'GoalsAfar', to design and manufacture the unique, patent-pending 'Back-Atcha' portable rebounding goals. They are lightweight goals, used as coaching tools and backyard solo practice aids, to develop shooting accuracy, ball handling and co-ordination skills during and away from team practice sessions.

I now think of Minnesota as my home. We've got our dream home on the golf course, I do love the game, I've got a 10 handicap. I play the game for enjoyment and I still take good care of myself.

I do a little scouting for Maritimo but I've never really seen myself as a potential manager. I would have a tough time dealing with players.

ALEXANDER BUNBURY

Now players are all about me, me, me, they really don't seem to think about giving something back. I used to do a lot of charity work when I was with Maritimo, but the other players didn't get involved in that kind of thing, I never understood that.

My parents have been the greatest influence on my life, although I like to read biography and have been inspired by reading about the lives of Malcolm X, Martin Luther King and Nelson Mandela. I also enjoy John Grisham and Mary Higgins Clark. I like to listen to R'n'B, jazz and I love U2.

I guess I was the prototypical centre-forward; tall and strong yet mobile, agile and skilful, dishing out delicate passes. I was what others might call an excellent all-round player, known for my commitment to Canada.

On 5 December 2005 Alex Bunbury was inducted into the Canadian Soccer Hall of Fame and Museum, in recognition of the contribution he made to Canadian international soccer between 1986 and 1997. Only John Catliff and Dale Mitchell, both already in the Hall of Fame, scored more (19 goals apiece). He is one of only 86 men thus recognised in the history of Canadian soccer. Alex played just five games for the Hammers, but he is proud of his association with the club and in particular its supporters. Given his distinguished career and contribution to the North American and world game, everyone associated with West Ham should be proud that Alex wore the Hammers over his heart.

DALE ANDREW GORDON

HAMMERS DEBUT: 14/8/93

'People don't even see me as being black ... I had a banana thrown at me once and I ate the bastard!'

I arranged to meet with Dale in Great Yarmouth and he decided he would talk to me while he was having his hair cut. When the cut was complete we were still talking. He suggested that I get mine done and we finished the interview with me in the chair. Dale, known to the fans as 'Reggie' (as he looked a bit like Leonard Rossiter's TV character Reggie Perrin) and 'Flash', was an exuberant and dynamic right-winger, who had gained wide recognition at Norwich City before becoming a star of the Glasgow Rangers side that won back-to-back Scottish Premier League titles, the Scottish Cup and the Skol Cup.

Dale runs a very successful soccer training school for boys and girls aged 6–15 that operates all over East Anglia.

I was born in Great Yarmouth [Monday, 9 January 1967]. *With my roots in Norfolk I always thought I'd come back here and retire. When the West Ham move come along, they had just been promoted to the Premiership. I enjoyed the experience of living in London, I really did.*

My wife Lisa is a Norfolk girl. We met when I was 16. We have a son, Remi. He was born in 1993. The year I signed for West Ham [that was in July]. *Little left-foot Remi ... he's shown signs. I think he was conceived with the help of a bottle of brandy. Courvoisier, it was, but I was gonna call him Courvoisier Gordon* [laughs]. *We've also got Paige. She's 16 and very theatrical. She's a very confident young lady. I won't say she gets it from me* [smiles].

146

DALE ANDREW GORDON

My mum and dad live in Caister where they've lived for many, many years, I was brought up there and went to the local school. Dad's still involved in what I do, mainly on the setting up of the business, helping out with the boys who work for me now. He was originally from South America, Guyana. He's been in Britain for close to 50 years now. He did go back there with a brother a long time ago but that was a bit of a mistake. So much had changed over time. I've got one elder brother and two sisters. My brother is an area manager for Debenhams. He takes care of four or five branches, including Lakeside, Bromley and Bluewater. My oldest sister is married with three girls. My younger sister works in local holiday camps.

I was an all-rounder at school. Athletics and so on. Later on I used to enjoy golf. As a young player I was impressed by Laurie Cunningham. It was awful when he died in that road crash. The West Bromwich Albion days, they used to call 'em 'The Three Degrees'; Brendon Batson, Cyril Regis and Laurie Cunningham. Laurie Cunningham, being a winger, his pace and his power made him someone I wanted to emulate.

Before I signed for Norwich I was approached by quite a few clubs and offered a fair bit of money as well. Man City, who at the time were one of the big sides in the old Div One, offered a nice brown paper bag [smiles] and housing. It was a period when that was happening quite a lot to the up-and-coming better boys. West Ham were also looking at me, as were Tottenham, Arsenal and Ipswich.

I started with Norwich as a schoolboy. I was offered an apprenticeship there. I served six months of a two-year apprenticeship. I went on tour with them as a boot boy, sort of hod carrier, but, with a couple of injuries they had on tour in Sweden, I was given the opportunity. That's where 'Disco Dale' was born. The Norwich physio called me that. I got up with Louie Donowa and did a dance, messing around completely. Then forever more you're John Travolta and accused of being out every night dancing, which is all a myth.

I was just gone 17 and came back and carried on being involved with the first team. In August '84 I made me debut v Liverpool on the right-wing. I was seven years with Norwich. Ken Brown, a former Hammer of course, put together a good side and I played 248 games

147

and scored 43 goals – that's brilliant from the wing, innit! I was Player of the Year in 1989. They were mostly good years for the club. Fourth in the old Division One and semi-final of the FA Cup in the same year. That was the year of the Hillsborough disaster. We were playing Everton at Villa Park. The fact that we were defeated was totally out the window with what happened at Hillsborough.

I have a lot of good memories playing against West Ham rather than for them [laughs]. *I've scored a couple of goals against West Ham.*

In the quarter-final of the Cup in '89 we played them at Upton Park and it was a 0–0 draw. I hit the bar. I had a good game. I nearly always played well against them. We won the replay 3–1 and I scored the final goal, which took us to the semi-final.

You know, when players have a purple patch against certain teams, it always seems to be West Ham [laughs]. *West Ham and Norwich games have always been very exciting.* We were involved with West Ham in a live TV game as well when Alan McKnight played in goal. I made my mind up when he came out of his penalty area. He should have put me in row Z, but he sort of waved his arms up in the air, saying I ain't going to let you go past, so I scored the first ever live goal for Norwich as well.

The transfer to Rangers, in November '91, was for £1.2 million. It was always going to be a challenge for me to adapt to, what with it being in a different country as well. I think I was the second or third black player to turn out for Rangers. The supporters were fine. Mark Walters had been there, but from me debut I set the house on fire; I scored two and we won five–nil at Dunfermline Athletic [9 November 1991] and was a first-team regular [28 games, five goals] *as Rangers won the Premier League.* But injury kept me to 22 games [one goal] *the following season. Rangers retained the Championship though.* There was the Scottish Cup and the Skol Cup wins. It was good. It was a great side. I had a slight ligament problem with the knee so missed the end of the second season I was there. I just missed out on playing in the Cup final again, but they were very, very successful times.

I'd spent two years at Rangers, I had a four-year contract. Walter Smith told me that they'd had an offer from West Ham; Rangers were about to go to Italy for pre-season training, he told me he didn't really *want me to leave but to go and see what West Ham had to say and let him know what happened. I came down to Heathrow the following day. I'd been left out of the Scottish Cup final team that year, which had disappointed me a bit, and it seemed as if I wasn't going to be central to things in Scotland. I wanted to go to a club where I was wanted and could show I was a top-class player. So I signed for West Ham within a couple of hours, I got the same arrangements as I had with Rangers, and I was looking forward to a new challenge. I'd spoken to the wife who at that time was in Great Yarmouth just having Remi.*

I look back on my career and it's good to say you were involved in something like the European campaign, the 'Battle of Britain' game against Leeds, the Old Firm games. I loved Scotland. I stayed at every championship golf course through football but was not allowed to play golf!

I was the first real major signing that Billy Bonds made. £750,000 was a lot of money at the time. I came in against Wimbledon and got a goal in the opening game. I got West Ham's first Premiership goal. It was a 40-yard tap-in [laughs] in a 1–1 draw at Highfield Road, which secured our first point of the season [21 August 1993]. It was a bit of a change from Scotland playing in the Premiership. The pace of the game in Scotland had been faster and I found it strange getting used to what seemed like the slower game in England. West Ham were holding their own.

The injury was just a freak accident. It started from a cartilage operation and just escalated from there. Getting an injury like that, so early on, just when I got to the club, being a big signing, yourself and everybody perhaps wanted to get back a bit too soon. There's a pressure to perform. People didn't really understand you were doing your best to get back.

At West Ham I was friendly with Mike Marsh, when he moved from Liverpool. He lived in Epping too. That helped with the women and the children settling in. Ian Bishop was a mate. Bish was a chap who was very friendly and would get on with anyone. It wasn't long after me knee operation, Bish, Mike and Jeroen Boere took me down to Epping for a drink in The Thatched House. I was pretty depressed and we got a bit pissed. I'm playing pool with empty glasses using one of me crutches as a cue, smashing one or two of course. Anyway, Jeroen decided to call it a night, but, just a bit after he left, he's come back in the pub effing and jeffing in English and Dutch. He had chained up his bike outside and Ian has got a hacksaw from somewhere and sawn the bike in half. We were helpless with laughter.

I picked up the nickname 'the Flash' at Upton Park. I was quick. One of my main assets was running with the ball at speed. I was probably the first to use the 'step-over'; it was always difficult to stop, even for players who knew about it. With the speed this helped to make me an exciting player. I was an intelligent player as well. My all-round game was very good. There was also the thing about playing for one of the sides that were interested in me as a kid, when John Lyall was around. I always remember going down there, to the gym, that's probably still there, and the sports hall at Chadwell Heath, and thinking, 'This is a nice club.' There were good players down there at the time. Going back and playing for a team that I'd been associated with when I was eight or nine, that I'd been down there as a kid, even though I'd been with a group of boys, was a good feeling.

Having to go on a Saturday and watching the team play when I was injured used to get me down. I'd rather be out shopping with the wife. I'm not a great lover of watching football. I hated going there and having to explain to supporters how long it was going to be before I was fit enough to play.

Even though we were in Epping, we were only half-an-hour's drive from the City. We went to the shows, we did the things you always do. You get the stretch limo out. I had a good time. I did enjoy that side of it, not the nightclubs and so on. I did that, not so much with the boys but with the wife. It was a bit of a release, a way to get away from the disappointment of the injuries. You needed something else. If not you'd go to the training, sit on a treatment bench, go and do your gym work, back on the treatment bench in the afternoon, go home and basically sit round and sulk. I was a nightmare to live with, an absolute nightmare. At one stage it put a lot of strain on us both. I kept on feeling, 'I want to play, I want to play!' Harry and Billy were upset because Bonzo signed me and how well the club is playing shows how well the manager is doing his job. But with a couple of key players crocked it's frustrating.

I don't think people realise how much you wanted to do a job for the club, especially as a big signing. When the consultant turned round and said to me, 'Well, I think you may have to retire, this is a career-threatening injury,' I wasn't down in the dumps, I wasn't too disheartened by it. By then, when the time came when it was certain that I'd have to come out of the game, I'd had three years to adapt to the situation. If it had been sudden, if I'd been clattered and told straight away that I'd have to give the game up, that would have been hard. You haven't got time to prepare. I'd had ankle injuries. I'd had a shoulder injury at Norwich, but an operation the first year I was with Rangers sorted that out. That wasn't a problem at West Ham. John Green the physio is still at Upton Park now, he was good; when you look at what medical support they get now! Most players have to have a scan. It's so thorough now. Also the equipment they've got to get players back to full fitness, it's a lot more advanced. They've not just got a physio, they've even got counsellors, and sometimes you need that, especially when you're dealing with a bad injury. When I was playing, it was an X-ray. Check yer knee joints, check yer shoulders, check if you've got a brain [laughs], that was it, you'd passed the medical.

Harry [Redknapp], in his book, describes me as 'the head of light entertainment' [laughs]. He said that I'd wanted to hire an open-topped bus and tour through the West End. Not being disrespectful to Harry but I think he said things like that to sell books. Harry was a bit like that. I wouldn't say that I always saw eye to eye with Harry, but I kept meself to meself. I knew his thoughts on me getting fit and right for West Ham. He knows how hard I trained as well in my last season and I did actually get fit, even though I did get another injury. Most clubs have a Christmas party and sometimes it makes the press. All we did was hire a minibus, we went to a restaurant and then we went on to a club. Where he got the open-topped bus from … [laughs]. No! That's just Harry being – how shall I say? – a little bit over the top. I was something of a flamboyant dresser. It's easy to say that about somebody when they've gone. Don't get me wrong, I've always been a lively kinda bloke ... but that has never dominated my life and caused me to lose sight of what I need to do.

I don't think Harry's very good at the man-management. His relationship with the players – I'll be blunt, he wasn't that well liked. You need a bit of banter, but you have to draw the line somewhere. Billy Bonds got respect from the players. He was black and white. Bill would tell you what he thought. Harry wasn't the same. That's why Bill done so well as a player. He was an honest player, with blood and guts and that's who he was. He took that across into management. I don't think Harry was like that. There's two sides to every story, of course, but, when you went and see Harry, say when you came back from injury, you came out thinking, 'Why did I go in there? What a waste of time that was.' You were banging yer head against the wall half the time with him. Other people would know Bill better than I do, there may be a different side to him but Harry gave the impression that he liked to keep some things covered up.

There was some bad feeling when Harry took over from Billy. A lot of it was swept under the carpet. Especially at the time when Bill actually left. Harry pulled us all together one day and said that it didn't feel as if he wanted the job, still had his house in Bournemouth. He had the opportunity to go back there. Going back to being honest, was that more of a cover-up? He maybe wanted the job but needed the weekend to think about it. I think that the players thought that the way things were dealt with, the way the new coaching staff came in, that there was a lot more to it than we were led to believe. But Bill's not the sort of person to do anything other than walk away from a situation like that.

I never go to Upton Park. I don't like watching football, not even on the telly. I get more enjoyment out of what I do now. Seeing the kids' teams perform and hopefully produce players that will go all the way. I get more satisfaction out of that.

I played for England schoolboys; England v Scotland at Wembley. The game didn't really light up – I played at every level apart from full. Youth [1984 and 1985], four caps at Under-21, one game for England Under-15s. Like a lot of young boys I had growing pains. I suffered for six months in one season. That again was my knees. I

DALE ANDREW GORDON

played a 'B' international against Wales and I went on a trip to Turkey.

In football you go to clubs to win things, because of ambition, but [laughs] it's money really. I've been quite fortunate. I've had two good moves. I've looked after meself financially. I've got a good business and I've won things, but I've seen the other side of it, when you have to come out early. I got crocked when I was quite young. If I was playing now, I'd be earning ridiculous money, but I'm not bitter about that, that happens. When I was playing, the money wasn't the same as it is now, but relatively it was probably equivalent to what some of 'em get now. That's just the way football has gone.

I signed on loan to Peterborough in March '95. I was recovering from injury at that time. In August '96 I moved to Bournemouth and did a bit of coaching down there. I was in Yarmouth one day and Harry [Redknapp] offered me another year. I decided not to accept it. I had an operation on me right knee just to clear up a cartilage problem. I was at home one day and the phone went and it was Mel Machin at Bournemouth. I'd never thought about getting involved in coaching. I knew Mel from my days at Norwich. He was the assistant manager when I made me debut when Ken Brown was manager. He offered me the position of player-coach down there on the south coast. I thought about it for a couple of weeks. Coaching is something you never think about at such an early age. In the end I said, 'Yeah. I'll go for it.' I went down there on a three-year contract. I started playing well and I was enjoying the coaching, taking the first-team training. I took the reserves on a couple of occasions. I think it stood me in good stead for what I'm doing now. I was there about eight months. Scored a goal, played 19 games. But the knee was getting to me; my wife and children were still living in Norfolk. After games I was driving home and I'd have to drive back late Sunday night. Being involved with the coaching you had to be in early on the Monday. I learned a lot off of Mel though. Also, at that time, the club went into receivership. That didn't influence my decision to leave but there was still the arrangement of a settlement figure with them, which I thought would be difficult with them going into receivership.

I'd lost my appetite for the game. I thought to myself, 'This is not really the standard that I want to be playing at.' The coaching was good, but the standard of football together with the fact that I wasn't doing myself justice anyway led me to call it a day. February '97, that was.

My wife was the one who suggested, 'Do something you're good at,' and that was with the kids coaching. We advertised and on the first day that the advert went out we had over 70 phone calls. We started with 168 kids a week and within a few years we were up to over 400 with 60 on the waiting list.

I've known Albert Jones for many years. Albert is the son of Jimmy Jones, who was vice-chairman at Norwich when I was playing there, he owned the pleasure beach in Great Yarmouth. Gorleston was his football club, they played in the Jewson League. They were in dire straits. They were at the bottom of the table and looking like they'd go down just before Christmas 1999. I'd been involved with the other team locally, Great Yarmouth, since May '97 but coaching the kids limited me in terms of doing as much as I'd have liked. I played a bit for King's Lynn but only on Saturdays again because of soccer academy and I was still Yarmouth's Director of Football. I offered to help Gorleston out in November '98 as Director of Football. They were one place off the bottom of the table. But on me debut at home to Histon I got a red card in the 52nd minute for retaliation and dissent and Gorleston lost 1–0 [laughs]. But it was a bit of a release from my work with children and everything had been settled with regard to my personal injury claim. I resigned from Gorleston in 2000.

I've been going with the business now for 10 years. Ipswich have used it to their full advantage. I scout for them as well around here. Now I'm also consultant at Great Yarmouth College of Further Education. It's really surprising the success of the academy, but we've worked hard to get a good reputation around the area. I left football wondering what I'd do, but the business got to be a full-time thing pretty quickly. I love the work and it's a bonus doing it in an area I know so well.

I've been asked many times if I would go into management. It depends on the job. For what I do in the week, me social life, I take the kids in the evenings, the weekends are busy, who would take over my business? I could expand the business and probably do very well, but then it's Dale Gordon's soccer academy. It's not Dale Gordon's soccer academy if you get a young YTS boy in to do the job. That's where a lot of the soccer academies and schools have gone flat. If you put your name to it, you've got to be there to do it. I think, if I was to get involved with a club again, I don't think the club would have it and I wouldn't have time to do the training anyway.

I think the business, the way it's gone, with the numbers and the quality that the children get, it would be hard to give it all up. I have me own tournament as well, which is in July; we have about 120 teams come down on a weekend, they travel from all over East Anglia and Essex. We've got fantastic backing from McDonald's. Nat West and Pleasure Beach are involved. It has become very, very big. I can't see myself in the foreseeable future walking away from that. Every year the teams grow. In the long term I'd like to have me own facility, me own centre, a full-size pitch and astro-turf pitch, with changing and community facilities, something for the children to use as a football youth club. That's my goal now. Maybe we'll have to get lottery funding.

I got on well with the fans at Upton Park. At the end of the day I didn't really have enough games ... they all knew me. They knew I was an exciting player who had played well against their team; they knew they were getting quality. I don't think the supporters were really made aware that it was such a serious injury. Being a big signing I was always under that little bit more pressure to get myself fit. Big money had been paid for me, they were paying me good wages.

You're more aware of racism when you're standing on the touchline. If, as a manager, you're standing on a touchline, shouting instructions about opposition players, with the supporters being so close to you, you're probably more aware of abuse. I had a banana thrown at me once and I ate the bastard! If you do it that way, it's amazing the response you get. They turn round and start clapping yer, saying, 'That's fair enough.' The lower in the League you go, the more you're conscious of the abuse. Yer Second Division and yer Third Division and some of yer First Division clubs as well, the ones that had been promoted over the last two or three years. Yer Burys, teams like Gillingham. In the Premiership you're in front of 30,000 people plus every week. But I don't know if that was more about a lack of awareness of the kind of problems players have from time to time with form and so on than it is about being black. I don't know if mentality is too harsh a word for trying to explain why things are as they are at lower levels. Maybe it's a financial thing stopping racism being stamped out at smaller clubs. If a club has got £20k, perhaps they'd think they can put that money to better use than spending it on preventing two or three idiots from offending people.

Now, in the Premiership, you've not only got the black players, but you've also got the foreign input as well. I think that everyone who comes to watch the Premiership now has adapted to the fact that it's now more cosmopolitan; the focus is much more sophisticated.

I never saw myself as a groundbreaker in terms of my colour at West Ham or Rangers. It's amazing, but people don't even see me as being black. I got a white mum, a black dad. My wife's white, my girl is virtually white, my boy's a bit dark but people wouldn't look on him and think, 'He's black.' Even round this area, when I was playing there was only about two or three of us that were black. Meself and Dion Dublin and his brother Ashley. Even in terms of socialising and that, you never thought it was going to be a problem. It was really strange, but I was never really seen as being black. Now results are the most important thing. Money is primary. Regardless if you're black or white or Chinese.

My fondest memory of the fans at Upton Park, the thing that has always stuck in my mind, was when I came on for only five or ten minutes, I'd got back from injury after about two years. Newcastle were going for the Championship, I came on and the supporters gave me such a warm applause. Within two or three minutes, I was one against one with Pavel Srnicek and I thought, 'This is really strange, what the hell am I doing here?' [laughs]. It was a Wednesday night, we were winning 2–0 and, because I'd been away from the game so long, I felt like a little schoolboy again. I heard the roar that wanted me to stick the ball in the net and I went through his legs and it just clipped his heel and went out for a corner!

I was never a nervous player, some players need to stick their fingers down their throat and be sick before they go out, some like a swig of brandy just to calm down, but I was never nervous. But that day I got a little shiver through me as I went out on the pitch. It was a feeling of relief. I'd battled against the injury, I'd got back into the squad and got on as sub ... it was like ... 'YES!' Of course, it didn't last for very long as I was soon to be back on the treatment table. The next morning my knee had blown up again. It was very disappointing, devastating at the time. I knew I'd lost a few yards in terms of pace, not good for a winger, and that I was not going to get back to where I'd been. During that last year I tried hard to give it a go. John Green probably got fed up with me being around him and I lost weight and trained hard pre-season. It did no good. The knee blew up regular. I'd played only 10 times for West Ham and scored that first Carling Premiership goal. I wish I'd had the chance to give a bit more. But that's life and that's football.

There was a good spirit there and you always miss the banter in the changing room. Do you know what, with all the ups and downs I had at West Ham, scoring that first Premiership goal is something that I'm proud of and it is something people seem to remember.

I told Dale I'd finished the interview. He replied,

Really? Shame. That was nice. I enjoyed that. And the haircut weren't bad either [laughs].

RIO GAVIN FERDINAND

'It's just the colour of your skin and it's just on the outside ... everyone is more or less similar in one way or another.'

Rio was born on 7 November 1978 in Peckham and was raised in South London by strict but loving parents. As is well known, his cousin is former English international striker Les Ferdinand, while his brother Anton is a central defender for West Ham.

Ferdinand the elder was signed as a schoolboy in January 1994, but got just eight starts in the 1994–95 term (Frank Lampard got 24 games in the South East Counties League) but was in the Youth League Cup final v Chelsea at the end of the season. The Hammers lost 5–2 in the first leg at Upton Park but at Stamford Bridge the young cockneys roared to 4–1 victory after a penalty shoot-out. According to Rio that was the moment he knew he was going to be a professional footballer – he had scored one of the goals and had the taste for success.

Demonstrating astonishing ability, Rio was almost immediately compared to Bobby Moore. However, he has flourished much better than the last player, Kevin Lock, to be thus hailed. He became England Under-18 skipper and in 1996 (five days before making his first-team debut) took part in the Youth Cup final against Liverpool, amongst his opponents that day were Michael Owen and Jamie Carragher. Rio remembered one aspect of his first experiences of football that had not been part of his life at West Ham;

I was at a football club ... I was about 18 ... sitting in the stands and there was a policeman standing behind me about three rows back.

Ade Coker

Clive Charles

John Charles

Ade Coker and Clyde Best

Paul Ince

Rufus Brevett

Paulo Wanchope

Marc Vivian-Foe

Matthew Rush

Jermain Defoe

George Parris

Ian Wright

Nigel Reo-Coker

Rio Ferdinand

Marlon Harewood

Samassi Abou

Leroy Rosenoir

Mike Smal

Alex Bunbury

Nigel Reo-Coker

Les Ferdinand

Danny Gabbidon

Zamora, Anton, Mullins

Bobby Barnes

Shaka Hislop

Andy Impey and Paul Ince

David James

Anton Ferdinand

Brevett, Sinclair, Defoe

Trevor Sinclair and Jermain Defoe

Chris Powell

Glen Johnson

Bobby Zamora

Trevor Sinclair and Fredric Kanoute

Hayden Mullins

RIO GAVIN FERDINAND

The visiting team had a few black players ... one of them scored ...
this guy right in front of me started saying 'you black this' and 'you
black that'. So I looked at my friend and said, 'I think I'm going to
leave, I can't sit here and listen to this all the time,' and the policeman
didn't say or do anything. The guy carried on shouting 'you black this
and that' and then he turns round and says to me, 'Oh, not you,
mate, you're all right, it's just these ones, they get right on my nerves.'
I just kind of laughed out of embarrassment for the guy and I looked
at the policeman and he looked away, as if to say, 'I didn't hear it.'
It just makes you shake your head sometimes, they haven't got any
self-respect to start talking like that ... it's something that, touch
wood, is being driven out.

After an 11-game loan to Division Two Bournemouth, Rio made his
first-team debut in at the Boleyn Ground in a 1996 League encounter
with Sheffield Wednesday, coming on as a substitute with 22 minutes
to play. By now he was a designated central defender, having
converted from the midfield role he had previously filled. Ferdinand's
first Premiership goal was scored against Blackburn in February 1997.
He had come on as a substitute striker and as such showed he was able
to play left-back, central defence and midfield as well as an emergency
forward. In the same season he was voted the Young Hammer of the
Year and gained his first Under-21 cap.

But in September 1997, after selection for a World Cup qualifier
v Moldova, Rio was sent home by Glenn Hoddle after a drink-
driving charge. But he was ready to 'repent' even to the extent of
consulting the 'Guru' who was instrumental in Hoddle losing his
England role:

I went to see Eileen Drewery ... It was something that was suggested
to me and I went to see if it would help me. Personally, it didn't really
do anything for me, but it didn't harm me and I don't regret trying it.

Perhaps more interesting was Ferdinand's view on individual
liberties in the light of Hoddle being vilified in the press for his
more 'esoteric' methods:

THE BLACK HAMMERS

It's all about individual feelings and some people find it very positive, some people don't. Who knows, I may go again in the future – it's not something I would turn my nose up at. Everyone has their own needs, the right to make free decisions, and I think that should be respected.

At the end of the 1997–98 campaign, at the age of 19, Rio was voted Hammer of the Year; he was the youngest ever player to get it. He commented at the time,

The West Ham supporters have been brilliant to me since I started playing and my relationship with them is fantastic – it's great to get recognition from the people who pay our wages and it's nice to know that they think you are doing the right things.

Rio made his full international debut in 2–0 win over Cameroon in November 1998 and was selected for the 22 that would compete in the World Cup finals in France 98, although he failed to be selected for a game in that tournament, he found it a valuable experience:

The World Cup was a great experience for me. If a player doesn't learn anything from being around the best players in the world for a month, then they don't deserve to be there.

Kevin Keegan didn't want Ferdinand for Euro 2000. But after the finals a £16 million bid was made to take West Ham's central defender to Barcelona. This was succeeded in August 2000 by £15 million from Leeds in August 2000.

It was only in July that Rio had pointed out that manager Redknapp had promised not to sell his best players. When asked about the speculation around his move to Leeds, he responded,

I'm not going to Leeds, I'm not going anywhere. I'm perfectly happy at West Ham and I will only be leaving if the club say they want to sell me … If the club sold Trevor Sinclair, Frank Lampard and Paolo

RIO GAVIN FERDINAND

Di Canio this summer, then I wouldn't want to stay. But that's not going to happen, so I can't understand why a big thing was made out of it.

It was hard for Rio to leave West Ham and he confessed that it was something of a surprise to him that the club had let him go. He told the world that he loved the club and felt he owed much to the coaches he had worked with since he had been a schoolkid. Indeed, time would prove that Redknapp had flogged one of the Hammers greatest ever players relatively cheaply. The pain of that retrospective insight was, of course, compounded as Harry set about frittering away the return on Ferdinand on players that had no affinity to the club and unsurprisingly matched this lack of identification in terms of loyalty and performance.

Having won back his England shirt by way of a 1–0 friendly defeat by Italy in November 2000, Rio's marketability went up and an £18 million transfer to Leeds United created a new British record. Within a year he was captain of the Peacocks and in 2001–02 Rio was voted into the PFA's Premiership team.

In the 2002 World Cup Ferdinand partnered Sol Campbell at the heart of the England defence. He scored his first goal for England in the game against Denmark and, having shown himself to be of the highest international class, after the World Cup, moved, on 22 July 2002, to Old Trafford. The £30 million fee was for yet another British transfer record, but also a world record for a defender. In his first season with United he won a Premiership Championship medal. FA Cup glory (2004) followed, as did runner-up medals in the League Cup (2003) and the FA Cup (2005).

It had been a glittering decade and a meteoric rise for Ferdinand but his capacity to handle fame and fortune came into doubt in 2003. It was Tuesday, 23 September of that year that Rio left United's Carrington training ground without taking mandatory routine drugs test. He claimed that he forgot, being preoccupied with moving house. Two days later he passed a rearranged test. However, the FA imposed a £50,000 fine and an eight-month ban from January 2004, which applied to all matches, at club and international level. An appeal was dismissed, but at the same time an FA request to increase the ban to a year was refused.

The ban disqualified him from taking part in all Euro 2004 and Chelsea's John Terry took his place. It was the worst type of punishment for Rio, who is not the world's best spectator:

> I'm an absolute terrible watcher ... I'd rather stay at home and blot it out of my mind. I only came to the game because injured players have to, but I get so frustrated and you do find yourself kicking and heading every ball.

Adam Newton knew Ferdinand would be a big star the first time he saw him play. They were both at Upton Park in the 1990s. Newton was a rising star in the club's successful youth team when Rio was in the ascendant at West Ham. Adam recalled, 'I first knew Rio when he was a first-year YTS scholar, but he was already training regularly with the first team which immediately proved what a talent he was. He was a couple of years older than me, but he was someone a lot of the younger lads at West Ham used as their inspiration. It was always pretty clear that Rio would go on to become a great player, but not necessarily as a centre-back.

'My first memories of him are as a skinny, tall central-midfield player. He had a great touch and great skills, but due to his height and pace it was decided to make more use of him at the back.

'I was never lucky enough to play competitively alongside Rio, but I did get called into the first-team squad for training a few times and figured in mini five-a-side matches with him. He was the complete package in his late teens and early twenties and you could see he was ready to shine.

'He'd had this hype about him when he was still in the West Ham youth team and it was always just a matter of time for that first big break to come. And once he got into the first team it was inevitable that he was always going to go on to big things, so I'm not in the least bit surprised by how far he has gone in the game.'

According to Shaka Hislop, a long-time colleague of Ferdinand's at Upton Park, Rio always wanted 'to make sure he's looking good at all times. He's got his own individual style and always looks pretty cool in whatever he wears. You can tell he spends a lot of time in top clothes shops making sure he's got all the right gear to wear to training and matches. He can be really smart but he's also got some pretty good casual stuff – he's got a wardrobe for almost every occasion.'

Ferdinand is a great advocate of the anti-racist movement within football. When asked about how to combat racism in sport he responded,

The way forward isn't violence. As much as you would like to turn round and hit someone for saying something ... and you could be within your rights to do that ... it's not the way forward and it's not the way to solve it ... I know it's hard, but it's something that makes you a better person ... you don't want to go down to their level of being ill mannered and having no self-respect. If you've got a bit of self-respect, you just rise above it and keep your mouth shut. On a football pitch you let the referee know that something like that has happened and then after the game he may put it in his match report and he could take it further after the game ...

If your parents are racists and they tell you certain things about different cultures, the best way to judge is to find out for yourself. If you don't know yourself, then you'll never know and you'll only go on what other people are saying. If you just sit around with someone ... you'll notice that there's not much difference between anyone, it's just the colour of your skin and it's just on the outside ... everyone is more or less similar in one way or another.

Rio put in some indifferent performances for club and country when he returned from the ban. But he was first-choice defender for England in the 2006 World Cup in Germany and, while others let themselves and their country down, he showed himself to be one of the best defenders in the tournament. He is crucial in Manchester United's ambitions to challenge Chelsea's dominance of English football in the 2006–07 campaign. He has shown on more than one occasion he has a propensity to mess up, but he also has the potential to be one of the greatest defenders ever to have gone through the Hammers system. He is certainly a candidate for the next black captain of England and maybe one day a great and well-experienced manager, perhaps at Upton Park. We shall see. To use Rio's own words,

Football is all about ifs and buts.

EMMANUEL OMOYINMI

HAMMERS DEBUT: 1/3/97

'I swivelled and shot and it went in.'

Manny was born in Lagos, Nigeria (28 December 1977). But when he was eight his parents moved to Custom House, part of the West Ham heartlands. He became an English Schools international and appeared a dozen times and scored twice for West Ham.

A product of the Hammers' youth academy, one of the young Irons that claimed the South East Counties League Championship at the end of the 1995–96 season, Manny was also in the side that contested the two-leg FA Youth Cup final that term alongside Frank Lampard and Rio Ferdinand.

Manny's name could give the Hammers a tactical advantage at times, as announcers made emergency calls to Carol Vorderman. He once said,

> *On away trips with the reserves they were always getting it totally wrong. We'd be doing our stretching exercises out on the pitch and all the players would pause when my name was read out and then start laughing their heads off.*

The 5ft 6in Omoyinmi made his Premiership debut in a March 1997 encounter with Leeds United. During May 1998, coming on for Samassi Abou, he scored two marvellous goals in the 3–3 draw at Selhurst Park against already relegated Crystal Palace. There was no time for celebrations though, as the Hammers were looking for a win that would give them a chance of a UEFA place. Manny recalled his contribution:

For the first one Trevor Sinclair played a ball into the box and I knew I wasn't going to get much time. I swivelled and shot and it went in. The second goal was fairly similar. The ball was played in from my right. I swivelled and the same thing happened.

But first-team football was not a regular expectation for the diminutive wing-back (who preferred an all-out attacking flanker role) and his career began to look like a patchwork of loan deals. In September 1996 Manny played seven League games for Bournemouth; during February 1998 he made four appearances for Dundee United; between March and April 1999 he scored one goal in four outings for Orient and in November 1999 he netted against Oldham on his debut for Gillingham. He also scored the winning goal for the Gills that stunned the Oxford United defence. But Omoyinmi's most remembered appearance was at Upton Park on 15 December 1999.

Manny had been on the bench at the start of the quarter-final Worthington Cup meeting with Aston Villa. The match ended 2–2 after extra-time and the outcome had to be decided on penalties. When Shaka Hislop saved Gareth Southgate's spot-kick in the shoot-out, it seemed that West Ham had made it to a Cup semi-final for the first time since 1991. But only hours passed before Villa lodged an appeal against the result. With eight minutes of extra-time remaining, in an effort to change the pattern of the game and perhaps take up a few precious seconds, shuffle-manic Harry Redknapp replaced Paulo Wanchope with Omoyinmi. 'H' would later say that the decision to use Manny would 'haunt' him 'forever'. Many Hammers fans who lived through that season will share his experience. The substitute had little if any influence on the match, but he had played in both legs of Gillingham's second-round tie with Bolton in the same competition. The game had to be replayed and it was Villa who progressed into the last four of that year's League Cup. The first head to roll was Graham Mackrell, the West

Ham secretary, but, although Harry had avoided any blame, this was not to be the end of the matter.

Hate-mail and threats began to be directed at Manny. He was shunned and ridiculed in an unprecedented way. This left the club with no other recourse than to effectively exile the player via loans. He had half-a-dozen games with Scunthorpe United (he scored a goal while at Glanford Park) and made six appearances for Barnet. In July 2000 Manny went to Oxford United as a free transfer, forever to be regarded as a pariah at Upton Park.

Omoyinmi could not regain anything like the form he was capable of and was not able to command a regular place in the U's side. For all this, he scored nine times in 77 run-outs. His first season for Oxford could have been better, scoring just three goals in 24 appearances, although two of them came in one virtuoso performance during a 4–3 victory over Rotherham, who went on to win promotion.

However, along with the rest of his teammates in the 2000–01 season, Manny sank to the foot of the Second Division. With 97 professional games behind him and 15 goals to his credit, in the 2003–04 term he was loaned to non-League Margate and then Gravesend and Northfleet, where he was given a contract starting on 25 May 2004. But in August 2005 Manny joined Canvey Island in the Conference and by December of that year he was with Lewes.

Although a tricky, seemingly tireless player with skill and pace, since leaving Upton Park Manny has been prone to injury and protracted loss of form at times. For the more thoughtful Irons fans, there is a feeling that Manny was destroyed as a player by Harry Redknapp's lack of organisation and preparation and the same carelessness robbed the Hammers of some much-needed glory.

ANDREW RODNEY IMPEY

*'West Ham fans like players who try and I always tried ...
You can talk about the East End spirit, but we were all very close,
we got on really well.'*

I met with Andy in a hotel lounge in Wembley.

I was born in Hammersmith Hospital [Monday, 30 September 1971]. As a lad I was an Arsenal fan [laughs]. There was a lot of people at my school that supported Man U and Tottenham, a lot of them supported Arsenal as well. I think a lot of the blacks in the area used to go to Arsenal, there used to be a little crew of us that used to go over. I went to Harlington School. I wasn't bad at tennis, I was supposed to represent the county. I had to go for a county trial but I couldn't be bothered.

I've got three brothers and six sisters. I'm the third oldest. My brother Lee was on Wimbledon's books when he was younger but he dropped out. Mum and Dad are from Jamaica. Dad runs a minicab place. Mum's living in America at the moment.

Mum said that when I was young, three or four, I was kicking a ball about. I played for my first football team when I was eight.

I'm with a lady, Maxine. I've got two kids, Daryon and Reanne — ten and nine. I'm trying to get them into golf, get some real money [laughs].

I started off with Yeading and went to QPR for £30k in June 1990. I done an apprenticeship at Wimbledon. I was only there for two weeks, something like that. I had an argument with them. When I left Wimbledon, I got a job as a window fitter. That was good. I enjoyed it. Then I went back into non-League. I still wanted to play football, but I was just pissing about really. The guy, who was the youth-team manager, Alan Burke, he said that you're getting to the age now that you wanna try and make it – this could be your last chance. So I half knuckled down and got into the first team. Then a few scouts started coming to watch. Wimbledon come again, Fulham, QPR, Luton, Southampton, Millwall. QPR were the first ones who said, 'We want you to come in for a trial.'

I was capped at Under-21. It was a 0–0 draw against Turkey. I was chasing around some guy, I don't know what his name was, but I didn't enjoy it. I'd asked about playing for Jamaica, but at that time they was only picking home-grown talent, so that was a no-no. A couple of years after that, they got in touch with me and said that they'd like me to play for them, but I'd played in the qualifiers for England and that ruled it out. I've always been a bit too laidback as a player. I also need a couple of more inches, I need to grow to about 5ft 10in [laughs].

At QPR I got 18 goals in 228 games. I moved to West Ham for £1.2 million in September '97. The transfer was a bit on/off at first. I had an operation on my toe. West Ham wanted to make sure that I could kick a ball and that everything was all right before they would sign me. Forest were sniffing, but they never came right in. I would have never considered Forest over West Ham. Coming to West Ham from QPR, I was almost an out-and-out winger. Playing wing-back at Upton Park was different. I played in that position a couple of times at QPR but I never really knew when to go, when to stay. I'd never actually been shown how to do it. So, at the start of my time at West Ham, it was also a learning period for me. I played in the same role at Leicester and I still didn't grasp it fully. I learned a bit more as time went on, watching other players and that, but I preferred to be on the wing.

In all I played 34 games for West Ham. I made me debut v Liverpool. I'd only trained with the lads on the Friday, so I thought I'd be on the bench. Harry had said he'd probably put me in as sub. I thought, 'That'll be all right to get on.' But as I was coming into the ground he pulled me and said, 'I want yer to play on the left up against McManaman.' I remember thinking, 'Cheers!' First game against speedy Mac! But it turned out all right. I nearly scored. David James stopped me.

I admired Ian Wright. One of the biggest influences on me as a footballer was David Rocastle. It was when I was playing centre-midfield. I used to go over to Arsenal and watch David Rocastle when I was a winger. I used to say, 'Yeah. I like how he plays.' Rio [Ferdinand] was an outstanding player at West Ham. He's got so much. He's so calm. He's always played like he was older than his years. I trained with Joe Cole. I've never seen someone with so much natural ability. Paul Gascoigne was good, but Cole!! [Andy blew out his cheeks.]

The initial phase at West Ham, with a lot of injuries, was one of my worst times. I done all right in my first four or five games, then we were playing Villa in a night game and one of the Villa lads stood on my toe and that put me out again. Before I came to West Ham I hadn't done pre-season training. I wasn't fit. Tendonitis of the Achilles. That was just because of the hard ground. Then missing five, six, seven games … So I picked up a groin strain – played two, missing four. I never got a run of games to get myself into my stride, which was a bit frustrating.

I never experienced any racism from the West Ham crowd when I was at Upton Park. I did when I went there and played for QPR. I got some racial abuse. It weren't the worst. You got more at Chelsea. You got a lot at northern clubs, Leeds and Everton. Not loads and loads, to the extent to make you pack in the game, but you got more comments up North than you got down in London. There could be some institutional racism in football. You've only got to look at the amount of good black players that have come out of the game and are not managers. I think that managers get paid well, but it's the players that are out there and the managers get the stick. It's too much like hard work. I don't want to be a manager. When I pack in playing, I hope to have enough money to spend six months here and six months in Jamaica. That would suit me fine.

You see some shit managers. Harry was as good as gold [smiles]. *He's very different from Martin O'Neill. Harry is not one of the lads, but he could be one of the lads. He talks to his players. I had no trouble from him at all. I got on with him really well. Martin is difficult to sum up. Harry used to be with the players all the time; friendly's not the word, but he'd have a laugh and joke with yer. He was serious when he had to do the serious things, but he could have a laugh and joke. You could have a laugh and joke with Martin O'Neill, but he's just different. They are completely different managers*

The first thing I heard about me moving away from West Ham, I knew there was an offer they had for me from Forest on the Tuesday. We were playing Derby on the Sunday. We were to have a couple of days off and we were going to be training Friday and Saturday, travel up Saturday for the game Sunday. I thought Harry would pull me on the Friday and tell me what was going on. Nothing! I trained as usual. I thought, 'That's a bit strange,' but I just carried on thinking nothing's come of it. I've gone in on the Saturday and Harry's pulled me after training and he's said, 'What's this about Forest have come in for yer?' I've said, 'What do yer mean? You're the manager. You're supposed to know what's happening!' He said that he didn't have a clue, that he knew nothing about it. Peter Storrie, the MD at West Ham then, had gone behind his back and done a deal. Leicester had come in on the Saturday. So, Harry said, 'I don't want you to go.' So I said, 'Well, not being funny, H, but I'm not in the team. Fair enough, I've been injured, lost a bit of form, whatever.' He said, 'Well, you're in the team for tomorrow.' So I said, 'All right then. Fair enough. I ain't played for two weeks, that'll do me.' So, I left the training ground, got in the car, and got a message from my agent: 'You're not playing Sunday.' I've gone back into H and said, 'What's this? I'm not playing.' He says 'You're playing.' He phoned up Peter Storrie. They had an argument. Peter Storrie's saying, 'I've got it from the chairman. He's not playing. We're gonna get £1.6 million for him.' Harry's saying, 'Fuck you! You can't tell me who's not playing. I want him in the team. He's one of my players.' It was going on like that from 12 o'clock to 5 o'clock. In the end Harry said to me, 'You can play the game, or you can talk to Leicester or Forest, whoever, but the game's on Sunday, you can talk to them Monday or Sunday night, but I want you to play.' I said, 'Well, I want to play anyway.' I hadn't played for two weeks. But Peter Storrie said that I couldn't play, in case I got injured. West Ham won the game. Played well. Harry went on the telly at the end and said that it could have been Frank or Rio, that the board couldn't do that sort of thing, going behind his back. Which is fair enough. I didn't want to go North. I'm from London, I'd rather stay in London.

The reason I left was nothing to do with the fans. The fans were used as an excuse. Harry didn't want me to go. When we lost to Arsenal in the Cup, I wasn't going to hide the fact that I'd supported Arsenal. I said that I was gutted that we lost, but happy because Arsenal had gone through. Some fans took it the wrong way. It wasn't like I was saying that I was an Arsenal fan and fuck West Ham. The timing was wrong. When things wasn't going too well, some of the supporters were shouting, 'Fucking Gooner, get back to Highbury.' That got hyped up, the papers got hold of it. 'The fans are on his back', blah, blah, blah. People were asking me, 'Have you got to prove 'em right?' But as many, probably more, took it as a laugh. They knew who paid me wages; they knew the shirt I was wearing. But, what with the injury and not getting a run, it looked like things weren't really going well, but, at the end of the day, you can be the best player in the world and some of the fans will still get on yer back. As many were good about it. The ones who understood the game, and they're the ones that really matter, ain't they? Like yerself, football people know 'bout that shit.

I used to like it when the fans got behind the team – when they sang 'Bubbles'. They get right behind the team. That was special to me. West Ham fans like players who try and I always tried. They saw that. At West Ham the fans were more intense, even though both West Ham and QPR fans were good, they got behind you at both places. [Andy turned off two mobile phones that were demanding his attention to make his point.] *They both sit close to the pitch, but the West Ham were more 'come on' kind of thing; got you going. Got you saying, 'Right! Let's go!'*

The reason I left is, when you've got someone who's above you, doing deals behind yer back, it don't make you feel too welcome. Any time they can say, 'You're off.' So, I said to H, 'Not being funny, I want to stay, but with him doing things like that … It don't make me feel too good.'

I've no regrets whatsoever about my time at West Ham. Just that I weren't there long enough. The East End was a good place to be. Especially as they're performing now. If I'd have stayed I'd have played in Europe! I never played in Europe, always wanted to. It would have been good to do that with West Ham. It would have been more my type of game. I keep in touch with Rio [Ferdinand] and Trevor [Sinclair]. I was friendly with all the lads at Upton Park. You can talk about the East End spirit, but we were all very close, we got on really well.

First game for Leicester was Saturday, 28 November 1998 in a 1–1 draw at Coventry. I lived close to Wembley Stadium and commuted to Leicester. Me and TC [Tony Cottee] met up at Toddington. One day he'd drive, the next day I'd drive. He lived in Chigwell. It took about an hour and 20 minutes. Sometimes it got a bit tedious, but it was better than living up there. I couldn't live up there. It's a different life.

We won the League Cup in 2000, or the Worthington as it was. Beat Tranmere 2–1. That was the last final at Wembley. I'd been Cup-tied for the 1999 final against Spurs.

Had, I think, 178 games for Leicester, then I went on loan to Forest in February 2004 in Division One. First game on 14th of that month. Got 16 games, scored once – same total as at Leicester, got the goal on me debut. Took 15 seconds. I think it was some kind of record. Then got a permanent move a few weeks later.

After just under a year at the City Ground, Andy went to Millwall (at first on loan) with Dennis Wise and finished his career at Coventry with Micky Adams who had managed him at Filbert Street. He said,

I was on non-contract terms at Coventry. I'd never been on non-contract terms before but it was a case of getting on with it really. It wasn't ideal but I just wanted to play football. I finished at the end of the season.

I didn't like playing wing-back. I preferred to get further forward and play as a winger; that is what I knew best. But if I want to stay in the team, then I had to play in that position; that's the way the team was playing. But at West Ham everyone was ready to do their bit. It was a team thing starting from the front, where Wrighty, Trevor [Sinclair] and

Johnny Hartson were. It was a good side. It was a pity we couldn't have stuck together.

As Andy left I wished him good luck for the weekend. He said laughing,

If it was against my team [Arsenal], *you'd have to watch out for the own goal.*

ANDY IMPEY TRANSFER HISTORY			
FROM	**TO**	**DATE**	**FEE**
Queens Park Rangers	West Ham United	26 Sep 97	£1,200,000
West Ham United	West Ham United	25 Nov 98	£1,600,000
Leicester City	Nottingham Forest	12 Feb 04	
Leicester City	Nottingham Forest	18 May 04	Free Transfer
Nottingham Forest	Millwall	11 Mar 05	
Out of Contract	Coventry City	16 Sep 05	Free Transfer

SAMASSI ABOU

'When you win a game, you win together. When you lose, you lose together.'

Born in Gagnoa in the Ivory Coast on 4 April 1973, Abou began his career with FC Martigues (not far from Marseille). He recalled,

I left the Ivory Coast when I was 14 … It's a beautiful country but I wanted adventure.

Scoring seven goals in 24 games, he showed himself to be a goal-maker as well as a player who could find the net on occasion.

He moved on to bigger things with Lyon as an 18-year-old and, although his first game in the French First Division saw his side lose 0–2 to Nantes (15 August 1992), Samassi spent two seasons as a first-team regular, netting 11 times in 58 appearances.

Abou's silky skills and dynamic forward play caused AS Cannes (then also in the top flight of French football) to pay £250,000 for his services for the 1996–97 season and he scored five goals in 37 games for the cultured south-coast side.

A £400,000 fee brought the French Under-21 international to Upton Park in October 1997. Samassi told of his relief:

I got to West Ham at last. The deal had dragged on for weeks and, even when the day finally came, there were last-minute problems … I thought it would be good for me to come to English football.

THE BLACK HAMMERS

As he introduced Samassi to the English game, Harry Redknapp described him as 'big, strong and sharp'. Abou was to score half-a-dozen goals in his 31 outings as a Hammer between 1997 and 2000.

Abou's debut was at Stamford Bridge. He came on midway through the second half for Steve Potts with the Irons one down from an own goal by Rio Ferdinand. Abou was a crucial element in events. His slick play left Andy Myers with only a rugby tackle as a retort. For Abou,

> There was no doubt that it was a penalty. He couldn't get the ball so he stopped me playing it.

John Hartson's spot-kick made it 2–1 with 85 minutes played. West Ham's chance of a point relied on Eyal Berkovic hitting home from a free-kick in the last minute of the match.

Abou, desperate to get the kick taken, tried to seize the ball from Celestine Babayaro, only to receive a booking for his urgency. Long after the event, he still felt the injustice of the moment:

> He had to drop the ball. That's the rule! But I couldn't explain that to the referee. I didn't speak English. He should not have held on to it! But I got a yellow card. The referee had blown his whistle; it was West Ham's free-kick. I just wanted to put the ball on the ground.

Samassi's commitment and affable truculence made him a popular figure at the Boleyn Ground, although the crowd's appreciation sounded like a hail of booing as they collectively eulogised the player with repeated choruses of 'Aboooo!' He proved to be a player of unpredictable even eccentric style and this, together with him telling Sky Sports' *Soccer AM* (live at 10am) that, when he was learning English, his West Ham teammates had told him that 'fuck off' is perfectly acceptable language for post-match interviews, made him a cult hero with the Upton Park faithful.

'Sam the Man' was probably at the zenith of his fame in England when he was sent off by David Elleray at White Hart Lane on 17 January 1998.

SAMASSI ABOU

Thanks largely to his penetrating runs and smart flicks, Abou had been inspiring the Hammers in a fight back (Spurs were leading by a Jurgen Klinsmann goal). Then, like a dying swan, Ramon Vega collapsed theatrically to the turf following contact with Sammy. Seconds later, as Vega recovered like a latter-day Lazarus, the man from the Ivory Coast was flashed a red by the slapheaded teacher from Harrow.

Now agitated, Abou attempted to express that he felt he had been provoked by the frustrated thespian Vega. At this point Harry 'Not a word of French' Redknapp entered the fray to act as interpreter. 'Arry's antics brought Colin Calderwood and then John Hartson into the 'debate' and in no time there was a merry old to-do on the sideline. But looking back Abou was philosophical:

I didn't blame Vega. At the time I was angry because I left my colleagues on the pitch, and that is a worry. I'm really sorry to have got involved. The referee was misled by Vega; I was too. He couldn't have done anything else.

I can't say anything against the referee. I was just angry because in the heat of the moment someone has acted on the pitch and it was me that ended up paying for it.

I didn't like leaving the team with just 10 men, especially as Spurs were winning. I think we would have equalised, but at 10 men versus 11 the task was more difficult.

But you have to stick up for your teammates. When you win a game, you win together. When you lose, you lose together. We lost that game and to some extent it was my fault. That's what hurts. But what Vega did to me probably happened to him at some time.

However, as time passed, although saying all he wanted to do was 'make or score goals for West Ham', Samassi didn't get on too well with 'Appy 'Arry. One of the few public comments Redknapp made about Abou probably says much: 'Samassi Abou don't speak the English too good.' While Abou was at Upton Park, his teammate David Terrier was recruited as translator by Harry Redknapp. Samassi laughed as he recalled,

THE BLACK HAMMERS

He put David between us to explain everything!

But maybe H's attitude to foreign players in general was most succinctly expressed by his very 'stereotyped' (and that's being generous) assessment of the same:

With the foreign players it's more difficult. Most of them don't even bother with the golf, they don't want to go racing. They don't even drink.

For all this, Abou wanted to succeed at Upton Park:

English football is still very different from other countries ... And West Ham play it differently to the average English club. I enjoyed playing in England and I liked West Ham. I also [laughs] liked the shops in England. You could dress how you want here and no one minds.

My English was not very good but I'm still learning. I've always liked English football. I'm a big strong player and I've always thought that I could play there. It wasn't easy fitting in, but West Ham were very good to me and the players are friendly. My wife Sandarine came to England while I was with West Ham. I wanted to get used to it there.

I liked to play with Hartson and Kitson, who are very English. In France the ball is always played on the ground and I had to always run on to it. In England the ball is used in the air and players like Hartson can use it so well that it helped my game. Hartson was a good player, he moved around a lot and even helped in defence. He could hold the ball up well and that's important. I tried to play off him.

I liked Berkovic, he was very clever with the ball. The technique is different to France, but it suited me. I was happy there and wanted to do my best. I liked the noise you make ... 'ABBBOOO!' [laughs]

While the West Ham manager allowed Abou's talent to rot outside the first team, with Ian Wright, Paul Kitson, John Hartson and Trevor Sinclair all competing for places in the Hammers forward line, the Bradford City manager Paul Jewel, backed by his chairman, Geoffrey Richmond, waded in with an £800,000 club record bid to take Sammy North (beating the record £625,000 they paid for striker John McGinlay from Bolton the previous November). Richmond commented, 'But the player decided he wanted to stay at West Ham to fight for his place.'

According to Richmond, 'At the end of the day it wasn't about money, it was about Abou's rapport with the West Ham fans and his belief in his ability to stay and play at Premiership level.'

Abou's agent Paul Miller said, 'The offer Bradford City made was the equivalent of what most Premier League clubs would offer so it isn't about money – it is all about wanting to stay at West Ham and continue as a Premiership player. He still feels he has a lot to offer West Ham where he has a great rapport with the fans and he wants to fight for his place at the club and prove to them that he can play.'

After refusing another chance of a move, this time to Hearts, the 6ft 1in, 12st 8lb forward was sent on loan to Walsall. The club had just been promoted to the First Division. Abou brought flair to the Saddlers game and he was an immediate favourite with the Bescot fans who were pleased to have a big name player at the club. His debut game was a 2–1 defeat to Stockport. Samassi partnered Andy Rammell up front showing why Lyon and West Ham had taken a chance in signing him. His unique style of play, the quality of his first touch set him apart from everyone else on the field.

As his stay in the North progressed, it became clear why Abou frustrated his managers. His work rate was not high. He would drift in and out of games showing moments of brilliance but long periods of seeming inactivity. Abou left Brescot without a goal after eight games. Maybe in a more productive team he would have found the net on a regular basis. But his goalscoring record over the course of his career was never huge. He was much more of a player to draw defenders and allow goals to be scored by other forwards than a prolific marksman in his own right.

Samassi's next loan move was to promotion-chasing Ipswich. His one-month stay in Division One at Portman Road finished with five appearances and one goal, scored in the 2–1 away win at Bramall Lane on Sunday, 20 December 1998.

After returning to Upton Park in 1999, Abou had another loan spell, this time in France with Troyes, before being consigned to West

Ham's reserve side. Kilmarnock in the SPL was the next loan stop for Samassi (where the local newspapers heralded the arrive of 'Abou Samassi'). But with no goals in 10 outings for the Killies nothing came of the move and he was released in the early summer of 2000.

Abou made his way back to France to find a place in the French Second Division side AC Ajacio, on the west coast of the island of Corsica. Sammy enjoyed a fair amount of success there, achieving promotion during his second season in 2002, getting five goals in 60 games. He signed for another Ligue 2 club, Breton-based Lorient, in 2002–03.

Samassi's life in football has been guided by pragmatics, but like many players this has been transformed into something of a philosophy of life for him:

As far as I'm concerned ... you can't stop ... not even during the close season. You have to keep yourself in shape ... If I score a goal or someone else does, that's not what matters ... it's the team that counts ... At first, in England the speed of the game made a big initial impression on me. I looked at it and thought, 'I will work at this.' It's a question of habit. I'd been used to French football and now I had to get used to English football. If you get used to doing something, you get good at it. For me that's football — habit.

In common with many players, Abou has fond memories of the West Ham fans:

The supporters! At Chelsea I hadn't even got on, yet they were chanting my name. I adored the West Ham fans for that. It made me feel I wanted to really go and play for them — like a kind of ethical responsibility. I didn't experience any racism. None at all at West Ham. Racism is a foolishness. It is a waste of energy. Teamwork is about making the most of differences and pulling together as one unit, one person. That includes the fans. That's why there is no room for racism in football or society. In the end segregation, discrimination, prejudice is a waste of resources on an inhumane level and is contemptible.

SAMASSI ABOU

If Abou could have applied his undoubted talent, perhaps with a more technically knowledgeable manager than Harry Redknapp (the likes of Paul Jewel perhaps), he might have been a big success with the Hammers. As it stands he was yet one more name in the long list of claret and blue 'might-have-beens'.

TREVOR LLOYD SINCLAIR

'After you've scored a goal, it's just orgasmic ... if you asked me just after a game, I'd say it's better than sex, but if you asked me just after sex I'd say, "Forget it, mate."'

Having played 206 games for West Ham and 'hit the rigging' 38 times along the way, while making many more, Dulwich-born Sinclair came to Upton Park for a £2,300,000 fee (plus Iain Dowie and Keith Rowland) from Queens Park Rangers in January 1998. Able to play on either flank, take the demanding forward role just behind a main striker or revert to midfield or defensive duties, he was always going to be missed when he moved to Manchester City for £2,500,000.

Although born in London (2 March 1973), Sinclair was brought up in Manchester and was a graduate of the FA School of Excellence. He started his League career with Blackpool, making nine appearances during the 1989–90 term when the Seasiders tumbled into Division Four.

For all this, Trevor was developing a reputation as one of English football's brightest young stars, and Manchester City boss Peter Reid tried to sign him but the £200,000 fee prevented Sinclair making the trip to Maine Road. City chairman and 'comb-over king' Peter Swailes seemingly wanted to save his dosh for another shipment of 'Grey Away'.

With Trevor's help Blackpool were promoted to the newly formed Division Two in 1992. Sinclair found the back of the net on 16 occasions during 140 outings in four seasons in the Bloomfield Road cause, before, despite interest from West Ham, he moved to Shepherd's Bush in August 1993 for £750,000.

TREVOR LLOYD SINCLAIR

Sincs (as he was known to West Ham colleagues and fans) was a big hit at QPR and scored some spectacular goals. When they were relegated from the top flight, he stayed with them until midway through the 1997–98 season, before joining West Ham in January 1998.

Trevor came from Loftus Road having netted 21 times in 190 appearances over five seasons as a Ranger, and had broken into the England Under-21 side, but he had stagnated in West London. However, he revitalised at the Boleyn Ground, scoring seven goals in the 14 matches he played in up to the end of the 1997–98 season. In his first full season at the Boleyn Ground, he shone, playing at wing-back, although his desire to ply his trade up front never diminished. But it was Trevor's utility that made him hard to resist as an England prospect.

A groin strain kept him out of the last part of the 2000–01 Premiership campaign, a time of poor results for the Hammers. In 2001, he put in a transfer request, hoping to move to a bigger club, but later withdrew it and was present in all but four games in 2001–02, playing at a consistently high standard.

Sinclair had been part of England squads mustered by Terry Venables, Glenn Hoddle and Kevin Keegan, but he finally made his England debut in November 2001 in the 1–1 draw with Sweden at Old Trafford.

Trevor played the second half of the 1–1 draw with South Korea in a friendly on Tuesday, 21 May 2002 in Jeju, South Korea. This was considered to be a preparation game for the World Cup in North Korea and Japan, but he wore the number 24 shirt in the match, even though only 23 players could go to the World Cup. England manager Sven-Goran Eriksson was to place the injured Kieron Dyer in the squad in preference to Sinclair, saying he would have preferred Sinclair to have stayed with the squad, as FIFA allowed replacements for injury up to 24 hours before England's first game on 2 June. Sinclair, however, wanted to return to England but remain on standby by training with West Ham. It was also the case, that Natalie, Trevor's wife, the mother of his three boys, was pregnant and had been ill at home in London. So he made the 8,000-mile trip back to Britain. The players' committee demonstrated their sympathy by agreeing that Sinclair would still share in their bonus pool worth a reported £75,000-plus.

While Sinclair was flying home on 22 May, Danny Murphy fell victim to England's metatarsal jinx and was obliged to withdraw from Eriksson's squad. Sven therefore sent word to Sinclair to meet up with the squad again at their new base in Awaji Island, Japan; this time he would be travelling as a full squad member.

Thus, Trevor made it 24,000 miles journeying and was named as a reserve for the second match of England's tournament. An injury to Owen Hargreaves after just 18 minutes got Sinclair involved in his nation's 1–0 win. He said that it was 'like a dream come true' and the greatest night of his career.

With outstanding displays for England against Argentina and Denmark, Trevor demonstrated his great eye for the goal and that he was one of a handful of players in England who could take on two or three players and make something out of nothing. He had a fine run of four matches up to the disappointing defeat by the winning finalists-to-be Brazil in the last eight.

A fan of Magic FM and the Superbikes circuit, Sincs signed a new contract at Upton Park in 2002, and, although the Hammers were relegated at the end of the season, Trevor seemed to be ready to remain loyal to West Ham, saying that he had no intentions of following Jermain Defoe and requesting a transfer, even though he was one of the favourites to move to pastures new. He confirmed that if the club wanted him to stay and fight for promotion then that is what he was going to do, having two years left on his contract, and that he was going to be up for the challenge and had no intention of 'going in and knocking on any doors putting in transfer requests'.

But Sinclair knew the club had to make savings, and as such there were going to be players leaving. He said,

I presume the players that are a bit older, like myself and David James, might be considered worth letting go if there are clubs interested, and if it is advantageous to the club to sell ... They will be trying to cut the wage bill and look for replacements.

TREVOR LLOYD SINCLAIR

In July 2003 Trevor moved to the side he has supported as a boy. Trevor scored in the first game at the City of Manchester Stadium against Barcelona, and also opened the scoring against TNS in the first ever competitive match at the arena in the UEFA Cup. The next time he was on the scoresheet was at the wrong end as he headed past David Seaman into his own net.

By his own admission, Trevor struggled to find the kind of form that had previously earned him a place in the England squad and was, for much of the time, a spectator on the bench as City slipped towards a relegation battle. Never able to get a consistent run in the side, his only other goal of the season came in the first Manchester derby at the City of Manchester Stadium.

The following season in Trevor's first start for City, a home game against Charlton, the Addicks keeper, a Dean Kiely kick rebounded off of Sinclair's legs and into the net. This contributed to City's 4–0 victory but it was Sinclair's only goal of the 2004–05 season. The next game against Everton saw him substituted with a knee injury. A subsequent operation would see him ruled out for the remainder of the season. He had played only five games.

Sinclair began the 2005–06 term in the right-wing berth. He put in some encouraging performances but was injured against Bolton Wanderers at home after an awkward fall. However, as the season wore on, he looked to be making an adequate contribution to the cause of the Manchester Blues, although he was out for the historic FA Cup quarter-final battles against the Hammers.

Trevor gained 11 England caps while at the Boleyn Ground; he was only able to add one more international appearance to his CV while at the City of Manchester Stadium. It is clear that his best football years had been those he had spent with West Ham.

Sinclair will be remembered at Upton Park as a player blessed with lightning acceleration and an individual who was likely to come late in games when an injection of pace could turn a match. As a Hammer he was able to provide and score goals, often in spectacular fashion. His mix of guile and graft in defence, midfield or attack made him a professional in the true traditions of the 'West Ham way'.

BERNARD PASCAL LAMA

'One of the beauties of football is the responsibility it demands individuals take for themselves and others.'

Small for a keeper, Lama was known as something of an eccentric custodian when he came to Upton Park, but he was a superb shot-stopper and acknowledged as having fine athletic ability, although his handling of crosses often left a lot to be desired.

He is a well-travelled player as his career path testifies:

1978–81 Montjoly (Guyana)
1981–82 Lille OSC
1982–83 Abbeville SC
1983–84 Besancon RC
1984–89 Lille OSC (Ligue 1)   played 93 (1 goal)
1989–90 FC Metz (Ligue 1)   played 38
1990–91 Brestois Stage (Ligue 1)   played 38
1991–92 RC Lens (Ligue 1)   played 36 (1 goal)
1992–97 Paris SG (Ligue 1)
1997–98 West Ham (Premiership)   played 12
1998–2000 Paris SG (Ligue 1)   played 177
2000–2001 Stage Of Rennes

But this has not stopped Lama accruing an impressive list of achievements. For France, he has been a World Cup winner (1998) and was in the sides that won the European Championship in 2000 and reached the semi-finals of the same competition in 1996. At club level, he helped Paris SG win the European Cup Winners' Cup

BERNARD PASCAL LAMA

in 1996 (defeating Rapid Vienna 1–0) and made the final again in 1997. He was a finalist in the Supercoupe d' Europe in 1997, won the French League in 1994 and has winners' medals from the Cup of France for 1993 and 1995.

It has been reported that he was born in Montjoly, French Guyana but according to Lama this is a mistake.

I was born in St Symphorien in France [7 April 1963] but I went to French Guyana in South America with my family when I was three. We lived near the sea. I learned to play football there, when I was about 12, on the beaches of Cayenne [the capital of French Guyana]. We used to go to Brazil with my dad. I really liked that.

I got known for my agility. I came back to France when I was 18. I liked South America. It was a good life, no problems. Guyana is beautiful; wild animals and nature are never far away.

My interest in football started when I saw the 1970 World Cup on the television. Pele was, and still is, my hero. From then on, I knew what I wanted to do with my life.

Outside football, I admire Nelson Mandela and the Dalai Lama, he has the same name as me [laughs], but that's not the only reason.

I went to Lille [France] when I was 18. I was a professional there for eight years. I used to play without gloves. As I started playing football on the beach I didn't need gloves. After that the heat in Lille meant that I could not stand wearing gloves and I started to rediscover the same sensations that I had when I was an apprentice when I took them off. I learned that a modern goalkeeper must be a 'superman' who can play both outfield as well as in goal. One of the beauties of football is the responsibility it demands individuals take for themselves and others.

My best years were with Paris Saint-Germain. I joined the club at the age of 29, probably the start of a goalkeeper's peak years. Less than six months after signing for PSG I was selected to play for France against Israel in Tel-Aviv [17 February 1993 – France won 4–0] and I have played 44 times for my country.

I got selected for the 1998 World Cup squad, but I didn't play. Who knows who will play in goal for France [laughs], but I am the best keeper in the world [laughs]. *There are some excellent keepers but to be able to play at the highest level you need to be very consistent and that takes a lot of time.*

But I made the mistake and was tested positive for drugs. There is drug-taking in football, as in any other sport. I lost my place in the French side. I regret it, but in life you make mistakes. No one should do what I did. I was suspended. Once my suspension was over, the fans and the players wanted me back, but the PSG chairman didn't. I had been there for 12 years anyway and I was already beginning to feel it was time to move on. I'd always wanted to play in another country. I had talks with Real Madrid but went to England to help re-establish myself and it probably worked out well.

I have been called things like 'flamboyant' and 'complex' but I have always looked to win all the competitions I played in. At West Ham I came into the Premiership side after Craig Forrest was injured. I performed well. In my first game Arsenal could not score against me at Upton Park [the score was 0–0]. *Soon after that I again faced Arsenal in the FA Cup at Highbury. It was 1–1 so there was a replay at West Ham. Arsenal won on penalties but I played well and in the following seven League games West Ham lost only once.*

London is a much bigger town than Paris and a lot more cosmopolitan. The stadiums are always packed and the public have good knowledge of the game. I regret not being able to continue playing there for a big club because medium-sized clubs like West Ham do not have the same facilities; they were not professional enough. The situation in England is completely different and my lifestyle was completely different. I had appeared in two European Cup Winners' Cup finals, played more than 500 French League and Cup games over 12 years with clubs like Lille, Metz, Brestois, Lens and Paris Saint-Germain and with West Ham I found myself playing for the reserves at Oxford! I was not a boy! I hadn't had to do anything like that for 12 years, but the coach said he wanted to see me play. I could not play for the reserves! That was not my place. It was good for me to come to West Ham. It was a good team with very good fans, but I could not help them sitting on the bench! Redknapp used to say that I had to be

*patient, but sitting on the bench was not where I should have been!
In France no one could understand why I should be a substitute.
I had to play to get in the World Cup squad; the coach had told
me that, when I played club football again, I could go back and
start playing for France. Fabien Barthez had always been the*
replacement [the substitute].

*I was in a hotel in Essex with my wife Vania and 10-year-old son
Levi, thinking it would not be possible for me to play in another World
Cup competition. It could have been my first and last finals and the
coach wasn't worried! I had been the French keeper for five years!*

*But wherever I have played, PSG, West Ham, anywhere, I thank
the supporters for their loyalty. As a player I have always worn their
jersey with pride.*

*After West Ham I went back to Paris Saint-Germain and played
65 more games in 1998–99 and 1999–2000 and played a few more
games for France. I then moved on to Stade Rennais FC in the
2000–01 season. I played 32 times for them. But when a player has
played at the top level it is hard to get used to a drop in class. I always
dreamed of playing in Brazil, in particular for Flamengo or Botafogo.
But God had not willed it. I stopped football when my wife had a
baby. It seemed the best thing.*

*Unfortunately, football is just business, business, business. Amongst
my best moments in football was winning Le Championnat with PSG
in 1994, and winning the Cup Winners' Cup in 1996. The club has
had quality players; the likes of George Weah and David Ginola.*

*I have some plans to develop a training centre in Guyana, which
would help improve the local level and help players move to
professional clubs. I always followed PSG, although I'm not really a
supporter, a lot of Africans have played for the club. There are and have
been a number of good players from Guyana in Le Championnat, but
there could be more, that's why I'd like to start a training centre for
Guyana players.*

*Racism is a problem that the whole of society has to deal with, not
just the supporters. Racism has no place in society and as such no place
in the sporting arena. The sooner we get rid of troublemakers, the better
the atmosphere in stadiums and the surrounding areas. Some players*

THE BLACK HAMMERS

like Anelka have converted to Islam. Everyone is free to choose their religion and it is not for me to question their choice. I would say if I have the opportunity to talk to them that they have to accept the implications of their decisions.

I sometimes think about going into politics. For the moment I am focusing on my job and my current projects before thinking about a political career.

Outside of football I like music, reading, travel and Guyana. I live in the Maison Lafittes area. I'm not enthusiastic about horses but it is good to see them outside. I have promised myself to get more interested in them because they are beautiful animals. Later in my career I went to bed late and so I got up late [smiles]. Now I can do more. I have a sports shop in Guyana and can go there when I feel like it.

In 2003 Lama signed for Birmingham City to provide cover for Steve Bruce's side for the last few weeks of the season.

In recent years Lama has started to make a name for himself in film and television. He has also played a part (alongside other French stars such as Patrick Vieira) in opening a sports training and educational centre located some 80 km from Dakar, Senegal, the Diambars Institute, designed to assist 13-year-old Senegalese children for a five-year period, combining football training with schooling with the aim of using 'football as a driving force for education'.

Twenty per cent of Diambars' students go on to become professional football players, but the institute looks to make sure that those who don't 'can still become champions in life'.

In the future the school will take in children from all over Africa. Perhaps with this in mind Lama has argued that

Africa should be allowed to host the World Cup as much for sporting as economic reasons.

Diambars – which means 'warriors' in Senegal's Wolof language – is funded entirely by charitable donations and sponsorship.

Other big-name players, including Marcel Desailly, El Hadji Diouf formally of Liverpool and now Bolton, Arsenal's Thierry

BERNARD PASCAL LAMA

Henry and Silvestre at Manchester United, have promised to boost funds through fundraising projects.

Bernard has taken an interest in water. French Guyana has vast reserves of water, but mercury pollution in connection with gold mining has caused tremendous problems. In response Lama has set up two water-purification plants. He says,

Water is life – when you have water you can live – I making water clean for people to drink.

NEIL SHAKA HISLOP

'Show every man the utmost respect … whether it is a teammate, tea lady or someone playing in the streets. I find that, when you do that, people respect you back equally and that gives you a warm feeling.'

I first met Shaka, a tall (6ft 4in), powerful (14st 4lbs) but easygoing man, at the West Ham training ground in Chigwell in September 1999. We went back to his new house near Loughton, Essex – it was the East Ender's dream palace. The interview took place as Shaka tended to his two children. Over the previous few years he had been one of the most popular players at Upton Park, winning the man–of–the–match award on numerous occasions, and on becoming Hammer of the Year 1998–99 by a landslide he said,

> *It's one of the highest honours you can get. Recognition from your own fans is important and there aren't many things that would make a player more proud. There are not too many awards to be won in football … To be appreciated by my own supporters was the highlight of my career so far. I'm so thankful and I felt so proud. Even now it's still hard to put into words six months later. It was tremendous.*

According to Anton Ferdinand, 'People don't realise how funny Shaka is until they get him on a night out. He's got top banter. He's a typical Trinidadian – they're mad. Sometimes he just acts like a big kid.'

Shaka's top TV show is *Seinfeld* and his favourite movie star is Denzil Washington. Holidays will nearly always be in Trinidad and he doesn't like ironing. In terms of food, for a starter fish broth is a winner for Shaka, main course would be seafood and for dessert cheesecake. He avoids beetroot with energy. Hislop admires Michael Jordan in the world of sport, but on a wider plain he has great respect for more politically influential figures:

Nelson Mandela ... his book A Long Walk To Freedom *... was a fantastic book and showed his history and how he was involved in the movement from day one. That's a real inspiration. I think that most people know all about his anti-apartheid views by now, but to know what drove him to that was a real eye-opener. I also read the autobiography of Malcolm X. I find, when I read these books, there is so much more that you understand from what is portrayed on the films. They are real inspirations and I find that I get to know these people a lot more intimately by reading their books.*

Hislop also has a taste for John Grisham novels. Ambitions outside football include taking a round-the-world cruise and to shoot a round of golf under par. His most embarrassing moment came when he caught a cross and fell in the net while playing for Reading reserves. Shaka's proudest moment was the birth of his children. If he could take one person on a desert island it would be his wife.

According to Shaka,

I'm not the best at karaoke, though, and you definitely won't be hearing my voice above all the others in the pre-match sing-song!

However, his taste in music is fairly eclectic, particular favourites at the time I first interviewed Shaka were 'Move Closer' (Phyllis Nelson), Bob Marley and the Wailers, in particular 'Jammin', and 'Lady in Red' (Chris De Burgh).

I was born in Hackney on 22 February 1969. I was christened Neil but I've always gone with my middle name. Originally we lived just a couple of miles from Hyde Park, but I was taken to my parents' home in Trinidad when I was two years old. My dad, George, was a lawyer and my mum, Gina, was a court reporter. My mum is an inspiration because I am a real mommy's boy. She has been a big influence on how

THE BLACK HAMMERS

I view life. It was in Trinidad that I first started to play football. I also tried my hand at a bit of cricket too. Football was always my game and I can remember back to the days when I was about 10 and there was an exceptionally good eight-year-old called Dwight Yorke.

When I was 18, I won a soccer scholarship at Howard University, Washington DC. I passed a mechanical engineering degree with flying colours. Of course, I always wanted to give football a try, but once I'd graduated all I was thinking about realistically was advancing on to a Master's degree and making a career for myself in engineering. I'd only dreamed about becoming a professional footballer. I'd never given it any really serious thought. But then one day I played in an indoor exhibition tour match for Baltimore Blast against Villa. A Reading scout was watching and I was offered a trial. Playing in England was always going to be my best option; being a British citizen I didn't have to get a work permit.

Less than two months after arriving back in the UK, I made my debut, during the 1992–93 season. My game at Reading was a 3–0 defeat, but after that we didn't lose for half-a-dozen games. I played a dozen games that season. The following couple of seasons I was always in the first team. We won the Division Two Championship and I was in the Division One side that finished runners-up. The team finished up just behind Middlesbrough. However, there was a one-up, four-down policy that season so we didn't get an automatic promotion spot. At Wembley in the play-off final, we were defeated 4–3 by Bolton. That was disappointing. But it was that season, '94–95 I got voted Player of the Year and selected PFA's First Division top goalkeeper. I was very honoured.

I went to Newcastle in August 1995 for £1,575,000, a British record fee for a goalkeeper at the time. I'd only been in England for two-and-a-half seasons and Premier League football had suddenly arrived much faster than I expected. I played 24 times for Newcastle in 1995–96, 16 in 1996–97 and 13 in 1997–98. I didn't concede a goal in my first four games. We were miles clear at the top of the table, however, slowly but surely, United started to close the gap. In early December I got injured and, by the time I got back into the side with just seven games to go, we were suddenly chasing them. We had to settle for runners-up spot.

NEIL SHAKA HISLOP

Then it was the Champions League. In my wildest dreams had I ever expected to play in the Nou Camp against Barcelona or face the likes of PSV Eindhoven and Dynamo Kiev. After I'd had a 20-game run, Shay Given came back after injury and I came to West Ham on a free transfer from Newcastle, on the Bosman ruling. I signed a four-year contract on 6 July 1998, the same day as the Dr Martens sponsorship was announced.

I made my debut at Hillsborough on 15 August 1998. My first game at Upton Park was a week later, v Manchester United. Ludo [Ludek Miklosko] was very supportive and full of advice. I learned a lot from him and we had a great working relationship. It was always going to be tough filling Ludo's boots.

After being on the bench for England 'B's' defeat against Chile at the Hawthorns, I found myself in the starting line-up as an over-age player in the Under-21s in March '98. We lost 2–0 to the Swiss in Aarau. I believe I'm the only West Ham player to have represented two countries. It was 28 March 1999 that I first played for Trinidad and Tobago against Jamaica. Trinidad won 2–0. It was great to start off with a clean sheet against the top team in the Caribbean, even though they didn't have too many of their France '98 World Cup team playing. It was a very good result for us.

I had previously rejected the offers to play for Trinidad because the 18-hour return flights were disruptive. But now I've accepted that a touch of jetlag is a small price to pay for an international cap. As you get older you get more accustomed to those long flights back. I never ever expected to get an England call for France '98.

There are and have been some good Trinidadian players in British football. Some of us pretty much grew up together and we've known each other for a long time. Desha, my wife, is from Trinidad and that's where I will retire. I want to have a presence back there. I think I've contributed to Trinidad and Tobago football and I want to carry on doing that. After Dwight [Yorke], I'm probably the most experienced player from Trinidad and it would be good to give something back.

Desha and I have two daughters, Maalana, born in 1996, and Khazia, born in 1998. Football has given us a good life, but I think

THE BLACK HAMMERS

I have been committed to the game and the clubs I've played for, so you tend to get what you work for in any field.

I've lived in Trinidad and I've lived in the US and various places in the UK. I've tried to understand the way of life of any countries and communities that I'm involved in. Football is quite universal in its appeal and I'm a footballer plying his trade. That has made me appreciate the fans that I am representing more and also the job that I am doing. My parents have always been quite liberal. My father would always say I should show every man the utmost respect. So I try and do that whether it is a teammate, tea lady or someone playing in the streets. I find that, when you do that, people respect you back equally and that gives you a warm feeling.

West Ham have a certain history, which was also a big, big plus for me. One of the first things you wonder when you join a new club is how the fans are going to accept you. The Upton Park crowd gave me a great reception when I first joined the club.

I'm an Honorary Patron on 'Show Racism the Red Card' [launched at Upton Park in November 1998]. At the launch I said that racism is not as bad as 10 years ago, but that doesn't mean we should not strive to remove it entirely. Thankfully I have not heard racist comments from my teammates or opposition and incidents are fewer and further between. But there are still odd occasions when someone says something particularly unsavoury in the heat of the moment, and we're trying to stamp that out. West Ham United were the first Premiership club to follow the Football Task Force recommendations on racism. Football grounds are much more pleasant places to come now. I've certainly not experienced any racism at all since I've been at West Ham. I would've been first out of the door if there had been any hint of prejudice. Anyway, just look at the characters who have played for the club. Do you really think that people like Trevor Sinclair, Rio and Ian Wright would stand for anything like that around the place? Not one of them had anything to say.

The future? I've never ever asked any manager for guarantees and I certainly ain't gonna start now.

NEIL SHAKA HISLOP

After Glenn Roeder brought England international David James to West Ham, Shaka resolved to fight for the keeper's jersey and, when James was injured playing for England shortly before the start of the 2001–02 campaign, Hislop pulled on the gloves. However, when James returned from injury Shaka was once more playing second fiddle. He recalled,

> *Glenn Roeder called me in and told me he was going to sign David James. He wanted me to stay at the club. He didn't expect me to be playing too many games, but I had to battle on and of course David got injured playing for England just before the season started and it gave me a chance to at least play a few games, which was more than I had expected.*

Hislop was to be reunited with Harry Redknapp at Portsmouth. Around that time he said,

> *You want to believe that the club is worse off without you, but you know better. It is an ego thing.*

Shaka played a big part in the south-coast side's promotion to the Premiership in 2003, being ever-present and walking away with 16 clean sheets. He was subsequently selected for the PFA Division One team of the season. Trinidad's veteran custodian continued to be first choice at Fratton Park at the beginning of 2004–05. With 100 appearances for Pompey to his credit, Shaka, in his own words, was unceremoniously shown the door at Portsmouth and was left trying to figure out what then.

He had two trial games with Crystal Palace, saving a penalty in one, before seizing the opportunity to return to his East End roots in August 2005, but was only third choice when the Hammers began their season back in the Barclays Premiership. However, injuries to Roy Carroll and Jimmy Walker gave him an opportunity. Reviewing the situation, he said it was a very exciting time and a big turnaround, whereas, a year before, he was wondering about his future.

However, in July the Hammers goalkeeping coach and former star Ludek Miklosko and Alan Pardew contacted Hislop and, having been on the point of leaving the game, he came back to Upton Park. Looking at the benefit of experience he brought with him, he commented,

When you get to my age you have a sense of acceptance.

With the goalkeeper injury crisis at Upton Park during 2005–06, Shaka played for the Hammers in their glorious if unsuccessful Cup final appearance of 2006 just before travelling to the World Cup in Germany. Hislop gained his 25th cap and played a vital role in Trinidad and Tobago's first game of the tournament against Sweden, coming into the side just before the kick-off after first-choice keeper Kelvin Jack suffered a last-minute injury on the way back to the dressing room after the warm-up session. Shaka kept his rigging clean, helping his side accomplish an historic goalless draw, the most impressive result ever achieved by Trinidad and one of the best performances ever by a Caribbean nation.

Among Trinidad's elated fans was the great West Indian cricketer Brian Lara. Shaka told of how:

He goes to all the games … I played in the Under-14 national team with Brian; myself, Dwight [Yorke], Brian, Russell Latapy played. As a footballer he was a striker but he was too small. I played cricket with him. I take credit – he mastered a lot of his strokes off my bowling.

Following the FA Cup final, Shaka had made around 150 appearances for West Ham, the highlight of those have been West Ham's one European campaign while Hislop was at the club:

… playing in the UEFA Cup, when we qualified through the Intertoto Cup … Upton Park is a place steeped in tradition. It was great to bring European football back there.

NEIL SHAKA HISLOP

In April 2005, Hislop was recognised as the recipient of the Professional Footballers Association (PFA) Special Merit Award for his continued involvement with the 'Show Racism The Red Card' campaign, which he helped start in 1996 as a way to keep racism away from soccer.

In July 2006 Hislop left West Ham for US side FC Dallas saying,

This is an exciting new challenge.

Shaka is one of the Hammers' finest ever keepers. His philosophy of life seems to be in line with his view of the lot of the goalie:

As a keeper you're thrown in at the deep end and you're expected to swim.

MARC VIVIEN FOÉ

'Sometimes it is not just about the colour of the skin. But we all belong to God and to God we are all the same. I think the West Ham supporters know this thing.'

A tall, muscular figure, blessed with athletic prowess and determination, Marc Vivien Foé signed for West Ham from French side RC Lens for a club record £4.5 million on 27 January 1999. He came to Upton Park with 54 caps for Cameroon where he was born on 1 May 1975 in Nkolo.

According to Marco (as his French colleagues called him),

I didn't have a dream to play football ... I thought I would like to be a pilot. My father is a teacher and he worried about me playing football. He never really wanted me to play. He wanted me to study. When I asked him for a pair of boots, he said, 'OK,' and then came back with some books and said, 'These are your boots' [laughs].

Jean-Pierre Sadi, Cameroon's Under-15 coach, saw me playing at school. My move to Lens was organised by Pape Diouf, he is from Senegal. He was in Marseille and became my agent. He's a good agent for many African players. He knows all the best young players and who is going to be big successes.

Foé was a Hammer for 14 months, scoring twice in 48 appearances. Notwithstanding his huge physical presence and massive fee, Foé strolled into the Boleyn Ground, wearing one of his dazzling wardrobe of Hawaiian shirts, almost anonymously as Harry Redknapp announced the signing of the mad, bad, brilliant and dangerous Italian Paolo Di Canio. In France Foé had been described as a 'monster' in the middle of the park. He was 6ft 4in tall and had an imposing physical presence. It had looked as if he might go to Manchester United but the deal fell through. Nevertheless, 'H' justified his club record purchase when he stated, 'Manchester United don't try to sign too many bad players, do they? Marc may be a very quiet family man, but he's also a big, strong powerful midfielder who likes to break up attacks and make tackles. He gives you a presence in the middle of the park and is a totally dedicated player. He's serious about his football.'

For all this, to those who were most familiar with him, Marco was a gentle giant who cared about the people he played with and for. Looking back on how he arrived at Upton Park, he said,

I came to West Ham looking to rebuild my career. I had broken a leg just 10 days before the 1998 World Cup in France. It got broken while I was training with my national team and I missed out on playing in the finals. It was that which stopped me signing for Manchester United. Alex Ferguson still wanted to sign me but, because I refused to have an operation on my leg, the Manchester United doctor stopped the move.

It was more disappointing, for me, not to be able to play in the World Cup finals for Cameroon in France. France was where I lived. It would have been an opportunity to show what Cameroon could do there. Playing for my country is one of the biggest honours in my life and to have done that in the World Cup in the place where I played for my club would have been good for me. But I am thankful. I am still young and have the chance to play in more World Cups.

Harry Redknapp [laughs], he was never happy about me playing for Cameroon, but he could do nothing about it [laughs]. He is a very funny man [laughs]. I think he complains about a lot. Sometimes people do not take as much notice as they should [laughs]. Harry is Harry.

There were stories that healers had said they would cure my leg, for example by burying it in the ground and putting fire around. People said I was using traditional Cameroonian massage with gorilla bones. But I am a good Roman Catholic, St Michel Archangel is my best

saint, for his courage. I would not do all that. For me God gave me everything; if he wanted me to stop playing I wouldn't be unhappy because I have so much already. I would still have my hands so I could work. Almost all footballers that break their legs automatically have an operation. Two doctors told me that I should have an operation, three others said no. God told me no as well so I just had a plaster cast and I healed myself.

That I think is the way God wanted it because when I broke my leg I thought more about the people who have to walk with the aid of crutches. I went to Burkina Faso with George Weah and Abedi Pele to support the 'Kick Polio out of Africa' campaign. I might have a lovely house but I know that there are so many people who have nothing.

That my move to Manchester United did not happen made me unhappy. But for West Ham to make me a record signing overcame my disappointment. I wanted to play football and make the West Ham supporters happy. I only look to the future. As with all the teams I have played for I was meant to play for West Ham. Everything in life is determined by God. I was disappointed not to play in the World Cup, but this is life. I believe in God and I was very unlucky, but I thank God for letting me play again. I think what will be will be. It is my belief that God has a reason for everything.

Other European clubs were interested in me, but I liked the sound of West Ham. There were many good players in the West Ham team and lots of young players with talent. The club looked very strong.

After matches I warmed down by dancing to the music of the African singer Koffi Olomide. I got everyone else dancing Cameroonian dances – the Dombolo, the Makossa, the Bikutsi and the Assik [laughs]. But only Samassi Abou could challenge me at dancing at West Ham. The team had a Costa Rican, me, a Cameroonian, a Chilean, a Frenchman and an Italian. We didn't speak great English but that was OK. I knew what every player was doing when we played or trained.

I did not find any racism at West Ham. The fans were always very good to me. At the training ground 'OK, Marc!' [laughs] 'All right!' And [singing] 'I'm Forever Blowing Bubbles' [laughs]. This is a funny song I think. Why do West Ham fans sing this song? 'Fortune's always hiding' [laughs]. The fans were very good. I cared about them and wanted them to like what I did. I think they did. I liked the West Ham supporters very much.

I think racism is everywhere. There is racism in Africa. Different groups do not like other groups. In Cameroon, there are 250 ethnic groups from five regional-cultural groups. Cameroon does not have much conflict but in some other countries people can say, 'He should not be in the team because he is this' or 'From there ... these are not good people.' So, racism is a big problem everywhere. Sometimes it is not just about the colour of the skin. But we all belong to God and to God we are all the same. I think the West Ham supporters know this thing.

At Upton Park Marco quickly became acknowledged for his determined tackling and his ability to distribute the ball with accuracy and intelligence. Above all, the qualities that shone through were his seemingly innate enthusiasm and enjoyment of the game, uncommon qualities in modern football. He recalled,

I found West Ham to be a very friendly club that wanted to face the challenges ahead. The players supported each other. The training was not strict or very organised compared to other clubs I have played for. This was good for me and some other players. I have the discipline to do what I need to do. Perhaps it was not the best thing for younger players.

Foé's hinted-at critique of Redknapp's training regime is interesting given Shaka Hislop's view of Marc's own attitude to training. The Hammers keeper observed, 'Marc has to be the worst trainer at the club – he's nearly as laidback as I am!'

For all this, it seems the big African could appreciate the contribution of his fellow professionals:

But players like Paolo Di Canio brought a lot to West Ham's training by being an example to younger players and he would instruct younger players too. At Lens the coaches were very highly trained and the training was organised. West Ham looked to the future. I liked that.

THE BLACK HAMMERS

Lens is a tight-knit coalmining town in northern France. The football club became professional in 1934 under the patronage of the Mines Society. It is a million miles away from Cameroon in terms of culture and climate, but Marco was never fazed by his first taste of European football:

I wasn't shocked by what I found. I was ready. I understood it would be hard and I knew the weather would not be good. Not like Africa, where there is little rain and sun shines every day. But I was a hero in Lens ... I lived outside of Lens because if I hadn't I would have been stopped all day! I'd go for a walk; people asked me to come to their homes! I'd go into shops to buy something and the people who owned the store would refuse to take any payment. Each season the club got stronger. When I started at Lens the budget was £6 million; when I left it had grown to £14 million.

My first game in the Premiership was against Wimbledon away from home. The conditions were difficult for me to adapt to. I enjoyed that first game in England, but the pitch was no good and Wimbledon had some very difficult players for me to play against. West Ham tried to play football, but we could not get a good chance to score. I was pleased that we drew in my first game.

It took me time to adapt but when I had played a few games I got used to English football. I found it very difficult to adjust to the way of life in England. It is hard when you arrive in another country, but I enjoyed the challenge of making a life and a career in the country. I am not the type of person to go back home if things are a bit difficult. God plays a big part in my life and my faith gives me the strength to deal with whatever comes my way. I always try to give of my best, and I am an adult, so I did not cry just because things were hard to get used to.

During his time at Upton Park, Foé lived within a Shaka Hislop goal-kick of Epping Forest, one of the green lungs of East London, in West Essex. He reasoned that 'the oxygen supply' was better there. A St George Cross flew high over the home of one of the neighbours and a couple of stone lions stood in front of the drive opposite, perhaps reminding Marc of his role as one of his nation's 'Indomitable Lions'. Looking at his domestic situation, he commented,

My English was not as good then. I grew up speaking French as well as Ewondo [the Cameroonian dialect]. *I like Woodford Green because it's peaceful. It's a nice area. When I'm in my house I always think I'm in the Cameroon. Some people prefer the fun and noise of London but I like it to be quiet* [smiles]. *I never want to say to people, 'Look at me, I am rich'; I don't want to force what I have down people's throats. I don't need a great big car. I want my family and friends to be happy, so the money I get is mostly used to do that.*

I met my wife, Marie-Louise, at school in Cameroon. We have a son, Scott Bradley [born 1996 and named after the man who composed the music for the Hanna Barbera cartoon 'Tom and Jerry' – Marie-Louise was an ardent fan during her first pregnancy], *and a daughter Lesley* [born 1998]. *They had to get used to living in England, so it was difficult. But my brother Emmanuel also lived with us and that helped. He is a talented footballer and played for Lens' B team. But he came to Britain to study English.*

I have a routine I stick to. I wake up at 5am on match days. At 10.30 Marie-Louise makes me rice or pasta for lunch, she's a good cooker [smiles]. *She generally makes African food; getting ingredients from Leytonstone when I was with West Ham, from the West Indian and African shops there. I do not eat red meat, I prefer rabbit, chicken or fish. I don't drink coffee, tea or alcohol and I don't go to nightclubs* [laughs]. *After a game I go home, have my evening meal and then I'll maybe watch a movie or a video of the game. Win or lose, I am strong in my head. I do not lose control. I just ask myself, 'Have I done my job?' And I have always answered 'yes' to that question.*

I always want to get better, as a person and as a football player. God has given me the ability to make myself stronger than the opposition. I am tall and strong and that has helped my game a great deal. I wanted Harry Redknapp to give me the time to prove myself and for the fans to enjoy me and what I had to offer. I don't think I got that time. That is my disappointment about my time at West Ham. I think the team could have done more if they had been kept together. It is hard for a team to win things if the team keeps changing. You buy a player and then you see another player so you sell the player you bought to buy the player you have seen. This is not 'managing', it is being a salesman! That is thinking that players will bring success. But it is teams that bring success — players that are given the time to learn to play together, to become good together. This is what coaching should do. No player ever won a thing on their own. But if you don't coach you have to rely on buying and selling.

As a child I used to play on the streets with my friends. We didn't always have a ball and would kick around other objects and always bare-footed, but I loved playing football all the time.

When I played for clubs in Cameroon, Nikoloii and Canon-Yaounde, it became my dream to play football as a professional. I wanted to be a midfielder and Frank Rijkaard was my hero. I saw him on the television playing for Holland and he always wanted to stop the opposition from scoring a goal and I could do that too. Then my dreams came true when I went to Racing Club Lens. I was 19 years of age. My time at Lens was very successful. I was with Lens for three seasons in the French League. While I was with Lens the team got to the French Cup final and won the French Championship in 1996 [it was almost a memorable double but Lens were defeated 2–1 by Paris Saint-Germain].

I was very happy for my family, and for me [laughs] *and the supporters of Lens that we won the French League. I enjoyed that a great deal. It was a very good team. The supporters were magnificent and we played in a great stadium.*

I had a great deal of success in France, but it was always my wish to play in the Premiership. I watched West Ham on television in France and the other Premiership clubs every Saturday. I think there are things about French football that are the same as English football, but in England there are more good players who are strong on the ball.

I liked to watch attacking players like Dwight Yorke, Andy Cole and Gianfranco Zola. They were excellent players. Yorke was very quick and scored many goals. I think that is very important for a team when you have someone who can score great goals. West Ham had Ian Wright and Paolo Di Canio and others who could do that. I knew Ian Wright and Rio Ferdinand before I played for West Ham. They are both very good players. I met Rio Ferdinand for the first time when Cameroon played England; he was a very good player then.

I played for Cameroon for the first time when I was 17 and it is very exciting playing for Cameroon in the African Cup of Nations. But everything I have achieved in life is thanks to God. I pray to God and thank him for everything. I go to church on Sundays and will never forget my origins. I believe that everybody has their bad times and when I broke my leg that was a very bad time for me. But I went through good times and I have enjoyed my life.

When Foé first came to Upton Park, African football was moving into a new phase. The nations of Africa were much more of a force to be reckoned with on the world stage than had previously been the case. However, when he arrived at the Boleyn Ground, Foé was still only one of just a dozen African players in the Premiership. He reflected,

I wanted to play in the big European Cups. West Ham were not quite ready to break through to that level, but everybody was strong within the club and wanted to win, even in training. I liked that. There were a lot of skilful young players and that is very important. I liked what I saw.

When he first came to England, Foé was compared to the likes of Patrick Vieira and Marcel Desailly. Considering this, he responded,

They are both very strong players and maybe it is true that I played a little like Vieira.

I think that Desailly was a very good player but I am a positional player who can also play in defence. Football is my work and, if I am of more use to the club I am playing for by playing in another position, then I will play in that position.

Foé was an honest, modest man, with a mental strength that matched his physical prowess. He always gave 100 per cent on the pitch, accepting refereeing decisions with the integrity of a true professional. He noticeably avoided confrontation with opponents and played with a focus on the team's benefit.

Marco had a warm and friendly nature and a habit of greeting everyone who crossed his path at the training ground with a warm handshake (including his teammates). But he did literally see red on occasions. On 3 October 1999 after two bookable offences, he was sent off in an ill-tempered London derby against Arsenal at Upton Park. In the same match Patrick Vieira was infamously dismissed for spitting at Neil Ruddock. However, unlike the Arsenal man, Marco took time out to shake referee Mike Reed's hand on his way to the changing room.

Marc found it hard to come to terms with the pace of the Premiership, and he soon found himself suffering from a severe bout of yellow fever. He picked up his ninth yellow card of the season in a controversial encounter at Highbury, which consequently resulted in FA charges. Marc then rounded off his Hammers career during injury time of the final game of the campaign against Leeds United at the Boleyn Ground. Everyone in the 26,044 crowd, apart from referee Graham Barber, saw Matthew Jones make 'intentional physical contact' with the African. The Cameroon international handed out his own justice, finishing with a kick at the floored Peacock in full view of the official.

Marco's first goal for West Ham was a thumping 90th-minute 10-yard header that rounded off a 6–1 aggregate victory over Croatian side NK Osijek on 30 September 1999 in the Hammers first sortie into the UEFA Cup. His first (and last) Premiership goal for the Irons was scored during the exciting 4–3 Upton Park defeat of Sheffield Wednesday in November 1999. While he was pleased to contribute by way of netting, the big African international was always a team player. Marco's celebrations were marked by a subdued joy that reflected the noble humility of the man:

I like to score goals, but I don't mind who scores the goals. The fact that

MARC VIVIEN FOÉ

I score or someone else scores is not too important to me. As long as the team win the match, I am happy. If I score a goal, when a game is over, the only thing I think about is that we won, not that I had scored a goal. Football is a team game and it is no good me scoring three goals but the team losing 4–3.

With Harry Redknapp always looking to make a fast profit in the transfer market, a lucrative £4.6 million, end of 1998–99 season bid from Liverpool manager Gerard Houllier seemed to mark an untimely end to his career as a Hammer. Marco recalled,

For me, it was a crazy time. Liverpool wanted me to play for them, West Ham wanted to sell me and make some quick money. I talked to Gerard Houllier and it seemed I would go to Liverpool. But my agent was telephoned by a director at West Ham who said West Ham did not want me to go. I telephoned Harry Redknapp and he said come back to training with West Ham.

To go to Liverpool would have been a great challenge for me. I didn't know what to do. Liverpool are one of the greatest clubs in the world and I was proud to know that they wanted me to play for them. But I thought I had work to do at West Ham. I had not asked to leave West Ham. My family had just begun to get used to things in Woodford Green and I had to think about them. But West Ham had agreed to sell me, so I went to Liverpool and spoke to Gerard Houllier. I thought I was going to go there and there was nothing I could do about that.

I didn't make a song and dance about all of this, and I still don't really know why I didn't play for Liverpool, but that is not for me to worry about. The important thing for me was to enjoy playing football, and I did that at West Ham. I loved the fans and I loved the feeling at Upton Park. The supporters were very close to the pitch and that made it special for the players. It is important that a team has the support of the fans, and at West Ham I, and players like Paolo Di Canio, wanted to play well for them.

West Ham worked as a team. The spirit was wonderful. Being at West Ham was for the best. This was God's path for me.

THE BLACK HAMMERS

After his first season at the Boleyn Ground, Foé was being tipped by many to be one of the 'Players of the Season' in the 2000–01 term, but, instead, ever with his eye on the cash till, Harry sold him to Olympique Lyonnais for £6 million, making a handsome £1.5 million profit on the player (in fact, the surplus was much more than this as Redders had used the proceeds of John Hartson's transfer to Wimbledon to buy the Cameroon player). The deal took Frédéric Kanouté to West Ham.

A bout of malaria caused Marco to struggle to hold down a first-team place at Olympique, but he was well respected by fans and players alike for his dedication to the club and his determination to regain his first-team place and he again won a French Championship medal in 2001–02.

Foé, together with captain Rigobert Song, formed the backbone of the Cameroon team that vowed to take African football into the 21st century and won the African Championships in 2002 in Ghana and Nigeria. Marc became the first Hammer since 1966 to win major international honours. Hardly ever wasting a pass, Foé was typically competitive and strong throughout the tournament. He scored twice in the run-up to the final against Nigeria; he was then left stunned as he side-footed wide in a dramatic penalty shoot-out that was eventually won by Rigobert Song's successful spot-kick.

Marco played in all three of Cameroon's group matches at the 2002 World Cup in Japan, but the 'Indomitable Lions' went out of the tournament at the group stage.

After Japan, Marco went to Manchester City on a one-year £500,000 loan deal. He took time to acclimatise but he managed to score nine League goals, including the last ever goal at the club's erstwhile home, Maine Road. He finished the 2002–03 season as the club's second-top goalscorer; this was his best goal tally in 10 seasons in Europe. He played his part in a successful season for City as they secured their Barclays Premiership status. Marco was especially impressive over Christmas when he scored six goals in as many games. Kevin Keegan wanted to make him a permanent feature of his side, but a £7 million price tag turned him off, although it did not deter Harry Redknapp, at that time in his first stint with

Portsmouth, from sniffing around, looking to create 'West Ham Lite' on the south coast.

The death of Marc Vivien Foé on Thursday, 26 June 2003 shook the football world. He fell to his knees then collapsed in the 72nd minute of his 64th international game (he had scored eight goals for his nation) in the centre circle, just inside his own half, as play had moved deep into Cameroon's opponents' half. The game was the Federations Cup semi-final against Colombia at the Stade Gerland in Lyon. No other player was within five yards of him. Immediately on noticing his condition, players from both sides and the referee called for a stretcher. But Marco sadly died, in the stadium where he played for Lyon between 2000 and 2002, shortly after all attempts to revive him failed after 45 minutes. He was just 28.

Foé left a wife and three children, the youngest of whom had only recently been born. His family watched him die from the stands. It was reported that he suffered a heart attack.

Cameroon won the match 1–0. After the game several Cameroon players fell to the turf sobbing. The Colombian players went to the Cameroon dressing room to console their brothers in football.

The following day Rigobert Song, the Cameroon skipper, said, 'It's terrible, yesterday at half-time, his last words were "Boys, even if it means dying on the pitch, we must win this semi-final", and he was the victim.'

There was some talk of not playing the final, however FIFA president Sepp Blatter said of the Cameroon side: 'They will do it for the honour and respect of their teammate ... I never say "the show must go on", but life must go on, and our competition and football must show it is part of our life, and life is sometimes marked by death.'

Marco's fellow midfielder and long-term friend Geremi (who later would join Chelsea) told of how: 'When we went to Marco's house, his wife told us to win the trophy on behalf of Marco – the main thing is to play and to win the trophy for Marco.'

As a mark of respect, the French team – many of whom had played with and against Foé in the French and English Leagues and at international level – observed a minute's silence prior to their semi-final against Turkey later the same day. Some of the French players, especially France's coach Jacques Santini, who had coached Foé at Lyon, looked distraught.

The final was transformed by the players into a tribute to Marco. Thierry Henry, the Arsenal and France striker commented, 'We know it is nothing, but it is all we can do.'

Before the game the Cameroon squad warmed up on the Stade de France pitch wearing green shirts bearing Foé's name and number 17 on the back. All the Cameroon players wore black armbands and white shirts, discreetly bearing Marco's name in black. Both teams walked on to the field for the final carrying a huge picture of Marco, which remained on the side of the pitch throughout the game.

It was a poignant moment as Thierry Henry and many of his teammates openly wept. Henry led the French players in pointing up to the sky when he opened the scoring for France, indicating that the goal and the game, won by France, were for Marco.

The victorious French captain Marcel Desailly invited his Cameroon counterpart Rigobert Song to share the trophy after the presentation.

A post-mortem examination indicated that Foé had died from 'sudden death syndrome', a condition which causes athletes to die during their regular sports activity without any warning symptoms. The final verdict on his sudden death was an enlarged heart.

Later Harry Redknapp revealed that the player had failed a medical before he had joined West Ham. Redknapp told the *News of the World*, 'At first it seemed as if his enlarged heart might be a problem. But when we sent him to a heart specialist we were told this was perfectly normal in African players and that we could go ahead with the signing.'

Manchester City 'retired' the no. 23 squad number used by Foé during his only season with the club and Olympique Lyonnais made a similar gesture and posted a touching memorial on their club website: 'Marc Vivien Foé will leave us the memory of a charming boy, the incarnation of the joy in life. We will keep of him with us, his bursts of laughter, the music which comes out of the changing room, and his kindness away from the ground. Marco, we will not forget you.'

The genial, gentle giant Foé was given a state funeral in the country's capital Youande on 4 July 2003 in recognition of his services to Cameroon.

After his death it came to light that, unbeknown to the media and general public, Marco had been involved in efforts to improve the lot of disadvantaged youngsters in his home country though football coaching. The West Ham physio John Green recollected, 'He also did a lot of work for needy people back home in Cameroon and I remember him buying £20,000 worth of crutches to ship back there on one occasion.'

This work continues to this day in remembrance and celebration of Marco's life. Good has certainly come out of Marc Vivien Foé running on to the pitch of life. There have been many arguments and accusations about how and why Marco died, causing a level of discord and recrimination that he certainly would not have approved of. From what very little I knew of him, I think maybe he would have wanted what happened to him to be understood in his own typically honest and straightforward words:

This was God's path for me.

PAULO CÉSAR WANCHOPE WATSON

HAMMERS DEBUT: 8/8/99

'When you play you have to think to play well, to play better.'

C osta Rican Wanchope was born into a famous footballing clan on 31 January 1976, one of three brothers who are well known within the game in Costa Rica and his dad was a professional.

Hailing from Heredia, the awkward–looking, 6ft 4in, gangly Wanchope, who twice turned down a career in basketball to pursue his first love of football, was an avid watcher of the game as a boy. He supported teams like AC Milan and Barcelona which were his inspiration. Van Basten, Gullit, Stoichkov and Romario stirred his imagination but Marco Van Basten was the one he pretended to be as he played his first street games.

It was Bob McNab, the old Arsenal defender, who 'discovered' Wanchope and it was on his recommendation that Jim Smith, then manager of Derby County, brought the young Costa Rican into the English game in March 1997, paying Club Sport Herediano, where 'Chope' started his footballing life as a fresh-faced, long-legged 12-year-old and made his first-team debut as a teenager in September 1994, £600,000 for his services in March 1997.

Although Paulo found the Derbyshire climate inhospitable ('too cold'), he made an instant impact on the Rams and improved his game steadily; his trademark loping style and twisting running impressed the Pride Park Crowds. He scored a remarkable goal on his debut against Manchester United at Old Trafford. After racing from the halfway line and beating half-a-dozen United players, the Costa Rican bamboozled Peter Schmeichel to score a stunning debut goal. It was a magnificent solo effort finished off coolly and summed up the very best elements of one of the game's most unconventional players.

In July 1999, Harry splashed out £3,500,000 to bring Wanchope to Upton Park, to pair him with the luminous Latino loony Paolo Di Canio. He was initially billeted at the Swallow Hotel in Waltham Abbey, not far from the M25.

Wanchope, who throughout his career has been able to inspire and frustrate in equal measure, made a fittingly eccentric debut: the semi-final of the Intertoto Cup. It was a first-leg encounter with Heerenveen of Holland at the Boleyn Ground in the same month as he signed for the Hammers. It was in the second leg of that tie that Paulo got his first goal as an Iron (the only goal of the game). He hit another in the second leg of the final at Metz (West Ham won 3–1) and was on target again in the 3–0 UEFA Cup first-round, first-leg victory over NK Osijet.

For all this, at West Ham, Wanchope went through the most frustrating period of his career. Davor Suker and Frédéric Kanouté were at Upton Park in July 2000 creating a situation wherein five quality forwards were competing for a first-team spot. At least one had to go, given what seemed to be a constant problem under the reign of 'Redders', the pressing need to cut the club wage bill. Paulo's inconsistent performances at Upton Park led to him being booed by sections of the Hammers support. He tended to miss more chances than he took, although he created more than most and far more than Suker the Fluker, but it was a good enough excuse for ever-ready Redknapp to offload him.

Wanchope had previously been the subject of a bid from Leicester City, then managed by Martin O'Neill, prior to transfer-deadline day. A last-minute effort from Bradford City was brushed aside and in early August 2000 Paulo signed for Joe Royle and joined his new striking partners George Weah and Shaun Goater at Maine Road for a record fee of £3,650,000 for the Manchester Blues. A hat-trick on his debut against Sunderland suggested as so many times before that 'winker-blinker, tokey-tic' 'H' had done a wrong 'un. Paulo went on to play an important part in the Blues' promotion to the Premiership. At the end of the 2001–02 First Division season, with

29 goals in all competitions, Chope was City's top marksman, a good send-off for his trip to the 2002 World Cup with Costa Rica.

After four years in Manchester, Wanchope had 75 games under his belt and 29 goals, but £500,000 took him to Málaga CF in Spanish Primera Liga in August 2004. Paulo had accrued 25 outings for the Spanish side, scoring half-a-dozen times, at the conclusion of 2004–05. He scored what was considered the best goal of the entire 2004–05 Spanish First Division against Numancia.

However, the Costa del Sol was not where wandering Wanchope wanted to be. He had done well, scoring six goals in 14 games, but told of what has come to be seen as something of a Spanish malaise over the last few years;

> *I've seen racism in almost every stadium in Spain. It's a shame that referees haven't abandoned a few games because of it. That would have set an example and cut the problem off at the root. What has upset me most have been the insults in my own stadium.*

Following a game against Real Betis during which his family were also abused, Paulo leaped into the crowd and struck a supporter. The rights and wrongs of that action can be debated, but there are a few of us in the East End of London that could see his point of view.

After rejecting a return to the Premiership with Portsmouth and a reunion with the now salty seadog Redknapp, Paulo opted for a lucrative one-year move to Al Garafah in the Qatar League. Wanchope described this sojourn as 'having a break'. He lasted just six months and used the January transfer window (2006) to return to Club Sport Herediano, in Costa Rica (despite interest from Cardiff City). He commented,

> *I have reached an agreement with Herediano to play in the Torneo Clausura* [The national League Championships is a tournament that is played twice a year: 'Torneo Clausura' from February to July, and 'Torneo Apertura' from August to December.] ... *I said some time ago that if I didn't come to an agreement with the teams I was negotiating with I would stay in Costa Rica.*

PAULO CÉSAR WANCHOPE WATSON

Paulo has been hugely important to the Costa Rican national team, not only in the 2002 World Cup but also several Gold Cups.[2]

In San Jose on 8 October 2005, Wanchope became the all-time leading goalscorer for *Los Ticos* when he scored the first goal in a 3–0 home win over the USA in the qualifying match that sent Costa Rica to the 2006 World Cup.

After helping to clinch qualification with a third-place finish in CONCACAF's final round 'Hexagonal' with one match still to go, Wanchope said,

> *My national team career will end in Germany ... Playing for the national team has filled me with pride and made me happy. I can't imagine the sadness I will feel the day I play my last match for the Tricolor.*

Following his two goals in the opening match of the 2006 World Cup finals in his country's 4–2 defeat by host nation Germany, Paulo's goal tally from 70 international matches was 45. This is a fantastic record since making his debut against Venezuela back in October 1996. He fired seven altogether on the way to Germany.

Wanchope has described himself as 'a happy person' but also 'a very straight person'. He admits to saying the things he has to say directly to the person and not behind their backs. He has thought that is why sometimes people fail to warm to him. He once said,

> *... people sometimes try to be my friend and then behind my back they say things about me. That is very irritating.*

At times a scintillating presence, it is sad that Paulo was lost to European football because of the idiocy of racism. Quick on and off the ball, dangerous in the air, his goals always seemed to come in

---

[2]The CONCACAF Gold Cup is the main national football competition of the CONCACAF nations. The participating nations are from North and Central America and from the Caribbean islands. In addition, up to three entrants from the other world football confederations are invited to play in the final tournament. The Gold Cup has been hosted by the United States and twice co-hosted with Mexico.

bunches as he veered wildly between the brilliant and the inexplicable. But Wanchope always seemed a natural goalscorer at every club he played for. I'm not sure anyone in England understood that his flair was a product of a sharp intellect and a personal philosophy; according to him,

When you play, you have to think to play well, to play better.

You could almost see that as he moved around the park. He looked laidback physically, but he gave the impression that every brain cell in his head was firing all the time. Those who revelled in the breath of fresh air that his exuberance brought to the English game miss his presence.

Paulo came to East London to play 55 times in West Ham colours and score 15 goals. His performances were nearly always entertaining if at times enigmatic; although he was most often described as 'unpredictable', it was that erratic quality that made Paulo something of a cult figure at Upton Park. He was, at the same time, an entertainer and an annoyance. Hammers fans, like myself, who enjoyed Paulo's contribution to the history of the Irons, will remember his storming giraffe-like figure producing moments of sublime skill, grace and awkwardness, and punctuated with errors that have made him the kind of flawed genius beloved of the Boleyn faithful. The thought of him in claret and blue will always bring a smile as he epitomised something of the spirit of the club.

PAULO WANCHOPE IN ENGLAND			
SEASON:	CLUB:	GAMES:	GOALS:
1997-1999	Derby County	83	28
1999-2000	West Ham United	46	15
2000-2004	Manchester City	72	25
Total		201	68

IAN EDWARD WRIGHT

HAMMERS DEBUT: 15/8/99

'You've got to take the rough with the smooth. It's like love and hate, war and peace, all that bollocks.'

Although a 'Docklander' by birth (he was born in Woolwich on 3 November 1963, and grew up on the same estate as the late David Rocastle, who would be a colleague when they both wore red and white), Ian Wright will always be associated with Arsenal and Crystal Palace rather than West Ham. He is a Highbury legend, being the Gunners highest ever scorer (in 288 games he netted 185 times) until Thierry Henry took that record in October 2005.

As a boy Ian admired Garth Crooks, Laurie Cunningham, Cyril Regis, Pele and Kevin Keegan. He once said,

Kevin Keegan was my biggest one out of all of them – obviously the rest because they were black. They were in the limelight and you'd say, God, they've made it. They were the ones that made me want to be a footballer.

Starting adult life as plasterer/labourer, Wright was playing for Greenwich Borough when he came to Steve Coppell's notice. The then Palace manager brought him to Selhurst Park in 1985 and he was the star of the Eagles side that made the 1990 FA Cup final against Manchester United, rising from the Wembley bench to score two spectacular goals and so force the replay. He recalled some of the less savoury aspects of his early days at Palace:

I experienced racism from the older senior pros. At the time it was quite disturbing, I didn't want to be there. I had a decent job then, it was in

219

my early days and a phase where I wanted to give up, but I had good
people round me who said, 'You can't give up just because of that or
they'll have won' … I couldn't even imagine what it would be like in
Cyril Regis and Laurie Cunningham's day because I wouldn't take it,
but I suppose it was harder for them to speak out then – and that is
why I'd now take any opportunity to speak that I can.

It was George Graham that took Wright to Arsenal for what now
seems a ridiculous £2,500,000 in September 1991. Ian scored on his
debut in a League Cup game at Filbert Street. In 1994–95 he
became the Gunners highest-scoring marksman for the fourth time
in succession.

In eight seasons with the Gunners the club gained winners
medals for the FA and League Cup in 1993, the European Cup
Winners' Cup in 1994 and the Premiership and FA Cup double
in 1998.

Wright contributed nine goals in 22 outings in West Ham colours
(a fair strike rate for a player well past his best) between August 1998
and August 1999. It might have been more if a cartilage injury
hadn't kept Wright out of action for three months of the one season
he spent at Upton Park. During his first game as a Hammer, he
scored the only goal of the match at Hillsborough. That term he
finished as the Hammers top scorer.

While Ian Wright was with the Hammers, Shaka Hislop said of
him, 'He's got the best singing voice at the club – and, as you can
imagine, he's not shy about using it. I didn't realise how good he was
until I went to see Lionel Ritchie at Wembley and Ian went on the
stage to sing a song with him. Ian was fantastic – I didn't know he
had such a good voice! It really was something to behold!'

Such was Wright's form while with the Hammers, he added two
more English caps to the 31 he already possessed before landing at
the Boleyn Ground (v Luxembourg and the Czech Republic).

For all this, for many fans it is still difficult to envisage him with
the Hammers on his chest.

Before his departure from the Boleyn Ground, Wright had a short
loan period with Nottingham Forest before signing for Burnley.

IAN EDWARD WRIGHT

This was followed by a brief encounter with Celtic.

Wright is a fan of Alan Shearer:

I think he's done really well — with some of the setbacks he's had in his career. I like Paul Ince and not just because he's my best mate!

Outside of football, Ian admires Malcolm X who he saw as a fantastic leader for black people and an inspirational man. For Ian, Malcolm did wrong when he was younger, but after he'd been to Mecca he 'realised that everybody should be together'. According to Wright, at that point, had he not been shot, Malcolm would have been a person that was able to lead not only black people but everybody. Ian also has a great deal of respect for Martin Luther King, but sees him as having more of a pacifying influence. For Ian,

You can't just turn the other cheek, that's why when Malcolm X said 'by any means necessary' — if you do this to me, I'm going to do this to you — I thought it was a better way ... You can't expect somebody, when they're being shot at to hit them back with a sponge or something. You have to do what you've got to do.

Wright retired from football in the winter of 2000 and now has a career in television that was premised on his demeaning antics telling Britain several times in an evening that he felt 'like chicken tonight' and 'fluttering' across the screen in 'hen mode'. It is not for a Hammers supporter to question the decisions of one of the greatest ever Gunners, but many an Goonster sat staring at the undignified performance and asked, 'Did you really need to do that, Ian?' The answer might be 'yes' if his current 'golf clown' role to Joanna Lumley's long-suffering caddy in the Privilege Insurance adverts is anything to go by.

GAVIN VICTOR HOLLIGAN

'I just want to enjoy my football and keep my feet on the ground.'

Born in Lambeth (13 June 1980), and having turned down a musical scholarship at a university to play football, 18–year-old Gavin Holligan, who had been brought to Upton Park from Conference side Kingstonian just a month previously, was on the West Ham substitutes bench at Anfield on 20 February 1999.

With 13 minutes of the game remaining, the pacey striker took the field before a crowd of 44,511. He took the place of Joe Cole who was forced to retire with cramp. Seconds later, Gavin faced David James, one-on-one; here was the opportunity to conclude a 36-year history of West Ham failing to win at the home of the Liverpool Reds. I was amongst those Hammers fans present who watched the ball rebound off of the legs 'Calamity'. *'And like my dreams ... fade and die ...'*

However, with the scoreline at 2–2, with just seven minutes on the clock, Eyal Berkovic played a pass that tore the Scousers' backline in half; Trevor Sinclair broke through, Holligan made it a two-pronged charge.

Striding on as if the sub didn't exist, Sincs sent in a bending drive; it sailed over the head of James but also over the bar.

Holligan had netted a dozen times in his first five weeks as a reserve and Under-19 player with West Ham, but he wouldn't get another opportunity at Upton Park.

Gavin started out on his footballing path in August 1997 with Walton and Hersham. At one stage in his career, 18 out of 20

GAVIN VICTOR HOLLIGAN

Premiership teams had representatives watching him. Following his short moment in the limelight with the Hammers, he was sent out on a series of loans that took him full circle back to Kingstonian, only to be involved in an ignominious campaign that concluded with the relegation of his old team.

Finally, Gavin got away from, what was for him, the dead-end of Upton Park. In May 2001 he was given a free transfer to Second Division Wycombe Wanderers. Holligan made an immediate impact at the Causeway Stadium when he scored two goals on his debut during a pre-season friendly at Crawley. He found the net on 10 occasions in a half-century of appearances with Adams Park Posse.

Gavin was back on the loan-go-round with non-League clubs. In March 2004 he was told his contract would not be renewed at Wycombe by former Highbury Humpty Tony Adams – the Anglesey Ass showed him the door with a free transfer at the end of the 2003–04 season.

Holligan signed for Conference South side Havant and Waterlooville where he teamed up with ace striker Dean Holdsworth for 2004–05 and was with Lewes at the start of the next season.

GAVIN HOLLIGAN – CAREER RECORD

DATE	CLUB	APPS	GOALS
Aug 97-Jun 98	Walton & Hersham	NA	NA
Jun 98-Nov 98	Kingstonian	17	5
Nov 98-Jun 01	West Ham	1	0
Sep 99-Oct 99	Leyton Orient (loan)	2	0
Oct 00-Nov 00	Exeter City (loan)	3	0
Mar 01-May 01	Kingstonian (loan)	7	3
2001/02	Wycombe Wanderers	24	5
2002/03	Wycombe Wanderers	10	2
2003/04	Wycombe Wanderers	16	3
December 2003	Crawley		
February 2004	Hornchurch		
2004/05	Havant Waterlooville	22	6
August 2005	Lewes		

ADAM LEE NEWTON

HAMMERS DEBUT: 25/9/99

'I'll just have to be patient.'

Attacking full-back Adam Newton looked every bit a potential West Ham star, with his startling pace and great ball skills. He was one of the young Hammers that trampled Coventry with an aggregate score of 9–0 after the second leg of the 1999 Youth Cup final. Sky TV covered the game live from the Boleyn Ground, but those of us in the 24,000 crowd at Upton Park to witness the match were confident that the future of the Irons was secure in the hands of the likes of Newton. But, alas, Adam, unlike his illustrious teammates in that encounter, Joe Cole and Michael Carrick, was never to bloom in the East End.

As is the custom and practice of the West Ham academy, as part of his learning agenda, in July 1999 Newton was sent on loan to Portsmouth in Division One. During his month with Pompey, he made one start and a couple of appearances from the bench. He returned to Upton Park to be catapulted into the first team on 25 September 1999, exactly three weeks after his 18th birthday, coming on as substitute in the 1–0 victory at Highfield Road. Five days later, he was in Croatia for the second leg of the UEFA Cup first-round meeting with NK Osijek. The Hammers were leading 4–0 on aggregate when Newton came on to replace Trevor Sinclair for the second half. West Ham went back to London as 6–1 victors over the two games. To round off a more than eventful week, the Essex lad from Grays was called into the England Under-21 squad.

As such, the prospects seemed rosy for the former Berkshire

ADAM LEE NEWTON

Schools player. But, after he came on as sub for the Premiership meeting with Coventry (another roasting for City 5–0) on the Boleyn Ground, Newton went out on loan to Notts County where he played 22 games from November 2000 to May 2001 scoring one goal. March 2002 saw Adam turn out for Orient 10 times, again getting a goal. He was signed on a free by Barry Fry on 1 May 2002, tying him to Second Division Peterborough United for three years.

Perhaps Newton's proclivity to run at and take defenders on with his speed and skill was not the stuff of the Premiership where defenders are inclined to take a more guarded attitude, one slip being the difference between success and failure.

Adam has played international football for St Kitts and Nevis, recently representing his ancestral homeland in 2006 CONCACAF World Cup qualifiers. Newton scored an 88th minute goal against Barbados but a minute later got himself booked. He was yellow carded again in the home leg, this time Barbados were beaten 3–2. Newton had helped his side into the semi-final round. However, it was Shaka Hislop's Trinidad and Tobago that qualified for Germany. The Soca Warriors defeated Newton's side 1–2 before beating St Kitts 5–1 in Trinidad.

GARY ANDREW CHARLES

HAMMERS DEBUT: 5/2/00

'There's nothing better in the world than being a footballer.'

Locally born (Canning Town, Monday, 13 April 1970) Gary, a former East London Schools player was brought to Upton Park from Benfica in 1999 as a cultured wing/right-back. There was no doubting that Charles had talent and class, but his mental and physical preparedness was always in question.

It was in 1987 that Gary became an apprentice at Nottingham Forest under the watchful eye of Brian Clough. He made his debut for Forest on 2 November 1988 against Coventry City.

Some time at Leicester on loan in 1989 was followed by a period struggling to get into the Forest side, but he was in Clough's XI for the 1991 Cup final. After only 15 minutes, Paul Gascoigne was stretchered off the field and out of football for over a year following a Charles tackle. This was probably the start of Gary's problems. Recollecting that incident, Charles said,

For most people I will be remembered only for being on the end of the tackle that wrecked Paul Gascoigne's knee in the 1991 FA Cup final.

Drinking was part and parcel of the game when I was playing. Managers didn't mind you having a few beers then – most thought it was good for team spirit. When I first joined Forest, I lodged with Roy Keane and we had some great nights out. Cloughie was fine about that, although he didn't like us drinking out of bottles for some reason. When I was 20, I moved in with my girlfriend, Michelle, and we soon started a family, so the nights out stopped. You could say I was a model

226

professional — in bed by 10, up early to take the kids to school and then off to work hard at training.

He was transferred for a £750,000 fee to Derby County when Forest were relegated. Gary had spent two years with the Rams when he was signed by Aston Villa in the Premiership on 6 January 1995. But at Villa Park he fell into a downward spiral:

It was when I got a bad ankle injury while playing for Aston Villa that things changed. I was out for two years… I started to drink just to get through the days.

After three years with the Birmingham Villains, it was something of a surprise when Graeme Souness, looking for a replacement for Scott Minto (sold to West Ham), waded in with the £1.5 million that would take Charles to Portugal.

Charles had won four Under-21 caps for England, been selected for two full internationals and was playing for one of the greatest clubs in football. However, everything fell apart when in training he twisted an ankle. Gary was out for six weeks; the season was practically over before he was fit enough to return to competition.

With Souness sacked and just five games for the Eagles of Lisbon under his belt, in October 1999 Redknapp gave Benfica £1.2 million for Charles. Gary signed a four-year contract. Playing for West Ham had been a lifetime ambition for him.

But, as was the way with so many signings made by 'Droopy', Charles was an unmitigated disaster. It seems Harry had 'lashed the cash' almost blindly. One local pundit in Lisbon had wrote of Charles, 'One of the worst players Souness brought to Benfica! One of the many!!! Four games, one goal, and a "Get the hell out of here."'

In November 1999, Gary made his debut for his hometown club as a substitute in a 3–2 League Cup win at St Andrews. Another appearance from the bench in the first home match of the 2000–01 season against Leicester City was his last as a Hammer. The Foxes went away from the Boleyn Ground 1–0 victors. Gary recalled,

THE BLACK HAMMERS

I wasn't fit and only played six times in two years.

The drinking continued.

Gary said goodbye to League football with three games on loan to Birmingham City. He recently admitted,

> *I was getting in trouble with the police … Michelle left me after 12 years, taking our three children with her. I missed my boys like hell. Then I set up a company selling windows, but it didn't work out. The hammer blow came a couple of years ago [2003] when my dad died of emphysema. He meant the world to me and died in my arms. After that, the drinking got so bad that I'd wake up in the morning with the shakes and would need a drink to stop them. In the afternoon, I'd go to the quietest pub in town, sit on my own in the corner and drink until closing time. Sometimes I'd wake up in a police cell because of something I couldn't even remember.*

In May 2002, Charles retired from the game on medical advice. It seemed that every time he was set to make a comeback he picked up a strain, knock or pull. Charles is a story of tragic proportions on a personal basis but this has overshadowed the fact that Redknapp, often portrayed as the master wheeler-dealer of English football, had spent £4.4 million of the club's money in transfer and wages on Charles.

In May 2003 he was also banned from driving for four years and in January 2004 at Derby Magistrates Court Gary was sentenced to four months' imprisonment having pleaded guilty to dangerous driving. In early May, on being sentenced for a common assault, he was warned he could be returned to prison if he failed to work towards beating his alcohol addiction. Gary recollected,

> *When the doctor told me I was killing myself, I knew that I had to stop drinking. People said I wouldn't be able to cope in prison … But I grew up in a tough area of the East End of London and didn't have it easy.*

At his best Gary was quick, good going forward and skilful, if more than a little lightweight in defence. He now lives quietly in a small house in Derbyshire.

FRÉDÉRIC KANOUTÉ

HAMMERS DEBUT: 26/3/00

'You look at the problems in everyday life, there are so many messages to convey to people … one of the central messages of the Koran is the respect of everyone and to work together as one community.'

Kanouté was born (2 September 1977) and grew up on the outskirts of Lyon, in the south-east of France, the second-largest city in the country, in a small town called Sainte Foy-lès-Lyon. His father worked as a mechanic there. Before that, Kanouté senior had been employed in Paris, which is where Fredi's older brother and sister were born. Fredi's father arrived in France from his native country at the age of 21 and married in Paris soon after. The mechanic was and still is a sports lover; he boxed and coached youth football and this is how the youngest Kanouté began to take part in sport.

Fredi first played football around the council flats where he lived in a quiet neighbourhood called Les Provinces. The Kanouté family lived in an eight-storey block. Between the buildings, there were playgrounds and grass for children to play on. That's where Fredi and his friends gathered every day to improvise small three-on-three games or more serious matches with designated kits. Those games taught Fredi to play in small spaces. Every day, as soon as he finished his school homework, he went out to play football and came back home only for dinner, just before nightfall. He remembers his childhood as a good one, although he commented,

I … was a little bit of a victim of racism like every other foreigner in France. When it's not directly, it's indirect. I've been a victim but I would like to choose another term because that's a bit strong. Sometimes

229

it's just between kids who are bullying or having fun on someone. It shouldn't happen but I think the person should take it on his or her part to be stronger. Unfortunately I think it will happen again. We have to work against that but until that we have to be patient, work for it and use it to be stronger.

But he dreamed football; in his bedroom he hung posters of Maradona and Abedi Pelé and he continues to have role models in his life:

As a Muslim my role model is the Prophet Mohammed: peace be upon him. After him I can admire a lot of people like Nelson Mandela ... in sport, Muhammed Ali. I admire a lot of people who have started from nothing and done very great things in their life by their own discipline.

The young Kanouté was recognised as a good player, but insists that some of his friends were more talented. It never occurred to him that he would one day be a professional player. As far as Fredi was concerned, it was all just for fun.

Kanouté joined his first 'official' club, Charcot, when he had just turned five. Fredi's parents had intended to enrol him in his brother's team, FSA, but Fredi was too young and had to wait until he reached six. Fredi was a big, tall boy, and was already stronger than any of the five-year-olds at the club. It was a very small football club, with few resources. Fredi remembered his team's shirts were old fashioned, red with cheesy white and blue stripes. He was envious of the more fashionable shirts others teams wore.

Every Saturday Fredi played in small seven-on-seven tournaments with other teams from the Lyon area, finding it great fun. He would take the ball, dribble round virtually everybody and score five or six goals in every match.

During one tournament, a coach from Olympique Lyonnais, the big team in the Lyon area, came to see Fredi and suggested he join the club. For the kids who played on Fredi's council estate, Lyonnais was *the* team to play for, and with them things began to get more serious for the young Kanouté. He trained three times a week with

Olympique, then played a game on Saturday. They won everything at regional level, but never became national title holders.

At 14, Fredi had a problem with his left knee, and had to have it in plaster for a month. This was followed by more bad news when it was decided that the lad from Les Provinces didn't qualify for the youth academy, which supported the best young players. There was a great deal of competition for places, as young players came to Olympique from all over France and coaches had their pick of some of the best young players in France. Then, at the very last moment, a coach decided Kanouté was suitable for the academy.

In the youth academy, aged just 15, Fredi became the focus of the full force of the French coaching system. Special schooling was arranged for all the players around daily training sessions. Lessons ended at 4pm (very early for France) and a bus would be waiting to take players to the training ground in Gerland. Fredi had great fun on these trips. He liked the atmosphere, although he thought that the coaches took themselves too seriously. He never thought he'd become a professional; he was still in football for fun. He was enjoying the life of the average teenager – he played basketball in the streets, practised Kung Fu, boxed and played rap music. He was still at school, trying to get good marks (but not too seriously).

Fredi's attitude led to problems with the management of the club and he was eventually told he would have to leave the youth academy; it was thought he was missing too many lessons. However, in the final tournament of the season, one coach decided Fredi should not be asked to go at that point. So he ended up signing his first apprentice contract. His mother, who was a teacher of philosophy, asked Fredi to continue studying. He took correspondence lessons, with his mother teaching him. Fredi was awarded a literary Bac (A-level equivalent) in English, Italian and Spanish. He started a university course in Lyon, but he left after three months, finding it boring. Fredi was not excited by accountancy or marketing.

In 1997 Kanouté joined the Lyonnais reserve team and played in the French Fourth Division and pretty soon, aged 19, he turned out for the first team; this was at the same time as some of his friends from the youth academy, including Hammer-to-be Christian

Bassila. Fredi found it very tough; no one really tried to help the young men. But they helped each other. It was during this period that Fredi devoted himself to Islam. He recalled,

> *I started practising when I was around 20. It's something that helps you in every aspect of your life and football is one of those aspects. Ramadan teaches you to be patient and make an effort. And it prevents you from eating too much and keeps you disciplined.*

In 1996–97 Kanouté stayed on the bench as a substitute all season. But he finally realised that he could make a career out of football. He began to see, surprisingly for the first time, making a living from the game as a reward for his hard work a natural, logical progression. At times things had been hard for Fredi at Olympique. He had regrets, but saw the experience as making him stronger.

For the 1997–98 season, Fredi made his first-team debut in the Intertoto Cup against Odra Wodzislaw of Poland. Olympique won 5–2 and Fredi scored. Lyonnais won the Intertoto Cup and had a great season that year, finishing eighth in the French top flight.

It was that season Kanouté won his first international cap with the Under-21 team in Sweden. He would achieve 10 caps at this level altogether, acting as strike-partner to Arsenal's Thierry Henry. Later, he was to comment that he wasn't proud so much of wearing the tricolor shirt, but was pleased that all his personal effort had been recognised and rewarded. At this time both Juventus and Monaco were taking an interest in the Sainte Foy-lès-Lyon lad.

But Kanouté's 1998–99 term was plagued by a groin injury; however, rather than resting it, he tried to continue playing and of course the injury worsened. After six months, he underwent surgery and missed the rest of the season because of the rehabilitation work. Fredi became disillusioned and Olympique did well enough without him, finishing in the top six.

During the 1999–2000 campaign, Kanouté found himself almost a permanent tenant of the substitute's bench. Three months before the end of the season, he finally decided to go. He had scored eight goals in 27 first-team matches in France.

FRÉDÉRIC KANOUTÉ

It was initially planned that Kanouté would go to Upton Park on a three-month loan deal, but this was cut short and he was signed for £3.75 million in March 2000. At the same time Marc Vivien Foé went to Lyonnais for a fee of £6 million. He made his first-team bow at the Boleyn Ground, just three days after his arrival in London, against relegation-bound Wimbledon and scored in the 2–1 Irons victory. Fredi knew the Hammers reputation, but the most important thing for him was to play. He was very impressed by the fans, claiming he was amazed how he was able to feel their support. He found the game less calculating than in France but demanding a more physical approach; he had never run so much.

Fredi chose the Hammers regardless of overtures from Middlesbrough, Glasgow Rangers, Chelsea and Bradford City. He had never found out the exact terms these clubs were offering, as West Ham had always been his first choice because they had given him the chance to play during his difficulties with Lyonnais; he had wanted to repay the Hammers' faith in him.

In four games over the Christmas and New Year period of the 2000–01 season, Kanouté scored five goals. At the end of the campaign he was the Irons' top marksman, with a tally of 14.

Though Fredi appeared unsettled towards the end of 2000–01 and apparently wanted a transfer, he openly commented that he couldn't go to Leeds, Liverpool or Manchester United as houses 'up North' were just too small!

The next season he had a run of four goals in successive victories against Southampton, Chelsea and Ipswich. His intelligent and focused work helped make Jermain Defoe the top scorer at Upton Park (14 goals) that term but he managed to finish just behind the young cockney with a dozen nets of his own.

Between 2000 and 2003, 6ft 3in Fredi scored 33 goals for West Ham in 92 games, proving to be a fast and powerful striker, with exceptional vision.

A succession of injuries in 2002–03 cost Fredi and West Ham dear. A groin problem forced him to miss over half the League games. After treatment in Canada in March 2003, he scored against Sunderland, Villa and the winner against Manchester City, but relegation was fated as was Fredi's £3.5 million moved to Glenn Hoddle's White Hart Lane in August 2003. However, he carried on with his scoring ways, starting with a home debut goal against Leeds, a spectacular overhead kick to win the Premiership clash. It was the first of seven in as many outings for Tottenham, but only five more were added to his toll in 2003–04.

Tottenham got annoyed when Kanouté decided to represent his ancestral homeland in the African Cup of Nations in Tunisia, absenting himself from League games at a point when Tottenham were fighting hard to save their Premierships status and pushing forward in the Carling Cup. But untroubled by his club's plight Fredi netted twice in his debut against Kenya, setting up a 3–1 win for Mali. He was top scorer in the tournament with four goals in the three games that took Mali to the last four. But, to the chagrin of Spurs Director of Football David Pleat, when he did come back to the home of the Totts, he had lost his goalscoring blessing. In the 14 games he played during the remainder of the season, not once did he hit the rigging. However, being on the butt end of the Cockerel Chorus must not have been to his liking as, at the start of the 2004–05, he turned down the opportunity to play in the Athens Olympic Games to do his bit for the Spurs.

In March 2005 Kanouté was obliged to make a quick escape from the Stade Modibo Keita in Bamako during a pitch invasion by angry supporters following a 2–1 defeat in the World Cup at the hands of Togo. He may now, after being capped five times, never again play for Mali.

By April 2005, he had scored nine in 41 games for Spurs which didn't appear to be enough for Dutch Troll Martin Jol; after going AWOL from Tottenham's 2005 summer tour to Mauritius, Fredi was sold to Sevilla for £4.4 million in August. His six goals helped the Spaniards lift the UEFA Cup at the end of 2005–06, but a foot injury three weeks before the final had threatened to endanger his team's chances of glory and he was obliged to start the game against Middlesbrough as a substitute. For all this, he came on at half-time in Eindhoven and was a decisive element in the destruction of the Premiership side. When Jesus Navas played him in, Schwarzer could only parry Fredi's shot and Maresca swept home a simple finish to make it 2–0. In the last minute of the game, Kanouté completed Sevilla's 4–0 victory, crushing Steve McClaren and his Teessiders and gaining his first major club honour.

Able to play left, right and centre, in attack or in midfield, Fredi, who once said he loved London, finding it a pleasant place with many things to do and see, will be remembered at Upton Park wearing his woolly gloves and waving his long arms about like a Gallic windmill in a hurricane. But his speed, awareness, loping run and occasional flashes of brilliance marked by apparent pique will also remain in the minds of Hammers fans. His blistering pace, alongside swiftness of thought, contributed much to the Hammers cause when he was present. But, if Kanouté impresses as a footballer, he is even more striking as a human being, showing the influence of his philosopher mother and thoughtful approach to faith:

> … respect the difference as long as someone has chosen a way to live. Islam, Christian or Jewish religion is just a way to live one's life. This is everybody's liberty to the soul, to feel better in every aspect of his life. We should respect that because it allows one person to act and be a better person so I don't understand why we should blame a person who decides to be better.
>
> You look at the problems in everyday life; there are so many messages to convey to people. I would say one of the central messages of the Koran is the respect of everyone and to work together as one community.

CHRISTIAN BASSILA

'I am at West Ham to do the best I can for the club.'

Bassila was born in Paris on 5 October 1977. He played four games for West Ham during the 2000–01 season. He might be thought to be the signing that cost Harry Redknapp his job at Upton Park. The tall (6ft 3in) midfielder came on a one-year loan from Ligue 1 Rennes as a French Under-21 international.

He was a former teammate of Fredi Kanouté when they were both at Olympique Lyonnais, and they had been acquainted since they were trainees as 11-year-olds and their days at the Lyon Academy. Kanouté recommended Bassila, likening him to Patrick Vieira.

Bassila made his debut for the Hammers against Manchester United at Upton Park in August 2000. He trotted on as a substitute in 2–2 draw in the 67th minute and wasted no time in ploughing into King Becks the Overrated. However, the new French Iron wasn't fit, having injured his knee the day before. After three more substitute appearances, Bassila had to go back to France for an operation – he was paid £720,000 for 85 minutes' playing time.

A spell at Strasbourg and a loan period at Espanyol followed before Bassila turned up on a free at Sunderland in August 2005. It was rumoured that both Auxerre and Fiorentina were after him, but he seems to have done little more for the Black Cats than he did for Merchant Banker Harry.

JERMAIN COLIN DEFOE

HAMMERS DEBUT: 19/9/00

'Style is important for me. I want to be different, and now, when I go out on the field, it'll be my choice what I'm wearing.'

Born just a couple of miles from the Boleyn Ground (although his parents were from St Lucia and Dominica) in Beckton, London, on Thursday, 7 October 1982, in 105 games for West Ham, Jermain scored 41 times before moving to White Hart Lane for £6.7 million–plus sending Bobby Zamora to Upton Park. Defoe departed East London just before the transfer window closed on 2 February 2004, leaving the newly relegated Hammers to their fate.

Growing up, Jermain was inspired by Brazilian legend Romario, admiring his goalscoring gifts and clever tricks. His approbation for the South Americans has endured into his adult life and he watches videos of their past and continues to dream of emulating them by being part of a World Cup-winning team.

Known for his lightning pace, fierce shot, lethal finishing and being one of the most deadly predators in English football, Jermain scored on his debut at White Hart Lane against Portsmouth on Saturday, 7 February 2004 (Spurs won 4–3) and added a further six for that season, scoring seven goals in 14 matches. He was Tottenham's brightest star in the 2004–05 season, playing 44 games and netting 22 times, including a hat-trick in a 5–1 thrashing of Southampton. His four-year contract will keep him at White Hart Lane until 2009, although in 2006 he was finding it a challenge to get into the Spurs side as a regular.

However, early in 2004, at Upton Park there was a deal of talk about 'rats leaving sinking ships' and bemoaning of the lack of loyalty in contemporary football, but Judas Jermain (as he was baptised in some quarters) was originally poached from South-East London rivals Charlton Athletic in 1999; the Addicks were left indignant over the £400,000 plus £1 million in appearance-related fees they got in return for Defoe following a transfer tribunal. The £1 million the Valley brigade got following the diminutive striker's migration to Spurs did little to relieve their feelings of being robbed of the player that had been with them since his schoolboy days. Jermain's retrospective response to the matter was:

I was 15 and I left the club to go and play with my mates at West Ham ... I had a lot of friends there and it was closer to home. I went to Lilleshall at 14 for two years and when I came back I made the decision to go to West Ham. I was away from home for two years, so that was just about my age and where I was at that time.

West Ham's chair Terry Brown famously said, following Defoe's transfer, that Jermain's 'head wasn't right'. This goaded the new Tottenham striker to comment,

I accept I was wrong to hand in the transfer request when I did, but I never withdrew it. I think my transfer request could have been handled differently. It was a mistake, but I would like to thank the West Ham fans who gave me great support since I joined the club as a 17-year-old. I really appreciated that. At the same time his [Brown's] comments were a shock and hurt me.

Later, he said,

Let's deal with facts ... If I'd stayed at West Ham, I would be the only player left there now, so I had to go.

But TB looked to be on the mark, given Defoe's contribution to the Hammers in his final months at the Boleyn Ground; his disciplinary record, performance and commitment were not commensurate with a maturing professional; he missed a dozen games due to relatively unnecessary suspensions. He seemed consistently ill-tempered and resentful and as such alienated himself from West Ham fans who tried hard to make allowances. However, in March 2006, he commented,

What I'd really like to do is go down to Upton Park one afternoon when the stadium is full ... I'd like to go out on to the pitch with a microphone and explain to the fans exactly what happened. I was young, I was badly advised at the time. I made a mistake. I didn't have enough experience to deal with what I was being told.

I wish I didn't put the transfer request in at all, never mind biding my time. People say to me that I should have waited a week and then put it in ... I just wish I hadn't done it at all. I try to forget about it but it's still at the back of my mind.

My mate Izzy Iriekpen, who I used to play with at West Ham, was staying at the hotel at Upton Park. He asked me if I wanted to meet up with him there and I told him I couldn't because, if people saw me there, there would be trouble. It's sad.

There have been times where I haven't played in a match and I have come in for training the next day still feeling down. But you still have to work hard and do your best. I stay behind for finishing practice every day.

Comparisons have been made between Jermain and the likes of Greaves and Pele at the same stage of development. Certainly Defoe had excelled in the Irons' Under-19 side that was victorious in the FA Academy play-offs in the 1999–2000 season. He demonstrated his potential, scoring the only goal in his first-team debut game; he came on as a substitute for Marc Keller with 13 minutes of the second-round League (Worthington) Cup encounter at Walsall to play – within seven minutes he had won the game for his club.

Glenn Roeder sent Defoe on loan to Second Division Bournemouth for the rest of the season. It was a decision that dismayed Jermain to begin with, but he scored on his debut for the south-coast side at Stoke and went on to break a Football League record by scoring in 11 successive games. Before coming back to the Boleyn Ground, in 30 League and Cup matches Defoe struck 19 goals for the Cherries. He made his first Premiership appearance, coming off the bench to replace Grant McCann in the 2–1 defeat at Middlesbrough in the last game of the 2000–01 season.

Just days before the start of the next campaign, the Beckton boy scored a brace for the England Under-21s against Holland; he put his first away within three seconds of the start of the match. Jermain was awarded the first of his 19 Under-21 caps v Mexico the previous season. He went on to gain 23 caps as an Under-23.

Defoe became the 1131st player to appear for England in his country's 811th match on 31 March 2004. Sweden defeated England 1–0 in that friendly game at Nya Ullevi Stadion, Göteborg. He came on as a 12th-minute substitute. Jermain scored his first goal for his country on 8 September 2004 in the 2–1 win over Poland.

Despite being mostly confined to the role of substitute in 2001–02, Defoe concluded the season as top scorer at Upton Park with 14 goals in all competitions, including the only goal of the game in the 1–0 Premiership win over Manchester United at Old Trafford.

In 2002–03, despite turning out in every senior fixture, Jermain managed just 11 goals. Although this tally made him top scorer at the club, it was part of a sorry tale for both West Ham and Defoe.

Jermain, who was a standby for the European Championship finals 2004 and was unlucky to be dropped from England's 2006 World Cup squad, although he was part of the pre-tournament training in Portugal, has said that financial rewards are not the main thing in his life and that it was more important for him to play and score goals. Defoe is not the stereotypical 'bling bling' Premiership footballer who is only interested in money, fast cars and nights out. Although he was kept out of the reckoning in Germany by his friend Wayne Rooney, Defoe, a devoted Catholic, said before the World Cup he prayed that the Manchester United forward would make a speedy recovery from his foot injury, wanting him to make the squad as he considered the Liverpudlian to be one of England's best players.

Jermain attended a Catholic primary school and secondary school and likes to go to church whenever he can, often with his mum, girlfriend, little sister and grandmother. But sometimes Spurs do a warm-down on Sunday and this prevents his attendance, but if he gets a day off then he gets a phone call from his mum, Sandra, at eight o'clock in the morning. She always made sure he went to church. Defoe sees his faith as giving him mental strength, putting situations and issues into perspective, especially when things aren't going well.

Defoe has made it public that his aim is to win everything: medals, trophies and individual honours. He has let it be known that he wants the Golden Boot (awarded to Europe's leading goalscorer) and to be Footballer of the Year. And one day he'd like to play outside of Britain, having heard David Beckham talk about his experiences in Spain with Real Madrid, while on England duty.

KABA DIAWARA

HAMMERS DEBUT: 23/9/00

'I will eat jellied ells!'

A sturdy and good-looking forward, born in Toulon, France, on Tuesday, 16 December 1975, Diawara scored on his debut for Girondins de Bordeaux in a 2–0 win at Lille OSC in the final match of the 1995–96 term. He netted seven goals in 29 French First Division games during 1996–97, emerging from the dug-out 23 times. The next season he managed just a single goal in 13 appearances. However, in 1998–99 he was in the Bordeaux squad that took the French Championship. Kaba's five goals in 17 matches convinced Arsene Wenger to pay £2.5 million to drape the red and white of Goonerdom on his French Under-21 international shoulders. He made his debut for Arsenal on Sunday, 31 January 1999 as a sub in a 1–0 win at home to Chelsea. But Kaba the Baba got homesick (or sick of Highbury) and never got a sniff in 15 run-outs with the North London knob'eads. He hot-footed it back to the land of coq au vin and, with relief, signed for Marseille for £2 million in July 1999 after just five months on Wenger's wonga wagon. But at the Velodrome Kaba's personal goal drought continued for another 15 games and he was unloaded boot-sale style (at a significant loss) to Paris Saint-Germain, where he rounded off the 1999–2000 season with 10 performances consistent with his last 30. Not a saucisson!

When Kaba's former Highbury teammate Nicolas Anelka arrived at PSG, the club quickly went for the loan option and First Division Blackburn Rovers took Diawara into their Lancastrian loins in

August 2000. But it seems tripe and trotters were not to his liking and his six outings under Laird Souness the McMiserable brought forth but a single Worthington Cup-tie goal that punctured the derisible defensive ramparts raised by a ramshackle Rochdale – he scored one of the half-dozen Rovers drove past the dumbfounded Dale in the 6–1 demolition. Kaba was given permission by Souness to bail out of Ewood Park early and take up an offer from 'daan saaf'.

Harry Redknapp, doubtless impressed with Kaba's ability to fire more blanks than a eunuch with a double vasectomy, snapped up the hapless French rover like a ferret would a bacon-wrapped mutton morsel. It seems Redders had been sniffing around Kaba for some time. According to the itinerant gauche Gaul,

> *The first time I heard that Harry Redknapp was interested in signing me was actually before I joined Arsenal … I was told that West Ham wanted to buy me but I don't think they could afford the price that Bordeaux wanted.*

Diawara started his sparkling career as an Iron on Saturday, 23 September 2000 as a sub in a 3–0 win at Coventry City. With staggering reliability Diawara failed to unload in 11 efforts. However, looking on the up-side, he was involved in five Premiership wins out of six between October and November 2000 and was only twice in a beaten West Ham side. So it seems he was not so much a passenger but more a semi-redundant bootlegger and it appeared as if the Toulon tourist had finally put his passport in for a service when he said,

> *I am living in Docklands, near the other French players, and it is very nice there. Now I am married and have many close friends at West Ham, so it is more comfortable for me and easier to enjoy life.*

But H had to make room to bring other players to Upton Park so it was once more on to France for Kaba, who by now was threatening P&O for the record number of channel crossings. He signed for Le Championnat new boys OGC Nice. In 2003–04 Diawara was the newly promoted club's top scorer, netting a dozen times in 37 games. In December 2004 he returned to Paris Saint-Germain before shipping out to El Quos in Qatar. He desert-hopped to the Saudi Arabian side Al Ittihad to do a double act with former West Ham teammate Titi Camara for a while, sort of Middle East End thing, before, guess what … going back to France!

Kaba, being of Guinean decent, chose to represent his ancestral nation at senior level. He scored two goals in the 2006 African Cup of Nations. The career (any bets he turns up at Southampton in the near future?) of Kaba 'King of the Gallic Romanies' looks thus:

1993–94	Toulon	
1994–95	Bordeaux	
1995–96	Bordeaux	1 goals, 1 game
1996–97	Bordeaux	7 goals, 29 games
1997–97 (June)	Rennes	3 goals, 12 games
1997–98	Bordeaux	1 goals, 15 games
1998 (December)	Bordeaux	5 goals, 23 games
1999–00 (December)	Marseille	1 goal, 9 games
1999	Arsenal	12 games
1999–00	Paris SG	10 games
2000 (December)	Paris SG	1 game
2000–01 (March)	Blackburn Rovers	5 games
2000–01	West Ham	10 games
2001–02	RC Ferrol	4 goals, 14 games
2002–03	Nice	12 goals, 37 games
2003–04 (December)	Paris SG	3 games
2003–04	Al Ittihad	
2004–05	Al Ittihad	
2005–06	AC Ajaccio	2 goals, 20 games

ABOUBACAR 'TITI' SIDIKI CAMARA
HAMMERS DEBUT: 23/12/00

'It is possible that I may stay here and play, play, play!'

This big, quick striker was born in Conakry, the Guinean capital, just a Yossi Benayoun throw-in from the Atlantic Ocean (on Friday, 17 November 1972). He was called 'Titi' by an older sister who had trouble with the pronunciation of Aboubacar.

Camara, who played eight times in the claret and blue of East London's finest, came to the Docklands with his family (wife Miriam, son Vekou and daughter Oumy) with a CV that included three African Cup of Nations finals.[3] But, with a mediocre record in the Premiership, there were those who asked, 'Why in the name of Ernie Gregory do the Irons need Camara?' He sashayed into the Boleyn Ground on Thursday, 21 December 2000 with 56 caps to his name, heaving a fee of £1.1 million, having scored 10 times in his 37 outings for the Scouse Reds in the 1999–2000 season. As such, Titi did not come to the Boleyn Ground with the reputation as a copious tormentor of the rigging. Camara hadn't played for his club in the 2000–01 season after asking Liverpool for a transfer in pursuit of regular first-team football.

But, of course, none of this troubled the ever-popular Harry Redknapp, the lovable cockney sparrow on whom Anfield had previously unloaded Rigobert Song and who had been responsible for signing such glittering prizes as Christian Bassila, Gary Charles

---

[3] Camara retired from international football after 15 years in 2004 following Guinea's 2–1 defeat and elimination at the hands of West African rivals Mali – Fredi Kanouté scored Mali's first goal of that game – in the quarter-finals of the tournament.

and Davor Suker in recent times. Nor was H shy about using the tank-like forward on the wing, apparently seeing him as the African Jimmy Johnston – what planet was that bloke on?

Titi was introduced into the Irons First XI on Saturday, 23 December 2000 in a 2–1 defeat at Leicester City. But his lack of impact made Titi's stay at Upton Park a brief one and at the same time did much to confirm Redknapp, still doing his *Minder* impressions, as little more than a flawed horse-trader who would bring totally random players into the West Ham fold in the hope that they would be successful. He might call that gambling, but in fact it is no more than wishful thinking, no matter how loud he could whistle 'I Could Be So Good for You'.

As a 15-year-old, Camara was with St Etienne, where he stayed from 1990 to 1995, playing 94 games and scoring 17 goals. He moved to Racing Club de Lens. He found the net 14 times in 63 outings for RC between 1996 and 1998. Then, with Olympique Marseille, in the 1998–99 season, he ran out in 61 matches (including an appearance as sub in Marseille's 1999 UEFA Cup final defeat at the hands of Parma) claiming eight goals.

In 1999 Titi became one of Houllier's Galloping Gallic Guard, parachuting into Anfield at a cost of £2.5 million to become the first Guinean to play in the Premiership, making his debut on Saturday, 7 August 1999 v Sheffield Wednesday; Liverpool won 2–1 at Hillsborough.

At the end of the 1999–2000 term, Camara finished runner-up to Michael Owen in the club's scoring table. But it is questionable if the English game was to Titi's taste. He once commented,

The game here is far more physical than in France and the pace is incredible. Referees don't penalise hard tackles here in the way they would do abroad and that took me a bit by surprise.

After he said his goodbyes to West Ham, Titi joined 'crack' Saudi Arabian side Al Ittihad on loan. In the winter transfer window of 2005, he joined Amiens SC in the French second flight on a short-term six-month deal. He scored half-a-dozen goals in 13 games before leaving at the end of the season. In December of that year, he was linked with the vacant manager's job with his national side.

Able to produce ferocious strikes at goal, Camara's power was not often enough aided by accuracy. Like many Redknapp 'captures', Titi was capable of the unexpected, but was also often predictable, and playing for the Irons he rarely troubled opposing defences.

DAVID BENJAMIN JAMES

'The bleach had gone a bit wrong.'

D avid was West Ham's custodian of the nets between 2001 and 2004. In that time he made 102 appearances for the Hammers. Born in Welwyn Garden City, Hertfordshire (1 August 1970), despite being considered one of England's best keepers, he will forever be known at Upton Park firstly for his blonde dye-job that inspired opposing fans to chant 'Urgh! Urgh! Urgh! He's got bird shit on his head!' (he once dyed his hair 'blonde then red, then orange'), and secondly as 'Calamity James', and there were many who breathed a sigh of relief when (on the recommendation of David Seaman) Manchester City paid a £2 million fee in January 2004.

David started his goal–stopping vocation with Watford in the old Division Two. The young man had a FA Youth Cup winners' medal to his credit and he impressed enough to be awarded Under-21 recognition and a £1 million move to Liverpool after 98 games for his local club where he had been since his school days. It was 1992 and the future looked bright for the lad from Herts.

It was at Anfield that David's penchant for messing up on crosses and high balls became evident. After conceding 20 goals in 11 games he was dropped by Graeme Souness and was to lose his place three more times during his initial season with the Scouse Reds.

On the departure of Souness, James found a supporter in Roy Evans, and became a fixture in Liverpool's team of the 1990s.

Despite winning the League Cup in 1995, Liverpool's side at the time had failed to oust rivals Manchester United as England's premier club, due to the team's poor defensive record that, of course, was related to James's high-profile gaffes. But, proving to be a consistent member of the first team, David earned full international recognition in England's 2–0 defeat of Mexico in a 1997 friendly match.

With the arrival of American goalkeeper Brad Friedel, David's place at Liverpool began to look insecure as he had never lost his reputation for losing focus at crucial points and, in June 1999, after 277 appearances for Liverpool, James was sold for £1.7 million to Aston Villa.

Although James resuscitated his international career at Villa Park, his inconsistency continued; he proved to be the hero in saving penalties against Bolton Wanderers in a 2000 FA Cup semi-final, but he was held responsible for Chelsea's winning goal in the subsequent final.

James, a constant critic of the regime at Villa Park, had played 85 times for the Villians when Glenn Roeder, James's former boss at Watford, made him his first signing at a cost of £3.5 million in July 2001.

David's debut was delayed after he'd been accidentally kicked on his knee by his fellow Hammer Martin Keown (while on England duty in a game against Holland). However, after Christmas, when James was finally fit enough to take up the gloves, he kept nine clean sheets in 26 games to the conclusion of the 2001–02 season, helping West Ham finish seventh in the Premiership, a placing that had long looked impossible.

As far as the international scene was concerned, James was not seen during the 2002 World Cup. He had made the trip but for several years James had been in the shadow of David Seaman. However, when Seaman was dropped after making a mistake against Macedonia in 2002, James became the new England number one, and played in all his nation's matches in Euro 2004, regardless of West Ham's desperate struggle to avoid relegation for the whole of the 2002–03 term.

With 10 clean sheets at club level in 31 appearances up to 10 January 2004, James seemed to be a keeper of growing stature; at Upton Park he appeared to have been set to make a future. But, after relegation, James seemed to want to move quickly back to Premiership limelight and in January 2004 he signed for Manchester City for a fee of £2 million. He made his debut for City in their 1–1 draw with Blackburn Rovers a week after playing his last game for the Hammers and helped keep the Manchester Blues in the top flight with two crucial penalty saves towards the end of the Premiership campaign.

David went to Euro 2004 and played in all the games up to the defeat by Portugal in the quarter-finals on penalty kicks. After conceding four goals during a 4–1 drubbing, England suffered at the hands of Denmark during a friendly on 17 August 2005, the worst defeat of an England side in a quarter of a century, James was displaced by Paul Robinson as England's first-choice keeper. He made the trip to Germany for the 2006 World Cup but was not called upon; from most perspectives he was included in the squad as an emergency third choice and it seems unlikely that he will make many additions to his 33 international caps.

In the summer of 2004 James was a guest at the training camp of American football team the Miami Dolphins. He worked out with the team and studied their training and conditioning methods. This has led to speculation that he is keen on a coaching role after he retires. He has an acute awareness of the position of black footballers in England and once left a PFA event when Warren Mitchell took the stage as Alf Garnett.

He was married to Welsh wife Tanya James and had four children, but later divorced, and she allegedly demanded £3 million. She also appeared in a tabloid newspaper discussing her financial hardship since the couple split and the breakdown of the marriage.

There is no doubting that James was and is a complex character. He is not a stereotypical footballer, having a love for portrait painting (he has completed studies of his teammates), yoga, collecting vintage Raleigh Chopper pushbikes and has an ambition to become a criminal psychologist when he retires. He has explored the field of sports psychology to improve his skills as a goalkeeper and has explained his lapses in concentration as a consequence of his passion for PC games. James once suffered a back injury while reaching for a television remote control. He has pursued a career in modelling since his Liverpool days and recently added to his experience on the catwalk with H&M.

David has visited the southeastern African nation of Malawi to help raise AIDS awareness and set up The David James Foundation in order to help farmers in Malawi develop better farming practices. He has also collaborated with Tony Blair on this issue.

During the last decade James has arguably been England's most naturally gifted goalkeeper. A commanding, athletic figure, on his day, he is a fabulous goalkeeper, with excellent shot-stopping abilities, while on a bad day James's errors can cost his team dearly.

EDOUARD CISSE

'French football is like the game in Italy – boring.'

C isse, who was born on Thursday, 30 March 1978, is the last of four brothers (Dominique is 12 years his senior, Philippe is 10 years older than Edouard, and Christophe was born in 1970) who all played football, although not at a high level. But they taught their baby brother everything they knew about the game, although they would often make him play in goal. Neither Edouard's father, Mamadou, nor his mother, Gracieuse, was a football lover, but they supported their youngest son when he started out with his hometown club Pau, in south–west France in 1997.

Moving to Paris Saint–Germain, Edouard made his Ligue 1 debut against Nantes in 1997 but was sent on loan to French First Division Stade Rennais FG (on loan in 1998–99).

He played in the same French Under–21 international team as Fredi Kanouté (he had 18 caps at this level) but Edouard's PSG career seemed under constant threat by changes of coach or failures of confidence. It wasn't until 2000 that he began to claim a permanent place in the first team and played in several European campaigns, in both UEFA Cup and Champions League.

Although linked to a number of Premiership cubs, Edouard was signed by the Hammers on a year's loan from Paris Saint–Germain in 2002. He was essentially a central midfielder, but had no problems filling in out wide if necessary.

The fifth Frenchman in the Hammers squad (Schemmel,

EDOUARD CISSE

Kanouté, Courtois and Sofiane were the others) seemed keen to be involved in English football saying,

> *The football in the Premiership is fast and furious with lots of goals, whereas French football is like the game in Italy — boring ... I am really looking forward to playing for West Ham ... I definitely want to stay here beyond the loan period and for many years beyond that ... It was a surprise in a way coming to West Ham ...*

As such, it seemed there was great hope placed in the young Cisse. He was a hardworking yet graceful midfielder with good ball control, poise in possession and was a tenacious tackler. The way in which his long legs helped him eat up the ground and cover from box to box brought comparisons with another rising talent at the time — Patrick Vieira.

Before coming to the Docklands, Edouard consulted his former French Under-21 colleague:

> *When it looked like I might be coming to England, I spoke to Thierry Henry on the phone to see what he thought about West Ham and he told me that it would be a good move for me ... He said that West Ham play attractive football and have some very good players.*
>
> *Here at West Ham, I have already noticed that it is a family club and that is what I love most ... Everybody has a smile on their face in the morning at the training ground here, and that wasn't the case at PSG. I think it is very important to enjoy playing football and I really love the characters here at West Ham.*

Cisse made his first appearance for West Ham at Roots Hall in a preseason friendly on Friday, 9 August; the Hammers beat Dutch side Vitesse Arnhem 1–0. He made his League debut on Monday, 19 August 2002 in a 4–0 defeat at Newcastle United.

Although not everything about West Ham was to his liking; he once said,

> *The food over here is OK, but we seem to have a lot of peas at the training ground, and they are not for me!*

THE BLACK HAMMERS

Edouard and his wife Sandra and their three-month-old baby daughter Jordane Leah were happy in their apartment in Chigwell, Essex (next door to fellow Hammer and French compatriot Sebastien Schemmel). However, Cisse was one of 16 casualties (players either sold or not retained) of relegation as West Ham strove to avoid liquidation by cutting the wage bill. He went back to PSG in May 2003 and was soon loaned to Monaco. In 2003–04, under the guidance of Didier Deschamps, Edouard enjoyed his best season of his career, making 33 League appearances and helping Monaco reach the Champions League final. He was in the Monaco team that defeated Chelsea in the semi-finals and gained a runners-up medal as a member of the side that were defeated by Jose Mourinho's FC Porto.

But, after returning to Parc des Princes, Cisse struggled and currently he not the smiling young midfielder that came to Upton Park.

EDOUARD CISSE – CAREER RECORD			
SEASON	CLUB	GAMES	GOALS
2004/2005	Paris SG	36	1
2003/2004	Monaco	44	3
2002/2003	West Ham	25	0
2001/2002	Paris SG	30	1
2000/2001	Paris SG	35	2
1999/2000	Paris SG	28	0
1998/1999	Rennes	28	2
1997/1998	Paris SG	14	0
1996/1997	Pau	0	0
Total		205	7

LESLIE FERDINAND

'I was surprised, but I always say nothing surprises me in football.'

Born in Acton, London (8 December 1966), Les made 14 appearances for West Ham (scoring twice). During his career he has taken the mundane with the exotic, the glory with the ignominy. For example, he appeared three times for Brentford while on loan but with Besiktas he netted 21 times in 33 matches, including the winning goal in the Turkish Cup final to help defeat the mighty Fenerbahce.

Although an England Youth international it was the QPR scouting system that found Les playing for Hayes in the Vauxhall Opel League. During March 1987 £15,000 took him to Loftus Road and he made his first-team debut a month later v Coventry. With the Super Hoops he became a West London legend; in 183 outings he hit 90 goals before an £8 million move in June 1995 took him to Tyneside and St James' Park. At Newcastle his career continued to be a glittering one. During the 83 games he wore the black and white, he contributed on 49 occasions to the Magpies' goal account.

Les was now the recipient of universal acclaim as a role model of the modern game as well as an exemplary performer and in 1996 he was presented with the PFA Player of the Year award.

'Sir Les', as he was now affectionately known across the realm of English football, moved to White Hart Lane in August 1997 for a £6 million fee. At Tottenham he became much more of an influential player in terms of his effect on the whole side, although his goal tally (39 goals in 148 games) was not as impressive as it had been with previous employers.

In March 2003 Les scored his first goal for West Ham. It was at the Boleyn Ground in the 2–0 defeat of his old North London club. That alone might have been seen by some supporters (me for instance) as enough to warrant his £200,000 fee.

Les bagged five goals in his 17 international games for England. He also has an England 'B' cap. When the Hammers were relegated in 2003, Ferdinand moved on to Leicester City. However, although showing his continuing value claiming 13 goals in 37 run-outs (his haul included him becoming the first City player to score six in one game), in 2004 he experienced his second demotion from Premiership.

Next stop for Les was Bolton and then Championship side Reading, who not long into 2005 lured Les with a deal rumoured to be something in excess of £70,000 a month. While the return in goals was not impressive (just one in 14 appearances up to the end of 2004–05), his influence and experience was invaluable to the side that would storm into the Premiership in 2006. Having done his bit in Bucks, Les joined Watford on 15 September 2005 on a non-contract basis.

Les has an active life outside football;

I like playing tennis and also enjoy listening to music. I listen to hip-hop and a bit of garage.

But he has been a tireless supporter of anti-racism in football. He recently said,

There were certain clubs you could go to, and you knew you were going to get racist abuse from start to finish … That doesn't really happen that much nowadays.

However,

Until enough is done about racism to get it completely eradicated from football, you just have to get on with your game and do the best that

you can. Throughout my career, I think the teams that gave me the most racial abuse were the teams that I was scoring more goals against than anybody else. So it gave me that impetus to go and do well against their sides.

Unfortunately, racism is definitely rearing its ugly head again. And it's becoming somewhat fashionable to chant at the black players. As we saw in England's qualifying matches for Euro 2004, and with some of our domestic clubs playing in Europe ... But at the moment I don't think that it's being hit harshly enough.

We've seen in recent years and months clubs being fined for that sort of thing. But the piddling amounts of money that these clubs are being fined is no kind of deterrent to supporters on the terraces ... They should be punished in the way that affects the team and affects the people that are following the team. Until those harsh lines are taken, you'll never eradicate racism in football.

The issue of racism is very important and needs to be constantly addressed. I think with the advent of campaigns like 'Show Racism the Red Card' and 'Kick it Out' there has been a huge decrease in racism among fans around the grounds. However, I do think a glass ceiling still exists in some clubs and that has got to be sorted as there are plenty of black ex-players with the qualifications and know-how to be great managers.

As to the future, although Les has said,

My face is the wrong colour to be a boss in English football,

he has indicated that he wants to stay in the game:

I'm toying with the idea of coming back and doing some type of coaching. I've spent a lot of time in this industry and at a later date coaching is the sort of thing that I want to do ... But there are definitely obstacles in my way and one of them is the fact that I am black — I am not afraid to say it.

GLEN MCLEOD JOHNSON

'Sixteen of us went round to John's [Terry] house to play a tournament on the PlayStation. We had loads of TVs set up and games going on at once. I don't mean to boast, but I won!'

Although Glen was born in Greenwich, South-East London (23 August 1984), he grew up in Temple Hill, near Dartford, in Kent. As a young boy he showed no interest in football, he had a pair of boots, but they had holes in them and he was a substitute for his primary school but that was as far as his participation in the sport went.

However, with the encouragement and support of his mother, Wendy, he took up the game as a 10-year-old. He was sitting on the sofa at home one day and his mum told him that the local YMCA boys' team needed players. She telephoned the organisers and Glen went along and enjoyed it. He didn't have a position, so the coach had instructed him to 'go up front and see what happens'. Glen scored a hat-trick in his first game.

Wendy Johnson brought up Glen, his younger brother Lewis (born in 1989) and elder sister Claire (born in 1981) on her own. Wendy did all she could to help Glen make the grade as a professional footballer. He said of her,

I have to thank my mum for pushing me … because I wouldn't have been able to do it without her.

After two games with the 'Y', a West Ham scout gave Wendy his card and asked her to telephone him. This led to Johnson joining the Hammers as a striker (he didn't move into defence until he was 14).

GLEN MCLEOD JOHNSON

When he arrived at Upton Park, Glen didn't realise that a young West Ham team existed, thinking that the club just fielded a first team.

Wendy took driving lessons and passed her test in order that she could take her eldest son to the training round. Three nights a week she would drop him off, drive home and then come back to pick him up.

When Glen was 13, he trained on Monday, Wednesday and Thursday, which meant he had to forgo going out with his friends and this caused him to tell his mum that he didn't want to go training any more. However, in a gentle but firm way Wendy helped Glen regain his focus. She saw his dislike for the academic side of school and knew he had to find another path. Johnson recalled,

They used to moan at me and ask me what I would do if I didn't become a footballer, but I just used to tell them that I would make it ... If I hadn't become a footballer, though, I'd probably be a builder − I wasn't the brightest!

His mother's guidance paid off and Glen was offered an academy scholarship. In November 2000, as a 16-year-old first-year trainee, Glen netted a hat-trick of headers in an FA Youth Cup third-round tie against Southend United. He was the only West Ham player to score in the FA Youth Cup that season. The young Hammers beat Southend 3–0 and then lost 4–2 to Oldham in the fourth round, Johnson scored one and the other was an own goal.

After Glen scored the hat-trick against Southend, Tony Carr, the maker of so many of West Ham's best players over the years, told Johnson that, even though he'd scored the goals, he had played rubbish. The youngster couldn't understand this reaction at the time, thinking it was better to play badly and win rather than play well and lose but later he said,

I realise now that it isn't very often that you play badly and win.

Glen had scored twice at the European Under-16 Championships in 2001 and went on to captain the England Under-19 side at the

THE BLACK HAMMERS

European Cup in the summer of 2002 and was voted Young Player of the Year two years in succession.

It has been said that Glen Johnson was a better player at 18 than Bobby Moore and Rio Ferdinand. How much this is about the hype that drenches the modern game is unsure, but what is true is that when the defender left Upton Park for Stamford Bridge after the Hammers were relegated in 2003 it seemed to confirm the fears of many involved with the club that a long-term decline had set in, starting as it did what seemed like a mass desertion of West Ham's future hopes.

Not long before his departure, Johnson had publicly asked his fellow Hammers to resist the temptation to be part of a general exodus from the Boleyn Ground following the last day of the season draw with Birmingham City at St Andrews that condemned the Irons to the Championship. This made the £6 million defection to Roman Abramovich's Frankenstein-like Chelsea (Johnson was the first major signing the Blues made under Roman the Doughman) in July 2003 all the more hard to take.

It had been the Russian's pal and best advert for Viagra, Sven-Goran Eriksson, who had recommended Johnson (along with Joe Cole) as one of England's top young players (the Swedish sex bomb had given Glen, already an Under-21 star, his first full cap in November 2003 in the 3–2 defeat by Denmark at Old Trafford).

However, in October 2002 Johnson was playing in the First Division with Millwall, on a three-month loan from the Hammers. Glen is able to play at full-back or at the centre of defence and in his eight games in the service of the Lions demonstrated a high level of calmly executed skills that quickly led to his recall to the Boleyn Ground, a month early, in December 2002.

Johnson was selected for the England Under-20s side to face Switzerland at Upton Park and within a month he made his first-team debut (coming on as a substitute) in the Premiership at the Valley. The Hammers lost (4–2). However, Johnson's first start in the Premiership saw his side defeat Blackburn 2–1 on 29 January 2003 at Upton Park. While substitute Jermain Defoe grabbed the headlines the next day after his memorable last-minute winner,

GLEN MCLEOD JOHNSON

Johnson had immediately settled into the right-back role, keeping winger David Thompson comparatively quiet. Glen's willingness to get forward was impressive and provided several decent crosses for fellow home debutant Les Ferdinand – the player whose poster image had adorned Glen's bedroom wall just a few years before.

Glen was to be ever-present to the end of that ill-fated season. Neither Moore nor Ferdinand retained their places after making their debuts, but as young players these two great West Ham defenders had much more competition for their places in the side than Johnson had to cope with.

After Glen was whisked away by the Chelski Child Stealer on 16 July 2003, the West Ham supporters trust commented,

> *The sale of Glen Johnson has been met by the fans with massive anger and disappointment. Subsequent to recent statements by the club on their own website, issued by Tony Gale and Trevor Brooking, it is apparent that the club are aware of the absolute need to maintain and build upon the core of young players that have come through the youth system and many fans have expressed misgivings regarding the cynical sale of Glen Johnson, hard on the heels of season-ticket renewals. The transfer has taken everyone by surprise and, given our defensive frailties during the first two-thirds of last season, a particularly poor footballing decision.*

That Johnson, so symbolic of West Ham's future, had been sold to London 'loads of money' rivals almost immediately after the body blow of relegation was for many the last straw.

Initially, Johnson enjoyed being at Chelsea, working under the Stromboli ice-cream-man-like Italian coach Claudio 'you wanta de nica flake?' Ranieri. Johnson was involved in seven of the Pensioners' first nine League games, scored his first goals at senior level v Newcastle and, in the Champions League, against MSK Zilina, he took the place of Mario Melchiot, one of the best right-backs in the Premiership. And, of course, he got his first cap from Uncle Sven (in November 2003, coming on as a substitute for the injured Gary Neville after 16 minutes). But his progress was halted by injury. However, in 2003–04 he had played in 19 League, two Carling Cup, one FA Cup and nine Champions League games in the baby blue of the Cheesey Chelsea Cossacks.

That was all before the arrival of big bad wolf Jose Mourinho. 'The Special One' (certainly special in the fact that he had never played professional football) failed to give Glen a match from the start of the 2004–05 term up to the end of September 2004. In a cost-per-match breakdown of the Chelsea 'Galacticos' undertaken by the *Daily Mail* based on the previous season, Johnson looked comparatively cheap at £3,068 a match, relative to the likes of Juan Veron at a staggering £19,133 (more than £2,100 per minute, over £350 per second) and Hernam Crespo who came out at a cost of £11,700 per game. This, for Chelsea supporters, constituted 'success'. There is another phrase for it often used in the East End that strikes the ear a little harder than being 'taken for a mug'. Certainly, England's Under-21 coach Peter Taylor was not alone when he expressed doubts if Johnson's transfer to Chelsea had been the best long-term move for the young defender. In early October 2002 Glen had not been given a single opportunity in the first team. Taylor commented, 'Maybe Glen needs to go on loan. There is an opportunity if the Chelsea manager lets him.'

With the 2006 World Cup in mind, Johnson commented,

This season I've only played for my country so obviously it's very important [to play international football] *as it's the only chance I've had so far to show what I can do.*

However, following injury to Paulo Ferreira, Glen got back into the Blues' first team and was involved in Chelsea's 3–2 Carling Cup final win over Liverpool in February 2005 and received a Premiership winners' medal that same season. But there would be no surety for Glen at Stamford Bridge, having to compete with the likes of Geremi and the versatile William Gallas, who was also able to play at right-back. In July 2006 it was reported that Glen was going to Harry Redknapp's Portsmouth on loan for the coming season.

Despite the relative lack of first-team chances, Glen has managed to maintain his England status (he has a dozen Under-21 caps and four at full international level). He is a strong tackling player, with fantastic vision. His eagerness and ability to push forward and contribute to attacks would be a valuable asset to any side. However, Johnson's temperament has sometimes been called into question. A red card picked up against Lazio in his Champions League campaign and early in the 2005–06 season breaking his hand punching a wall in what has been described as an 'unspecified incident' (keeping him out of the game for two months) being testament to this volatility.

Johnson's growing reputation for belligerence is in danger of obscuring his thoughtful and intelligent nature. Talking about racism, he said,

The world would be a better place without racism. The more people we have against it, the better ... People usually think of racism as a black and white issue but it's also against different cultures so it's nice to see everyone mix ... you see a lot of different people but deep down they're the same.

I had a few comments at school like most people do. But the main problem was when we played against Spain. It doesn't affect me at all, I'm not fused; I just ignore it. But it can affect some people. It was just getting on everyone's nerves because we didn't expect it from Spain. They're a decent country normally ... I've always just ignored it and said, 'Do you ever get bored of saying that?' It just shows you're not bothered and if you're not listening then it's not going to bother you.

Wendy continues to attend all the games Glen is involved in.

RUFUS EMANUEL BREVETT

HAMMERS DEBUT: 2/2/03

'Whenever I'd spoken to my old QPR teammate Trevor Sinclair after matches against West Ham, he'd always said good things about life at Upton Park.'

This attacking full-back was born in Derby, Derbyshire, on Wednesday, 24 September 1969. Rufus was signed from Fulham by Glenn Roeder during the January 2003 transfer window, his arrival at the Boleyn Ground alongside the budding Glen Johnson helping shore up a formerly unimpressive defence that helped the Hammers all but avoid relegation. 'Brev' was a talented and committed full-back and fierce tackler, but swift in attack, although when under pressure he did, occasionally, have a propensity to panic. He also preferred to pass the ball in field rather than take on his marker. This perhaps evidences his technical weakness. But, this said, his strength on the ball and eagerness to be part of everything that was happening on the pitch more than compensated for his shortcomings.

Although at the Baseball Ground since the age of 14, Brevett was unable to make a mark with his hometown club Derby County and he almost decided to give up football and go into the electronics industry, but Rufus made his League debut with Third Division Doncaster Rovers in August 1987 against Sunderland. Although experiencing relegation in his initial season, he was to make 118 appearances for the Belle Vue Brigade, claiming three goals in the process and learning from the likes of Billy Bremner, Dave Mackay and Joe Kinnear on the way.

Brevett jumped two divisions when he moved to Loftus Road for a fee of £250,000 during February 1991. At first Rufus found it difficult to break into the first team as a regular, but he was one of the 'Bush Boys' that gained a trio of top 10 Premiership finishes. But the 'Super Hoops' faced increasing financial difficulties and he was again part of a relegation side as the Loftus Road crew fell out of the Premiership in the 1995–96 season. But he was in good company with Hammers-to-be Andy Impey, Trevor Sinclair and Les Ferdinand all wearing the blue and white of West London at the time.

After 170 games (scoring a single goal) at the end of January 1998, Kevin Keegan took Rufus to Fulham, paying £375,000 for his services. This meant dropping into the Second Division, but promotion followed in 1998–99.

Brevett came back from a series of hamstring injuries, having missed much of the 1999–2000 campaign, to be part of the 2001–02 Fulham side that broke back into the top flight of English football; Rufus was back in the Premiership and, as Fulham were ground-sharing with QPR, he returned to Loftus Road.

Father of Jada (born 1998) and Georgie (born 2002), Rufus was impressive in the Premiership season of 2001–02, making 38 appearances and helping Fulham avoid the drop. As a Cottager, he won an Intertoto Cup medal and as a consequence played in the UEFA Cup in 2002.

Having made 203 appearances and hit two goals in the Craven Cottage cause, Rufus joined the Hammers, signing a two-and-a-half-year contract for an undisclosed fee close to the transfer deadline (he was obliged to fight through snowdrifts to make it to his medical). He recollected,

I'd trained with Fulham in the morning and then, at 6pm on the Thursday evening, I suddenly got a call to say that West Ham were interested in signing me. All the bad weather and traffic jams meant that I didn't get to the hospital until 4am and I didn't finish my medical until eight o'clock in the morning ... I still hadn't had any sleep by the time I finally signed at lunchtime ... The move had come out of the blue and it was a big surprise to me, but it had never been a case of me asking to leave Fulham. Jean Tigana told me that he didn't want me to go. At the end of the day the final decision was down to me and if I hadn't wanted to leave then I wouldn't have come to West Ham United ... West Ham are a bigger club in terms of their stadium and their support ...

Rufus learned a lot working with Tigana in West London, and came to Upton Park as an educated and thoughtful professional. But for most of the 2003–04 term an ankle injury kept him out of action, and his side missed him as they lost in the play-off final to Crystal Palace. Things didn't begin well for Rufus at the start of 2004–05; he was sent off on the opening day against Leicester City. When Chris Powell arrived and made the left-back slot his own, Brevett found himself sidelined.

Rufus moved to Plymouth and in 2006 joined Leicester on a one-year loan contract.

YOUSSEF SOFIANE

'West Ham is like a peach ...'

Born in Lyon, France (8 July 1984), Sofiane was one of many less than impressive Frenchmen entertained by the Hammers. The forward had looked good in pre-season matches following his engagement by Glenn Roeder (his first summer signing of 2002 beating off continental competition) from AJ Auxerre (from the French Le Championnat). Sofiane, who represented his country at Under-15, Under-16, Under-17 and Under-18 level, had not broken into the Auxerre starting line-up, but Roeder saw enough potential to pay an undisclosed fee to secure his services.

It seems it was the lure of possible first-team football that was the main reason why Youssef chose the move to East London ahead of other European destinations.

The aim was not to go to a massive club straight away, as I wanted to make a more gradual progression. West Ham is a club at a good level which will allow me to break through much more quickly than at, say, Arsenal or Manchester United.

My aim is to get in the side next year as quickly as possible, and I have a greater chance of playing here than in France — the style of play suits me more here than there, with the speed of the game.

The French striker looked a powerful, pacey player but he was unable to cut the mustard in the English Championship beset as he was by injury, although when he performed he might have been compared with Jermain Defoe given his swift reactions close to his opponents' goal and was thought of as one of the most exciting prospects to emerge from the successful French youth-development programme in recent years.

Sofiane made his First Division debut as a sub in the 2–1 opening-day victory over Preston at Deepdale in August 2003. He held on to his place for the next game against Rushden & Diamonds in the 3–1 Carling Cup win at Upton Park. But that was the extent of his first-team career.

According to Alan Pardew (December 2003), 'He has not really done much here and his attitude has been that of a foreign player not in the team … he has not impressed too much in training or in the reserves.'

Sofiane spent part of the 2003–04 term on loan back at Auxerre, but looked sharp in pre-season training and games, good enough in fact to be hopeful of breaking into the first team early in 2004–05. However, in September 2004, Sofiane was loaned to Notts County at the foot of League 2. Sofiane was back at Upton Park at the end of his month-loan spell in October 2004. At Fans' Forum, Pardew declared himself 'disappointed with the lack of progress' that the player had made during his managerial tenure at the Boleyn.

A loan period with Lille in the second half of 2003–04 was followed at the start of 2004–05 with a trial at MK Dons. Then Sofinae went on loan to Dutch club Roda JC between January and May 2005, however, this arrangement was mysteriously terminated due to 'personal reasons' before his contract was terminated (by 'mutual consent'). He then played for Coventry City on a non-contract basis. A period with Lorient was followed by a move to Louviéroise in the Jupiler League (Belgium) in 2006.

In the end Youssef's most notable contribution to the English game was his relationship with a former *Big Brother* housemate, the now long forgotten Tania Do Nascimento.

It seems problems follow Sofiane. In 2006 Louviéroise was one of the most frequently mentioned clubs in a gambling scandal that rocked Belgian football. It was alleged in the Belgian press that several players, board members and manager Gilbert Bodart had accepted large sums of money from Chinese businessman Zheyun Ye, who wanted to influence the results in matches so he could manufacture high profits in gambling. At first the club strongly denied the allegations, but on 21 February 2006 Bodart resigned as manager.

ANTON JULIAN FERDINAND

HAMMERS DEBUT: 9/8/03

'I will believe to achieve. If you don't believe, you will not achieve in nothing, not only in football but in life generally.'

M any of West Ham's black players have been Hammers to the core, but Anton Ferdinand is the first I have come across who just couldn't imagine himself playing for another club. When asked if there was another team he might join, he answered,

> *That's a hard one that, you know! I'd like to play with Brazil! The ability they've got all around – it's like sexy football. They play football. They're frightening.*

Perhaps part of his reticence to choose another club is the love the man at the heart of the Irons' defence has for his own 'manor' and the respect he gets from the people who live in the area:

> *I think I'd miss being out on the street and people recognising you – in a good way – as long as it is for the good things that you've done. I'm from London and the people in London know you for the good things you've done, whereas if you are in Spain or another country them people are just going to acknowledge you because of who you are. Over here they acknowledge you because of who you are, but they also know where you come from and they know what you've done to get there.*
>
> *I do a lot in the community, especially in Peckham. I like to let young people know that I come from the same background as them. I come from a worse background than some of them, and I still managed to reach where I wanted to go and if I can do it then they can definitely*

270

do it. They've just got to make sure they choose the right path to go on — make sure they work hard and believe in themselves because if you don't believe in yourself then you're not going to achieve your goals in life — I will believe to achieve. If you don't believe you will not achieve in nothing, not only in football but in life generally.

'Believe to Achieve' — that is the motto tattooed on the arm of Anton Ferdinand, and it seems he lives according to that courageous and challenging maxim.

Anton was born to Janice and Julian in Peckham, London (18 February 1985). Family has been a constant in his life and it was through this consistent network of support that he was introduced to organised football. He told me,

I was about six when I started playing with my uncle's team, Bloomfield; it was a Sunday-league club based in the Peckham area. Me and my brother both played for that club. I went to see my brother play on a Sunday, had a little kickabout and it made me want to get involved and my dad started taking me. I was always playing football over the park and always wanted to play professionally since then.

Then I played for a proper league team called Athonlea in Peckham Rye [Ben Watson, who made it into the professional ranks with Crystal Palace, was also in that Sunday-league side]. *I was there for about a year and then I started training at West Ham.*

I was playing for my district, South London, when I was in primary school; I went to Camelot and then Pilgrims Way. A man named Dave Goodwin, he brought Rio to West Ham, he had an eye for young talent; he picked up on me straight away and took me and Kieron Richardson, who went on to play for Newcastle and Manchester United, to West Ham. We were with the school of excellence since we was nine. I trained with West Ham, was on trial with them for a little bit, but from the age of nine to eleven I was in the school of excellence, in Beckenham, training there.

Then for about a year I wasn't with them. I was growing at the time. My body was all disjointed and didn't know what it was doing. I was going through a bad spell, but my dad kept me at it. I had the

THE BLACK HAMMERS

Osgood Slatters[4] a bit, the lump on the knee. Not a nice pain that. I just played my Sunday-league football. The local team was Millwall, and them and a few other clubs were sniffing. But Dave Goodwin saw me again and took me back over to West Ham. I was 12 and was playing for the Under-14s. I wasn't playing Sunday league any more – for the Under-14s upwards, you played proper matches.

As a young player I won everything in the district and the county. At West Ham we won everything in the League.

As time went on, sport in general and football in particular became central to Anton's young life:

My secondary school was Blackheath Bluecoats. I looked forward to sports at school and apart from football I was good at basketball [a game Anton still takes an interest in – he has a decent jump shot] *and athletics, sprinting, but the long distance, I left that to my friends* [laughs]. *Academically, I suppose I was average. I enjoyed school, being around my friends mainly. The teachers that made the lessons enjoyable, fun, with a little bit of laughing, little bit of a joke, I'd do more work with them.*

It seems that music-making is a part of Anton's life. When reflecting what he might have done if he had not made it in football, he said,

I like to sing in my spare time. I would have been trying to do something in music. Maybe doing a bit of singing.

Indeed, he almost took this path early on:

Just before signing YTS forms, I was going through another bad growing stage and I didn't think I was going to get a YTS at West

---

[4]Osgood Slatters is common in boys who play football. The symptoms are pain and inflammation below the knee. It can be due to lack of flexibility in the quadriceps, and stress placed on an area called the tibial tuberosity, which is where the quadriceps attach to the tibia. If this is not treated correctly, it can develop into more serious knee problems. But with the right therapy and exercise (stretching, active release technique) children often resolve this problem within a short period of time.

ANTON JULIAN FERDINAND

Ham so I said to my dad, 'I don't want to play football any more, I don't want to do it, I'm not enjoying it.' I said, 'I want to do singing – I've had enough.'

My dad said to me, 'You know what, you're just going through a growing stage at the moment, everything'll come round for you, but I think, if I was you, you're good at both things, football and singing, so you could even have a shot at both. You can do singing after football, but you can't do football after singing. You don't want to regret not taking up the football, so it may be better if you do get the YTS to go with the football. If that don't work out, then you could go into the singing.' I listened to his wise words.

Glenn Roeder signed Ferdinand as a professional at the age of 17, the same week in which his older brother completed his £30 million move to Manchester United. According to Anton,

Glenn played in the same position as me, centre-back, that was good for me. He gave me my chance in football and I'll always be thankful for that. He's a wonderful person. He'd always have time for you. Whether it was to do with football or not, he'd always have five minutes of his time for you. On the training pitch he was good. A lot of what he's done for me is starting to come out in my game now. There'd be times where after training I'd want to go in and he'd be saying, 'Where you going? You've got things to work on!' If it weren't for people like that, I wouldn't have improved the way I have. He put it in my mind that I need to work on things. He put it in my head if I don't work on those things then I'm not going to get better. He was good for me. Alan Pardew is a little bit different. They've both helped me in different areas. Alan Pardew has helped me a lot with my concentration, he's always said to me, 'You've got all the ability, all the attributes to be a great player, but you've just got to work on your concentration.' That's why when he first came to the club I wasn't in the team because my concentration levels weren't as high as they should have been.

Apart from his former and current manager, Ferdinand cites a number of other influential figures from his time at the Boleyn

Ground, but also sees the overall atmosphere of the club as being important in terms of developing talent:

> *Shaun Newton's been good for me. Obviously Teddy [Sheringham], Christian Dailly and Elliot Ward. I've played with Elliot since I was 16 and we clicked straight away. We grew to know each other's game. We've played at every level – Under-17s, Under-18s, Under-19s, reserves to the first team. We've played together at every professional level at West Ham. That's a great credit to the youth-team staff. Tony Carr, Kevin Keen, Paul Heffer and Peter Brabrook, he always kept the teams working hard. It's great for them and it's great for us. We always wanted to play in the first team together and we made it possible that we could do that. West Ham is a family club. If they see a young player that wants to learn and wants to better themselves in football, then they will more than help you. That's the way the club is.*
>
> *This year, Danny Gabbidon. He's been excellent. Different gear! I thought Hayden Mullins was the best player this year, but Danny weren't too far behind. He's been a great signing. Him and Benayoun have been the best signings this year. But me and Danny don't have to worry about each other the way we play together. If the ball goes over the top, on either of our sides, we know we are going to be first to the ball so we don't have to worry, we can just concentrate on our game. I think that's what's been so good about us two this year.*

However, Ferdinand has little hesitation in naming the best players he has taken the field with while with the Hammers:

> *Joey Cole; it's frightening. He's unbelievable on the pitch – he just likes to express himself. I like to see skills and he's got them in abundance. But to play with, also Jermain Defoe. Being a centre-back and having the ball, you want movement up top and his movement at times in unbelievable. You know where he wants the ball because he'll make certain movements, meaning he wants it a certain way or into a certain area, and he's got it down to a 'T'.*

ANTON JULIAN FERDINAND

Speaking with Anton, who has been nicknamed 'Lips' by his fellow players as he tends to kiss his teeth constantly when he's tired, is a pleasant experience. He has a mellow, soft voice in conversation, with just a hint of the accent of his dad's St Lucian homeland; the gently pronounced consonants confirm his natural sincerity; he strikes his listener as a very honest person.

My birth sign is Aquarius and my mind drifts sometimes. If you want to get to the top, you've got to be able to listen to people and take criticism, and take in what they're saying, otherwise you're never going to better yourself.

People don't see what happens behind closed doors. How hard you work on the training pitch. You've got to work at things. But it's also to do with the way you were brought up as well. My dad would tell me how it is. That made me stronger mentally. Not just in football, but in family life. People will butter you up. When I've played for West Ham, they'll say [whispers] 'Oh yeah, you were good today.' But if I didn't play good I'll get in the car and know my dad's going to tell me I was rubbish; he'd sort out what I needed to work on, what I was rubbish at, and I guarantee next week, because he's told me about it, when I'm playing the game, it'll be going through my head and I'll make sure I'm doing this right and doing that right. I always used to say to my friends, 'My mum and dad don't let me do anything, they don't let me out,' but now I realise that was for a good cause.

Anton was an admirer of John Barnes as a youngster so had a soft spot for Liverpool, but as soon as Rio started to play for West Ham he supported the Hammers so it was something of a dream come true when Anton made his first appearance for the first team in a pre-season friendly at Leyton Orient. Although he was taken to Old Trafford as a substitute by then West Ham manager Glenn Roeder for a Premiership match in December 2002, where he would have come up against his older brother Rio had he been brought on, Anton was still considered to be some way from becoming a first-team regular. That would have been a proud day for the young men's parents.

Ferdinand proved himself in the team's relegation fight, but following relegation the England Under-18 international was plunged into the first team for West Ham's opening match in their First Division campaign. Preston North End were defeated on that ninth day of August 2003. Anton completed the season with 25 outings and at the end of that term was voted Young Hammer of the Year by the Hammers supporters.

One lasting memory of Anton's early accomplishments was in a tense game at Watford on the final day of the 2004–05 campaign, when he opened the scoring with a superbly executed left-foot volley that drilled the ball into the bottom-left corner as West Ham booked a play-off spot; this was his very first goal for the club and a strike any forward would be proud of. But none would have matched his celebration dance in front of the Hammers fans at the other end of the pitch!

Anton became an established presence in the Hammers first team under Alan Pardew in 2004–05, notching up his first Barclays Premiership goal with a last-minute injury-time equaliser at White Hart Lane in November 2005.

Anton celebrated his 50th senior League appearance against Ipswich Town in the home leg of the play-off semi-final. This of course this led to the meeting with Preston North End at the Millennium Stadium. Amongst his most memorable moments with the Hammers, Ferdinand chooses his debut and his goal against Fulham in 2005–06 but by far and away Anton cites that day in Cardiff as the highlight of his career thus far:

It put us on a pedestal, it put me on a pedestal. Unbelievable feeling when that final whistle went. Just unbelievable to know I'd be playing in the Premiership the next season. For the whole summer I was floating. I only had about two-and-a-half weeks off because I went away with England straight after the game. But for the whole of that time, right the way through pre-season, I think people got annoyed with me because every two minutes I kept saying, 'Ahh! Premiership, what!?' Premiership! It was just a buzz for me to know I was going to play against players like Thierry Henry and Wayne Rooney and finally I'd get to play against my brother.

ANTON JULIAN FERDINAND

As Anton told me about that great milestone in West Ham's history and his own career, his attention turned to the supporters of East London's finest:

I was one of the only players playing in the games where West Ham went down. I've grown up in this club, I understand what it meant for the fans to go down and what it meant to them when we're going up; I've been there at both ends — that day I didn't want to leave the pitch. I think I was one of the last ones to leave the pitch. I just wanted to stay on and celebrate with the fans. I'd been through both situations. And I was part of the team that got back.

The fans are second to none. I grew up sitting in the stand at Upton Park watching Rio, so I know what it's about. I've grown up in it; very, very passionate. A lot of players that haven't experienced being at a big club, they have a real awakening when they come to Upton Park because the passion is so great, and if you don't put 110 per cent in you'll know about it! They'll tell you straight away. That's the way it is; it's tough pressure playing at West Ham but for me they've been just the best, unbelievable. They've watched every step I've made coming through; the reserves, coming into the first team. At the start when I first came into the first team and I was playing right-back, a lot of the fans expected a bit more from me because of Rio. I always used to say, 'Wait till you see me in my proper position, at centre-back, then you'll see a different player,' and to be fair to the fans they done that and didn't question my ability.

I got friends at other clubs and they've gone through the same situation that I gone through — saying to the fans 'wait till you see me in my rightful position', their fans wouldn't give two shits about that; 'You get paid to play, you got to do it now!' The West ham fans weren't like that with me. They went like, 'OK then.' Now that I'm playing in my best position, they understand where I'm coming from and I'm very grateful for that. To be stepping out in front of them week in and week out, it's unbelievable. They get us through the hard times and they've got me through hard times.

When we play at away stadiums it's almost like being at a home game! The away fans are just tremendous. Everyone talks about

THE BLACK HAMMERS

Newcastle being the 'Toon Army', they're supposed to be loud, but when we played them up there at the start of the season all I could hear was our fans and they was up in the top corner! That just shows how good the fans are.

When the ball's around me, I don't hear anything, I just hear familiar voices, but when the ball's up the other end I'm still concentrating but I can hear things. Especially when you are in the tunnel and you hear 'I'm Forever Blowing Bubbles' as you come up the stairs and you start to see the fans and you hear the roar, it's unexplainable, man! Unless you've experienced it, you don't understand what you go though. It's unreal.

When I questioned Anton about what he saw as the best part of playing for West Ham, he replied,

Stepping out in front of the fans – knowing it means a lot to them and it means a lot to me playing in front of them. Growing up in the club it's made it extra special for me.

The last day of the 2005–06 season was unbelievable. Everyone knows about the hatred between West Ham and Spurs. Beating them and knocking them out of a Champions League spot was one of the highlights of my experiences at Upton Park. Another was scoring against Fulham there, because I got to do something that Rio never done in a claret shirt – score at Upton Park and I've done it! It was against Tottenham and I knew how much it meant to the fans.

As if having a famous brother to live up to is not exacting enough, Anton is a cousin of Les Ferdinand, and this lineage suggested that his selection for the England Under-21 side (a 3–1 friendly victory against Ukraine at the Riverside Stadium) on 17 August 2004 would not be his last international honour. Wearing the three lions was another wish fulfilled; the first football shirt Anton owned was an old England one, the type Keegan used to wear.

Although now a crucial element in the Hammers side, Anton has a clear view of his own strengths and how he might develop as a player:

The reading of the game plays a big part for me. I used to be awful at

heading the ball; I've worked on it so much that it's just got better and it's been the high out of my play, definitely this year.

But as a player the reading of the game and heading are the things I excel at I think. A lot of the boys say that I'm hard to beat in one-on-one situations.

But there's poetry in his description of his perception of his own game:

It's the timing of the jumping. The first thing you got to do is pick up the flight of the ball straight away, if you can't do that you're going to struggle. You've got to read where the ball's going to drop and to do that you've got to watch how it's moving in the air. You've got to get that all put into perspective and then the timing of the jump comes. You've got to meet the ball at its highest point, and go and win the ball.

I just love being on the ball. I love touching the ball, I love playing long balls, I just love always having a ball around me, because I know, when I've got the ball around me, I can look a different player. That's what I want to get across to people. That I can play.

Anton's sensitivity and feeling for the aesthetic side of the game is reflected by his habit of drawing inspiration from music; he brings these two great passions in his life together in his preparation for competition:

I have a ritual. Going to away games I have to listen to an album by Lyfe Jennings. He was from the streets. That whole album is about his life; about him having to do certain things to get where he is. I grew up in an area where it was like that but my mum and dad kept me out of that side of things, but I still had to do something to get where I had to get. Towards the end of the album he's talking about how he might be doing what he is doing but he will never forget his friends. He says that in his last song. That is the last thought that I get from that album. He starts reading off all his friends' names saying they ain't forgot, and that's exactly the same thing that goes through my mind before I'm taking off my iPod ready to get changed; all my friends and my family.

THE BLACK HAMMERS

*And my friends, a lot of those guys I used to play football with when
I was young, they were good enough to make it, but maybe didn't have
the discipline.*

*I'm going out there to play for my friends, I'm representing them and
my family and West Ham.*

Ferdinand signed a new four-year contract just before the start of
the 2005–06 term and, such was the rate of his progress during the
Hammers' superb start to the Premiership campaign, he was
rewarded with a new deal in January 2006 that keeps him
committed to West Ham until 2010 and is rumoured to make him
one of the top earners at Upton Park. Alan Pardew commented,
'I'm overjoyed that we have signed another of our top young
players on a long-term contract and Anton fully deserves the
new deal.'

Anton was named the Barclays Premiership Player of the Month
for January 2006, after a fine run of results. West Ham beat Aston
Villa and Fulham in the Premiership, and Norwich City and
Blackburn Rovers in the FA Cup. The unbeaten run eventually
came to an end after a 1–4 away loss to Bolton Wanderers on 11
March 2006. But that month will also be remembered for
Ferdinand's spectacular turn and volley goal against Fulham on 23
January 2006, his second net of the season.

Although delighted and shocked when Pardew told him about
the award, he dedicated it to his fellow players because, as he said,

Without them, I wouldn't have won it.

Ferdinand has been described as a tremendously confident and cool
character. I asked one of his closest friends, Ben, what Anton was like
as a person: 'He's laidback, easygoing, just himself, just Anton. He's
not fake; you either like him or don't like him. I used to live in
Birmingham but moved to London at around the age of four. I met
him in primary school, Pilgrims Way. Believe it or not, me and him
used to be the same size. I'm 5ft 6in now and he's 6ft 2in! We used
to wear the same clothes and we used to be as thin as nothing! Over

the years he's shot up out of nowhere. He's cool, laidback. He's the same guy.

'Anton is a very generous person. Go to him with any problems and he's there for you. Regardless of the football, he doesn't look down on you. We, his friends, are willing him on. He's one in a million. There was loads of us that could have been footballers, but all of us are proud of him. That inspires him even more to progress even more. He's been given that chance and he's took that chance with two hands.'

Anton is certainly 'laidback' in terms of his sartorial taste:

> I like to dress down, in a tracksuit. When I go to training I'm always in tracksuits. I like to wear just comfortable trackies. When I'm going out I might wear labels but I just buy what I fancy; if it looks good, it looks good, no matter what it is — it's the way I was brought up — I was brought up wearing clothes from Tesco's; if it looks good on me it looks good on me, no matter what it is.

This says much for Anton and, like many of his views and beliefs, shows an impressively wise head on young shoulders. It would have been easy for him to come out with a list of designer names like many of the pumped-up young professionals that inhabit the Premiership. But, not for the first time, he made the point that his roots have informed him and he has not forgotten the lessons of his youngest years. One cannot but respect and admire that. However, his taste in cars is just a tad more extravagant:

> I drive a Cadillac Escalade but I have two ultimate cars; one day in my life I want a Rolls-Royce Phantom and an Aston Martin Vanquish S!

Ferdinand's earliest sporting memory is watching the 1990 World Cup on television and the first goal that sticks in his mind is the Maradona 'hand of God' that defeated England. While John Barnes and Paul Ince are two of his footballing heroes, when asked about the greatest player he has seen, he had no hesitation in saying,

Maradona, he had perfect balance and quick feet and was so strong on the ball.

And Diego el drago is one of the four people he would invite to his ideal dinner party. The other guests would be Jessica Alba, Pele and Michael Jackson. Although he is a lover of R'n'B as a genre, according to Anton,

Michael Jackson inspires me a lot. All of his music has meaning to his life and what he's about.

I asked Anton who was the most influential person in his career and he answered without hesitation:

My dad. He's been there through thick and thin for me. He picked me up when I needed picking up, and has given me an ear bashing when I've needed it.

Not for the first time I was struck by the closeness of the Ferdinand family and asked him to tell me more about this part of his life:

I'm too young for a steady girlfriend right now.
My dad's from St Lucia, but he was brought up in Peckham. My mum did cleaning jobs. My dad was into clothes, tailoring. Later, my mum ran a nursery for a little bit, Sunrise day nursery in New Cross, but now my dad's got his own business and my mum looks after my little brother and my sister Sian.
Rio is my only full brother. My dad's got Chloe and my two twin sisters. Chloe, she's nine, she's very intelligent, probably the quietest one of us, she don't want to do something that's not in the spotlight. The twins are four.
My mum's got Sian and Jeremiah. Sian's 13 she wants to be a singer. She's also into acting, theatre; she's good, very strong minded, when she wants to do something, but she's got the support of everyone for whatever she wants to do, same as all my brothers and sisters.
Jeremiah, he's seven, he just wants to play football all the time; he

could be an actor, he likes play acting. But he's been kicking a ball well for several years and has been to soccer training camps. It's all about enjoyment at his age, just learning your trade and enjoying yourself, and wanting to kick a ball about every minute of the day, that's what it's about for him. He don't like losing, that's the same with every kid. He's just football through and through.

At his age, like I said to my mum, I want to go and watch him, but because I've been through so much having Rio as my big brother, people comparing us, I just want to let him come through. So because of that I don't go and watch him. If I go and watch him and all the attention goes on me, you are not going to be sure if he is going to be accepted for himself and people could want to be his friend because of me and Rio. It's hard. I understand how it is.

My dad asks about Jeremiah, it's like a big family.

It has been reported that the question asked most by supporters of Anton is 'How is your brother?' And of course people compare him to Rio; he is to some extent used to that. When I asked if he had modelled himself on any other player, he answered,

My brother; he's never more than a phone call away, he's always around me. Rio and I have a good relationship. He wants me to do as well as him if not better than what he's done; that's the type of brother he is, that's what he's about. And he'll go through anything to help me reach the heights that he's reaching. We have a friendly rivalry, being from Peckham, it's 'bragging rights' [smiles]. We've got a big group of friends round there; if you don't come correct then you're gonna know about it. Last season [2006–06] we had a little bet on who would score the most goals. I scored first against Tottenham, I think that triggered him off, he scored three in about two months; we have a bit of banter about it. If one of us scores, we're on the phone straight away – it's good.

Early on in Anton's career, Glenn Roeder said of him, 'Physically, he's from the same stamp as his brother. If you watch him running, from a distance you could mistake him for Rio. Unfortunately, people will compare him to his brother. That's wrong because he should be judged on what he can do … I'm very conscious of that and it's up to us as a club to protect him to some degree. But it will be tough for him because he's a Ferdinand.'

However, the younger of the Premiership Ferdinands is philosophical about his situation:

> It's made it more difficult to come through the ranks because Rio come through first; some of the things I used to go through as a kid like hearing people as you go to get the ball, 'Oh, he'll never be as good as his brother,' but I've grown up with it and it's made me a stronger person and I don't care what people think. I'm confident in my own ability and I got people around me, my friends and family who make me know that I'm Anton Ferdinand, not Rio's brother, and that's all that matters to me.
>
> It's my mum and dad's dream to see me and Rio play together for England and we both want to make that dream come true for them and I think once we've made that dream come true then they'll die happy.

Looking to the future, West Ham's most promising central defender seems to have picked up an Upton Park trait of seeing the need to share his understanding and insights about the game:

> I'm not too sure about management but coaching, yeah. The knowledge I'm getting at the moment I definitely want to pass it on to other people, to people that want to learn and want to succeed in what they do. Not just for my benefit but for the club, for England. The more people that pass on their knowledge the better the young crop are going to be. That's the way it is.

Considering the challenges that black players face with regard to getting into management, Anton demonstrates a thoughtful and intelligent attitude that seems to fit in with his general philosophy of 'Believe to Achieve':

> It's a hard thing for a black man to get into management, but one of the most successful managers at the moment is Frank Rijkaard and he's a black man. That could be the start of something good.

ANTON JULIAN FERDINAND

I've experienced racism in football, but you get that everywhere — it's a very small minority at West Ham.

Ben, who regularly attends matches at Upton Park to watch his friend, commented, 'Away supporters are more racist than home supporters. It was noticeable at Wolverhampton in the Championship and a couple of games up North there was quite a bit of racism.'

I asked Anton what could be done to continue the efforts to eradicate racism from football.

Do a lot more publicity to make ethnic minorities feel more welcome to come and watch games; if they saw more things around the ground or happening outside the ground on match days, then they'd feel more comfortable to come in. To know their club is supporting them. If you see things happening before games it's got to make a difference. Like at West Ham they've done stuff about getting a job before a game, because they were sponsored by JobServe; they're putting that across a lot over there and I can guarantee that a lot of people have found a job because they've seen people advertising JobServe before a game.

While the game has had many highs for Ferdinand, the 2005–06 produced his greatest disappointment and regret to date:

Missing the penalty in the Cup final — I was devastated. I wasn't tired, I was fine — penalties are like a lottery. I've always taken penalties throughout my career. In training I was on fire doing penalties. But maybe it was the pressure. But I wasn't nervous stepping up for the penalty. Jose Reina has a good record throughout his whole career of saving penalties and it was just one of those days where it weren't for me to score.

I just wanted the ground to open and swallow me up. I wanted to click my fingers and be back home and be with my family and have all my friends and family around me. It was the reverse to the year before where I didn't want to leave the pitch ... I just didn't want to be there. I gave my runners-up medal away to my little brother; one day it'll mean something to him — I didn't want it — I want winners' medals;

my heart weren't in it to have that medal. That's just the way I am.

But the fans were quality after the game; if they had acted different, it might have been worse. I didn't know what to expect but they gave me that lift; even now, walking along the street West Ham fans come up to me and say, 'Don't worry about the penalty' and 'We're proud of you. You had the balls to step up and try to take a penalty and you played well and we should have won the game in normal time.' A lot of the fans say, 'In our minds we didn't lose that game.'

As one of those supporters I can only agree with Anton; how can you lose a game in which you are never behind?

But, for all this, it seems Ferdinand looks to what is to come:

But I tell you what, it's made me a lot stronger mentally and more hungry to want to step up and take another one in a big game like that again ... and put things right.

I got the Hammers News Player of the Year at the end of the season so the trophy cabinet looks all right! Things happen that people don't see at West Ham. A lot of things happen in the changing rooms and so on and it's just brought us closer and closer together and it's showing on the pitch.

But it seems that he is still able to learn from the past. When looking at what he might have done differently in his time as a professional, he said,

I'd work on my concentration. I think I would have been in the side at centre-back a lot earlier and if I'd have done that I might have been a bit closer to being in the World Cup squad this year [2006].

HAYDEN IAN MULLINS

'The crowd is guaranteed to get any footballer up for a game that he'll want to go out and enjoy.'

Hayden was born in Reading, Berkshire (27 March 1979), one of a family comprising of three sisters, three stepsisters, a brother and a stepbrother. He started his career with Crystal Palace as a trainee in 1996 and, as a YTS graduate, secured his first full contract in February 1997.

However, he had to wait until August 1998 to get his chance in the first team; he made his League debut for Palace in a 2–2 draw against Bolton Wanderers on the opening day of the 1998–99 season. By March 1999 he had won his first England Under-21 cap, coming on as a substitute in the young Lions' 5–0 win over Poland at Southampton.

Mullins was swift to prove his mettle in the Palace side, scoring five times in 40 League appearances in his inaugural campaign. This was Hayden's best season with the Eagles; he won the club's Player of the Year award.

Hayden captained Palace for most of his career at Selhurst Park and joined the ranks of the elite group who have gained the Player of the Year honour more than once when he won it again in 2003. He was regarded as one of Palace's crown jewels but, following interest from the likes of Birmingham City and Portsmouth, Mullins made his Hammers bow on 22 October 2003 in the 1–1 draw with Nottingham Forest.

Following a loan period, Mullins was Alan Pardew's first signing (£600,000). He was still just 25, but with 246 Cup and League games, plus 20 goals during his time with Crystal Palace, Hayden was an experienced professional and knew the game well, having worked under the likes of Ron Noades, Mark Goldberg, Joe Jordan, Steve Coppell, Attilio Lombardo, Terry Venables, Alan Smith, Steve Bruce, Trevor Francis and Steve Kember.

Being the near-perfect example of a 'utility man' has had its problems for Mullins, as Pardew admitted towards the conclusion of 2005–06: 'I was fire-fighting when I came here and shifted Hayden around. I was doing him a disservice. His spell in midfield coincided with our run at the end of last season and he has been terrific for us. He thinks it goes unnoticed but I don't agree with that.'

During his career Hayden has filled almost every outfield position. Although deployed at centre-half, right- and left-back, as well as wing-back and wide midfield, he feels his best position is as a central midfielder. It is in this berth where he has made the most of his ball control, his ability to play a holding role and so shown his ability to pass with accuracy and intelligence. However, it is likely that his many talents might prevent him showing what he can do playing in what is potentially his most influential role.

According to the West Ham manager, Hayden is 'quick, good in the tackle, comfortable in possession' and capable of bringing 'calmness and sureness to the side'. Mullins can also score wonderful goals.

Although defeated by his former club in the 2005–06 play-off final, Mullins was philosophical, keeping faith in his own and his new club's prospects. This focus was reflected in Pardew's impression of Mullins: 'You know you're going to get seven or eight out of ten from Hayden every game and I feel sure he'll be a good player at West Ham for a number of years.'

Failure to hold down a regular position lead to irregular spells on the bench in the promotion season of 2005–06 but, when the Hammers reached the Premiership, Mullins silenced his critics with a string of accomplished performances in partnership with Nigel Reo-Coker in the centre of midfield.

Mullins and his wife Stacey, together with their son, Maxwell (born in 2002), now seem to be a long-term fixture in the West

Ham arena and the ethos of the club seems to suit Hayden. He said of the home of the Hammers,

> *West Ham is such a nice ground to play at. As soon as you climb off the coach, the first thing that strikes you is just how big the stadium is, and once you're inside ... the crowd is guaranteed to get any footballer up for a game that he'll want to go out and enjoy.*

Possessing a quiet, reserved nature that serves him well in the heat of battle, Mullins developed into one of the Hammers' most consistent performers in the Premiership in 2005–06, attracting much praise for his tidy, no-nonsense displays in the centre of the park.

Just before West Ham's FA Cup semi-final match in 2006, Anton Ferdinand said of Hayden, 'The lads call him Youssef Safri because he looks like the Norwich player. He's a nice lad and someone I talk to a lot off the pitch. He is very laidback. That's his character and the way he plays his football. Hayden has been probably our best player this year. He picks up a lot of the loose balls that people try to play into the forwards. He doesn't get a lot of publicity, but he is one of the players who has taken to the Premiership very well.'

This last sentence probably says how much West Ham missed Mullins in the 2006 FA Cup final. Along with Liverpool's Luis Garcia, Hayden was suspended after the pair were punished for their involvement in a fracas in a League game shortly before the sides met in Cardiff. Of course, it was a body blow to Hayden:

> *It is absolutely devastating not to be playing ... Who knows? It could be my only FA Cup final, and to not be part of it is absolutely gutting ... These opportunities do not come along often. You want to be part of it.*

BRIAN CHRISTOPHER DEANE

'It is a challenge, I had other options but I wanted to sample the culture here.'

The widely travelled and experienced 6ft 3in forward Brian Deane came to Upton Park on a free transfer from Leicester City in November 2003 to provide Alan Pardew with cover and a level of attacking options in the drive towards the play-off final. Brian had a record as a strong, good finisher, who was also able to distribute the ball with intelligence and accuracy. He had won three senior and three England 'B' caps while with Sheffield United in the early 1990s. His first game for the Blades was in an 8–1 victory against Skegness Town. His first League goal came in the Third Division in the opening game of the 1988–89 season against Reading. Deane scored the first goal in the English Premier League for Sheffield United against Manchester United after five minutes on 15 August 1992.

Brian continued to cast a hex on the Manchester Reds. After joining Leeds, he scored against them at Elland Road in successive years, which made him quite popular in his home town, but the goals never came with the regularity they had at Bramall Lane, where he moved back to after four years with the Peacocks.

However, half a season later, Deane was in Portugal: it was a surprise to many that a traditional English centre-forward was wanted by Benfica. It took nine months for the incongruity to be confirmed, although his record at the Estádo Do Luz was pretty good and for a section of the fans he became something of a cult figure.

BRIAN CHRISTOPHER DEANE

Deane commanded an intermittent presence at Middlesbrough for a couple of years before moving to Leicester.

In his debut at the Boleyn Ground against West Bromwich Albion, Deano scored twice as the Irons built a 3–0 advantage, but his third goal was slotted into the back of the Hammers net and motivated a comeback by the Baggies who went home 4–3 winners. Given he cost the club nothing in transfer fees, Brian was a good servant of the Hammers, benefiting the Irons' crop of talented younger players and providing a good example of professional conduct.

At the end of 2004–05, Brian was assisting Sunderland's charge back to the Premiership. But, after a spell in Portugal, he joined Perth Glory in October 2005 in the Australian A-League. He left the Members Equity Stadium mid-season after failing to make an impact and sustaining a long-term injury. He stated that he did not want to prevent Perth from signing another striker due to salary-cap and squad-size restrictions imposed by the League. Deane re-signed for the third time at Sheffield United.

Deane has been called a gifted and natural professional. He has been a very underestimated centre-forward, who at times was a joy to watch. He also advanced the cause of black players in an era and an area (Yorkshire) rife with soccer racism. Awareness of his footballing brain has led to talk about him moving to Halifax Town as player-coach. Certainly, we have not heard the chant 'Deanoo!!!' for the last time.

CLUB	FROM	TO	APPS	GOALS	FEE
Doncaster Rovers	14 Dec 1985	19 Jul 1988	76	13	£30,000
Sheffield United	19 Jul 1988	14 Jul 1993	239	106	£2,900,000
Leeds United	14 Jul 1993	29 Jul 1997	168	38	£1,500,000 (record fee for Leeds)
Sheffield United	29 Jul 1997	15 Jan 1998	29	13	£1,000,000
Benfica	15 Jan 1998	16 Oct 1998	18	7	£3,000,000
Middlesbrough	16 Oct 1998	29 Nov 2001	95	19	Nominal Amount
Leicester City	29 Nov 2001	31 Oct 2003	49	19	Free Transfer

THE BLACK HAMMERS

CLUB	FROM	TO	APPS	GOALS	FEE
West Ham United	31 Oct 2003	30 Jun 2004	32	7	
Out of Contract					Free Transfer
Leeds United	21 Jul 2004	24 Mar 2005	33	7	Free Transfer
Sunderland	24 Mar 2005	23 Jul 2005	4	0	Free Transfer
Perth Glory	23 Jul 2005	1 Jan 2006	7	1	Free Transfer
Sheffield United	1 Jan 2006		1		

MARLON HAREWOOD

'I'm not sure where it came from but I'm very happy.'

According to Anton Ferdinand, Marlon is 'the black Homer Simpson. He's my roommate, and someone who will do anything to help you.'

Harewood was born on 25 August 1979. 'Marvellous Marlon' signed for the Hammers at what retrospectively seems like a ridiculously low fee of £500,000 from impoverished Nottingham Forest in November 2003, scored twice on his debut v Wigan Athletic and went on to be the top Hammer in the Upton Park scoring chart, having come to the Boleyn Ground with 11 goals under his belt for the season.

Admiring the likes of Gary Lineker, Jurgen Klinsmann, Ian Wright, Alan Shearer and Matt Le Tissier, Harewood joined Nottingham Forest and went to live in Nottingham at the age of 15. He was obliged to grow up quickly, needing to live almost independently from the first. Emerging from the youth scheme at the City ground, Marlon made his League debut, the first of his 182 League appearances for Forest, in the final game of the 1997–98 season, a 1–1 draw at the Hawthorns.

Stanmore's only asset, Dave 'Harry' Bassett, was the Forest manager at the time, and during the summer he sent Marlon on loan to FC Haka, in Finland, which was not too far from the capital Helsinki. It was there Harewood became a devotee of Michael Jackson and Usher, seeing them both in concert in Finland.

After his time in 'the land of a thousand lakes', the boy from

Hampstead, London, made his first Premiership appearance for Forest, a 0–0 draw against the visiting West Ham. Marlon was again out on loan in January 1999, this time to Ipswich, but in 2001–02 he was the second-best goal-getter at the City Ground, with 11 nets to his credit; he nearly improved that tally by 100 per cent the following season. He claimed 21 goals to help Forest to the Championship play-offs in 2002–03.

But Harewood was more than a goalscorer; he was also able to play wide and hold up the ball when necessary and had a knack of laying off intelligently, showing an uncharacteristic generosity for a natural striker. He has been used frequently on the right side of the Hammers midfield, allowing him space into which he can drive with his surging attacking runs but, whether playing there or as a front-line striker, Marlon's powerful physical presence and speed make him a handful for any defence. His 22 goals in the Irons' promotion campaign of 2004–05, 17 of them in the Coca-Cola League Championship, and a vital one in the home leg of the play-off semi-final against Ipswich, showed him to be a consistently good forward.

Marlon probably makes at least as many goals as he scores, none being more important than both goals Bobby Zamora scored in the 2–0 victory at Portman Road in the second leg of the play-off semi-final.

Harewood's class was confirmed by his impact on the top flight the following season when he was amongst the top goalscorers in the Premiership for much of the campaign and went with West Ham to the FA Cup final, where he was desperately unlucky not to score and win the Cup for the Hammers. Certainly, it was only injury that kept his name from the scoresheet.

Marlon admits that after training he likes nothing better than to sit on the sofa and watch television or possibly his favourite film *The Italian Job*. He is also often to be found riding decks in a DJ booth. Anton Ferdinand told how he and Harewood are 'always listening to music – he's a DJ and he likes to think he has more R'n'B tunes than me, but he doesn't.'

Marlon took up DJing around 10 years ago. He has an imposing record collection at his home in Epping, Essex, and says he would be keen, when his playing days are over, to become involved more deeply in what started out as a hobby when he was 17; it was what kept him at home at a time when he probably was going out a few more times in a week than was good for his football. He is into all kinds of music: classical, rock to pop, and loves 'a bit of Motown', but listens mostly to R'n'B, hip-hop, some soul tunes and funk. Marlon is sometimes responsible for choosing the music in the dressing room before a game and he tries to play tunes that some of the other players like and that will get them mentally prepared for the match.

Harewood married his wife Alison in December 2003; they have one child, Pharrell, who was born early in 2006. Marlon's dad, a big fan of the West Indies cricket team, would probably have liked his son to have become a cricketer. The senior Mr Harewood used to play cricket and Marlon often went to watch him. In fact, the summer game was the only sport he really knew for some time. He played for his father's team and reached a good standard. His dad is still a great spectator of the game and continues to support the West Indies. As such, of late, occasionally, he has not been very happy with the sporting aspect of his life and Marlon likes to wind him up by saying, 'What are you watching it for? They're rubbish!'

Marlon's parents were both born in Barbados and were anxious about their son's safety as a child, to the extent that he was rarely permitted to leave the house in the evening to hone his footballing talent. As such, Marlon didn't really start playing the game until he was about 11. The family didn't live in a bad area, but the Harewoods were wary of the North London environment. Harewood Junior went straight from school to home.

For all this, Marlon wasn't interested in football until one of his friends asked him to come and play for his team. He missed his first match because his dad didn't know where to go, and neither did he. Marlon didn't know his way about much at all because he wasn't allowed out. For the second game, the manager had to come and pick young Harewood up; he scored seven goals in his first game.

Marlon has been really appreciative of the West Ham fans, seeing the support at home and away as giving his side 'an edge'. He has often been seen enticing the fans to sing 'easy, easy'. He has a vast collection of football boots, his favourites are a pair of gold ones but he doesn't want to wear them all the time in case they get ruined. These are the boots he scored his hat-trick with in the 4–0 defeat of Aston Villa on West Ham's return to the top flight. He generally wears a pair of boots for a few games and then gets a new pair so his footwear is always in good condition.

NIGEL SHOLA ANDRE REO-COKER

HAMMERS DEBUT: 31/1/04

'Every action has a reaction, and you have to be careful with your actions and think about what you are doing and how it will affect other people.'

It was 23 April 2005 at the Withdean Stadium as a crowd of around 7,000 watched West Ham United play Brighton and Hove Albion. Nigel Reo-Coker, the Hammers skipper, scored the first goal of the match. The few travelling Irons supporters began to hope for the three points that would push their side into contention for a Championship play-off place. But in the last minute of the game the home side pulled level and to many it looked as if the pride of East London football would be obliged to dwell in the second rung of English football for at least another season and probably longer.

Just over a year later, at the Millennium Stadium, West Ham were preparing to run out in front of 74,000 people to play in the FA Cup final for the first time in 26 years. Many involved with the club found it hard to believe. The Hammers had not only made the play-offs, but also won the final in May 2005 and smashed their way into the Premiership, and now they faced the European Champions to contest the most distinguished title in football. Back in the finest League in the world, the boys from the Boleyn Ground not only survived, they thrived, spending much of the season in the top half of the table and qualifying for Europe.

Reo-Coker is anything but the archetypal professional footballer. He believes in true love, attends church regularly, loves deep-sea fishing and the first thing he does every morning as he gets out of bed is listen to the news. He is unable to understand how people deny they are racist while supporting the BNP, whose parliamentary candidates he knows to include convicted criminals and football hooligans. He understands how people might feel about asylum seekers who commit crimes yet have not been deported and sees how this can exacerbate racial and religious tensions and help the cause of far-right movements. At the same time, he feels that the likes of the BNP creating fear about 'the growth of Islam' is a disgrace.

I asked the man who scored the goal at the Withdean to compare his feelings about that seminal game against Preston at the Millennium Stadium with what had become known as the 'greatest Cup final in history' encounter with Middlesbrough in the semi-finals of the Cup:

Of course, the FA Cup is one of the biggest Cup competitions in the world and it has such a great history. It's a fantastic competition. The fans appreciated what we'd done, as we did. We didn't expect something like that this season. We've exceeded our expectations. The atmosphere in the semi-final was electric. We have a great fan base. The 20,000 West Ham fans made a fantastic occasion. We will prepare for the final in the same way that we would for any other game. As a team, we've had big games and we're always learning as players.

But winning promotion and captaining the side, being the person that picks up the trophy, to get promotion to the Premiership ... that was a dream that I've always had from a very early age. To play in the Premiership, not only that, but to win that right, not to be bought by a Premiership side, but win it with a club like West Ham was the best thing. Especially after all the criticism and the bad press we suffered throughout that year. I think that makes it one of my best achievements so far.

It's a game that will stay in my mind till the end of my career when I can sit back and reflect on it. Luckily I was involved in the final the year before, when we lost to Crystal Palace. I knew what the expectations were on the day and we knew what the expectations were on West Ham as a club. We knew we had to win the match, we knew it would be a very tough game. But for me it is one of those things that I don't really try to reflect on at all. After my career I might, when I

*can sit back and be proud of what I've achieved. It was a great day. We
got fantastic support from the West Ham fans; it's something that will
stay with me for the rest of my life.*

Like many of the Hammers' massive army of supporters, West Ham's
youngest ever captain believes that his side, in 2005, got 'back where
they belong':

*From when I first came to the club I have thought that West Ham are
better suited to the Premiership than the Championship. Some didn't
think we would survive, that we didn't have the players capable of
performing at Premiership level. As a team we've shown we deserve to
be in the Premiership.*

*The Championship is more physical than the Premiership. In the
Premiership you need more technical skill and tactical awareness as
every week you are playing against world-class players and mistakes
are costly.*

Nigel was born in Thornton Heath, Surrey, on 14 April 1984. Both
his parents were from Sierra Leone in West Africa. His mum, Agnes-
Lucinda, is a career nurse. He told me,

*She's started her own business looking after the mentally ill. I have two
older sisters, Natalie and Vanessa, 30 and 29. I have a nephew called
Devon and a niece called Tandy. My family weren't interested in
football, but they took interest when I started to progress.*

Although he was born in London, Nigel spent the first six years of
his childhood in Sierra Leone, where his father, Ransford, worked as
a doctor. In 1990, his parents separated and Agnes-Lucinda returned
to England with the children and a small, dingy one-bedroomed flat
in Elephant and Castle.

Agnes wanted her children to get a British education and to
spend their teenage and adult years in the UK. But the first years
struggling as a single-parent family were difficult. They moved close
to East Street market where the family were burgled on three

occasions. Agnes had to work incredibly hard to get her family out of their situation, but eventually they moved to a house in Thornton Heath and things got better from then on.

Agnes telephones her son at least once a day and remains the driving force of his life. Witnessing how hard she had to work, and not having a father figure or role model in his life, for Nigel made him stronger and more resolute to succeed. For him he had the option of letting himself fail life on the pretext of his father's absence, but chose not to use that as an excuse, feeling that would have been too easy and it seems Agnes-Lucinda was never up for the easy route. Natalie and Vanessa were put through college and emerged with degrees in law and business. However, although Nigel was doing well at school, he had the ambition to be footballer. His concerned mother did her best to dissuade her son, but his love and talent for the game were obvious.

Reo-Coker came into football for probably the best of all possible reasons. He remembered,

I never did recognise that I had talent for the game. It was always playing for fun for me. It was only when my schoolteacher thought that I could be good enough to make a career out of the game that I began to take it slightly more seriously, but at the time, at that young age, it was mainly just playing for the fun of it.

However, the future Hammers FA Cup final captain seemed to be blessed with a natural gift for physical endeavour:

I was very athletic at school. I was good at athletics, tennis, rugby, any other sport that I participated in. I would say I was either naturally good at a sport or I could develop until I was able to participate in that sport.

For all this, from his earliest years he was aware of where his passion lay:

But football was my one and only true love.

NIGEL SHOLA ANDRE REO-COKER

This said, Nigel kept his life in balance, with some parental 'input':

I had to be good academically or I'd see the back of my mum's hand! [laughs]. I was good academically. I left school with 11 GCSEs, all As to Cs, went on to college and got four or five qualifications at college as well, while I was YT at Wimbledon.

Standing just 5ft 9in Reo-Coker is a sturdy, fast, battling, hard-working midfielder. Looking at his own qualities as a player, he said,

I would say people describe me as powerful and explosive. I've always tried to look at the top players that dominate games, those who are all-round midfielders; Steven Gerrard, Roy Keane, Patrick Vieira mainly. I try to take bits from all their games and model myself on them really, because I think they're all very similar players. They're all powerful and explosive, but they can also dominate a game, and that's what I try to do.

Few would argue that Reo-Coker is probably the best buy Alan Pardew made in his first few seasons at Upton Park. He came to the Boleyn Ground following speculation that the likes of Spurs and Portsmouth would take him into the Premiership. But, according to his agent, Tony Finnigan, 'Once West Ham came in there was only one place he was going to go. The nice thing for the Hammers fans is that he really wants to wear the shirt.'

When I asked the young skipper of the Irons about this, he told me,

From a very young age I followed football, especially when the Premiership started. I saw West Ham as a big, big club, one of the biggest clubs in London. When you looked at the history of West Ham, the Cups and the players who played for West Ham, you are impressed. As a club, West Ham has always looked to the future, been innovative – the club's past helps it look to the future. So it was my personal choice that it would be best for my career to move to West Ham.

THE BLACK HAMMERS

It takes Nigel about an hour to get from his home in Tadworth, Surrey, to the West Ham training ground at Chadwell Heath in his black sports Mercedes CLS via the M25, Dartford Tunnel and A13. He has a bowl of porridge prepared by Tim, the club's resident chef, for breakfast when he gets there. If you were to meet him at that time in the morning, he might be wearing a designer (Bathing Ape) T-shirt, jeans, unlaced trainers and a baseball cap twisted sideways on his closely shaven head. But his good taste in terms of his choice of club is reflected in other aspects of his life:

I'll wear anything that looks good – I'm not too much of a designer freak – if something is not a name brand and it looks good and I like it then I'll wear it.

In terms of cars, I've always been a big fan of Bentleys. I'm probably gonna get a Cadillac Escalade.

Music? Well, I first started listening to Tupac around 1996, when he released 'All eyez on me' and got into his music [one of his favourite numbers is 'Dear Mama']. He was a very talented musician and, in terms of hip-hop, he is certainly one of the greats. It's a shame that he died because he wasn't a typical gangster rapper; his music wasn't about guns and violence; he tried to educate young people and tell them not to make the same bad choices as him. Tupac's music appealed to me, he was a great lyricist and he spoke out about black youth culture and the choices we have in life. At that time hip-hop was big in England. He has a song for all moods and for every aspect of life and there was and is a lot that I can relate to in his music.

The first of a triumvirate of Wimbledon players to move to East London within the space of a fortnight in January 2004, Nigel was the only one to remain at the club for a significant time and was dubbed 'the new Paul Ince', a simile he has little problem with:

I feel great about that. I was always a Paul Ince fan from a very young age. He was and is a fantastic player, one of my role models. Growing up watching him in the Premiership, what he's going to have, the career he's going to have and how successful he's going to become, also playing for West Ham and England was terrific. So I'm pleased that people compare me to the likes of Paul Ince.

Nigel donned the claret and blue on 22 January 2004; taking squad number 20, he made his debut a week later at Upton Park in a 2–1 defeat of Rotherham.

However, Reo-Coker played his initial first-team game for Wimbledon in April 2002. He went on to score six times in his 64 appearances for the club he had joined from school and played for as a youth. He recalled how he became involved with the Wombles:

> *I used to play Sunday football for local sides in the Croydon area. Then I was lucky enough to represent Croydon Borough and then the County of Surrey. I was playing one game for Surrey, when Roger Smith, the Wimbledon academy director at the time, was at the game. I had no idea he was watching the match. After the game a Fulham scout approached me and asked for my phone number. He said he was going to call me that night and that he wanted me to go on trial to Fulham. So I was excited. But when I got home I didn't receive the phone call from him, but I did get a phone call from Roger Smith. He'd been at the Surrey game checking out another player that Wimbledon already had on the team. He invited me to go on trial and I went on trial to Wimbledon and, pretty much, the rest is history.*

Nigel's mum had watched her son's excitement waiting for that call from the Fulham scout. Every second of the hours he waited, she lived through with him. When the Wimbledon scout spoke to her, Agnes could have put an end to Nigel's ambitions in a moment, but she must have understood something of his passion. However, Nigel was conscious of his responsibility in things. He didn't want to be the failure of the family, to see his sisters achieve and be successful while he was a failure. He was interested in graphic design and multi-media and knew it would be harder to be successful in football than in industry, but he was determined to succeed and resolved to work hard to make a future for himself in the game he loved.

Nigel was probably the most talented of the players that Wimbledon were obliged to sell as they plummeted towards relegation from Division One. The cost of bringing Reo-Coker to Upton Park was around £575,000 but this was a relative bargain, seeing that the Irons were getting an England Youth and Under-21 international and, as the youngest captain in the First Division, a proven leader. When I asked him about what qualities made for a good leader, he responded with an answer that demonstrated wisdom beyond his 22 years:

There's many qualities I'd say. I think that nowadays, in today's society, you have to be quite a good people person; you have to know the people you're working with and you have to know what makes people tick, because people tick off different things. You have to be able to dish out the dirt, but you also have to be able to take it back. It's a bit of give and take. I think for me the main philosophy I've learned is treat others in a way you'd like to be treated. If you can do that, you are more than halfway to becoming a leader.

For Nigel, captaining club and country call on the same qualities and have the same demands. As a skipper, Reo-Coker is not prone to being in players' faces or getting excited. He tries to let his football do the talking, winning tackles and driving forward with the ball and passing and shooting.

The responsibilities are the same whether I'm playing for England or West Ham. I think being made captain puts a lot of pressure on you. Not only do you have to perform, but you also have to be the inspiration, the person that people generally look to lift the team when needed. It's not an easy responsibility and it's not just a responsibility on the field, it's a responsibility off the field. There's so much pressure on today's generation of young people and footballers. The game, at top level, is very pressurised.

NIGEL SHOLA ANDRE REO-COKER

Being West Ham's youngest ever captain is something you can't really put into words. It's a tremendous honour, something I'm very proud of because of the history of the club and the players that have gone on to become legends who've captained the club. It's something I have for the rest of my life. You can look back on your achievements after your career, but you can't stand still and admire them now. They are something I'm glad I'll have to reflect on when my career is over; something to share with my kids and grandkids. But now I've got to perform in every game. You mustn't get complacent.

In his first England Under-21 game as a West Ham player (October 2004, against Azerbaijan in Baku), he was sent off. Reflecting on that incident, he said,

I don't really feel anything about what happened. I was unfairly sent off but I should have known better not to react as a player. It wasn't the best of conditions the game was played in. It's a learning curve for me, I have to keep my head and stay cool.

But that set-back was more than balanced by the huge part he played in helping the Hammers fight their way to the Championship play-offs in 2005 and their subsequent promotion.

Not long after he arrived at Upton Park, Nigel commented,

It annoys me when I hear young kids who claim they live in a ghetto. They are all living in brick houses. Then you look at Jamaica or Africa and there are people living in huts. That's the ghetto.

When I questioned him about this, he commented,

It's just annoying sometimes when I see kids saying that their life is worse than what it actually is. If you look at England and other countries around the world, England is a wealthier country compared to the likes of Jamaica or Brazil. In Rio people are living in huts not proper houses. They are having to fight for food and go through rubbish for food. I'm not saying life is easy in England, but, sometimes, saying it is harder than it actually is can just be an easy way to get out of things, especially for young black youth.

I think young blacks can find it very hard to find many role models so they can say, 'Look at what he's achieved, what he's done.' It is hard for them to find role models that have achieved and kept it real; who haven't changed the way they are or who they are to become that achieving person.

But saying, 'It's just so hard', it's always like it's the easy way out. For me, in football, I've achieved, and it's not the fact that I'm happy I'm a footballer, it's the fact that it's a dream I've had and have had to work hard for. I've had to go through a lot to get where I'm at now — but I'm not satisfied and I'm not finished. I still want to achieve more. And I know, if you want to do anything in life or win or achieve anything in life, you have to work hard for it.

This honesty and to-the-point attitude was nothing new for Nigel, who has always been a leader, a captain (those closest to him have nicknamed him 'Skip'). At school, it was common for him to be chosen to head a project or be a spokesman for the other pupils. On leading West Ham in the Premiership at the age of 21, he said,

There aren't too many people who can say that … Sometimes I can be a very dominant person when I need to be. I like to get my point across, have a force of personality — but most of the time I'm quite quiet and laidback.

I questioned him about this just before the FA Cup final of 2006 and he elaborated:

My closest friends would describe me as being very 'moany'. I think that is the one word that everyone uses. My closest friends that have known me for a very long time always say that I'm moany. Even though I play in the Premiership and am captain of West Ham, they always say, 'You ain't changed one bit!' So that's [laughs] their favourite word to describe me.

NIGEL SHOLA ANDRE REO-COKER

Anton Ferdinand confirmed this, 'Nigel is Mr Moany and Mr Miserable. He's the person you just can't talk to in the morning – he won't talk to you until after midday and he'll just bite your head off. But once he gets past that stage, he's fine.'

This said, Reo-Coker has no complaints about the Hammers supporters. For him there is 'having fans and having West Ham fans'; he has experienced the passion and vocal nature of the Hammers' support as potentially daunting and realises that, if they're not happy, the players know:

> The West Ham fans are passionate. That's the best way to describe them, they're passionate. And it's in the blood. It's a very, very family-orientated club – if the father supports West Ham, it's most likely that the son and the daughter and the mother will support West Ham and the newborn will support West Ham – I think they are very passionate fans.
>
> They, and the history behind the club, make playing for West Ham special. When the fans want to support you, the support they give you is tremendous. They are one of the best set of fans in the Premiership, the best you'll ever play for.

Nigel is very conscious of the privilege of being a professional footballer. Just before the Irons went out to play their FA Cup semi-final in 2006, Alan Pardew read his side a letter from a fan that touched the Hammers skipper. The supporter asked his team to think of the fans as they played and how they were the parents that buy boots for their kids and support them on cold Sunday mornings, but that it was through the players that the fans live their dreams. Nigel realises that West Ham have always been seen as the underdogs, 'the people from the wrong side of the river', and he empathises with that, because that is how it was for him. His mum and sisters used to buy boots for him; looking back, he recognises that they couldn't afford it, but managed to find a way and put him where he is:

> Every day, eve-ree day, is a memory. Every day is fantastic and is something you've just got to learn from. You take every day as a gift.

It would be nice if players did a bit more for the community. It's hard because we don't have as many schemes set up over here as they do in America. In America you've got a lot more famous athletes doing more for the community, helping youth and so on. So I think we could do more, player wise, not just football in the community. I haven't really been asked to do anything, apart from being involved as a patron for charities [he was a patron of 'Hope and Homes for Children'].

Early in 2006, Reo-Coker again showed his no-nonsense approach by revealing he, now the skipper of the England Under-21 side, could play international football for Sierra Leone if he is not picked by England's next manager.

Nigel was named by Sven-Goran Eriksson in December 2005 as a possible gatecrasher to his World Cup squad but Reo-Coker told how he was becoming increasingly frustrated at his lack of full squad recognition, stating that he could

... still change my allegiance ... As soon as you stop playing Under-21 football, you have a year to change if you want to. There is an alternative. I could play for Sierra Leone, but I've not thought that far ahead. I just want to see what happens and my main focus is West Ham.

Obviously, with Sven-Goran Eriksson leaving after the World Cup, I will have to see who comes in.

Late in the 2005–06 season, when thinking about the situation, Nigel told me,

It is a possibility. I think the rules have changed with UEFA. An Under-21 player can change allegiance to his parents' background after they've finished playing at Under-21 level, so I can still change and play for Sierra Leone. But the issue came from an interview that went wrong, shall I say. They took my words out of context

My main criticism of the England set-up at the moment is that there is a backlog of young players. I feel that players who are doing well, or players who deserve their chance, don't really get their chance until too

late in their career. I think they should be getting experience. It's always the same old case. Look at the England side now. Players that have been in the Under-21 set-up and the senior set-up have not been able to get themselves established and get a good run of games behind them.

There are players who I and some of my colleagues have played against who've played for Holland and Spain and France; we've played against them and they are making their full senior debut now, playing a few games and educating themselves.

Playing for Sierra Leone is an option that is in my hands and it's in my mind that I could represent a total different country and build awareness of what is going on in Africa at the same time. There are a lot of young African players playing in the Premiership who are representing their countries and doing well.

At the end of the day I make my decisions on the basis of what I feel is right for me. I'll get other people's opinions and consult other people that I trust in the game, but no one makes decisions about my career but me.

At the time of writing Reo-Coker remains the skipper of the England Under-21 side and is showing that he has a rightful place in the top flight of English football. It would be a tragic loss to the national side if he were to change his allegiance. As his fellow Hammer and international teammate Anton Ferdinand has it, 'Nigel should be going to the World Cup, because he is a born leader and would bring those qualities to the England team.'

In the short time Reo-Coker has been at Upton Park, he has made a tremendous impact, but he is the first to give his fellow Hammers credit. This was evident when we spoke about the player he sees as the most outstanding he has played with at club level:

It would have to be Hayden Mullins, my current midfield partner, 'cause obviously we've played together for a while now and we've known each other from a little bit back. I remember watching Hayden when he used to play for Crystal Palace. He's someone I've formed a partnership with so to speak, and we've gone on from strength to strength really.

Nigel has no hesitation when asked to name the most impressive player he has seen – Ronaldo de Assis Moreira:

> *I'd have to say it's Ronaldinho for me. The best way to describe Ronaldinho is a gift from God, because he's unbelievable. The things he does with a football, you just never dream about it, and he keeps showing it more and more all the time.*
>
> *I really don't know who has had the biggest influence on me at West Ham. So I'll just have to say that everyone has played their part in influencing me at West Ham.*
>
> *I've not been there that long and there's been so many changes. I'm grateful to Alan Pardew for bringing me there, for giving me the opportunity to play for West Ham. He's helped me a lot and he's brought a lot out of me really, leadership qualities that I really didn't think I had. It hasn't been an easy ride, but we're managing to get a bit of an understanding now. But all the people at Upton Park have had an influence. It's the same sort of atmosphere that I grew up in at Wimbledon; it's more a family-type atmosphere.*

Of course, Reo-Coker is still a young man, but he is aware that his playing career is limited and he keeps an eye of the future. However, he has strong views about the structure of football management in Britain and he is cautious in terms of his own managerial ambitions:

> *It is something that people have seen in me and said that I would make a good manager or a good coach. People have complimented me on my knowledge of the game so far, even though I'm very young. It's something I'd consider but I find it so hard to say, 'yeah, I would' because there isn't too many black role-model managers out there, so I think that not many black players think that they could go into management because they wouldn't really get the opportunity or the chance to be successful.*
>
> *There are some institutional limitations on the advancement of black players in the game and it's something that might put me off coaching; it might just lead me to walk away from the game totally when I finish playing. Being a young black male, it is sometimes nice to see black*

males achieve things. In the United States there's a lot more black role models. Even though they might come from bad backgrounds, they've still managed to change their lives and achieved things, so the young kids in America can look up to the likes of Puff Daddy and Jay Zee. Especially in their sports trade, it's always past players that are managing sides in the MBA and baseball. In America there are always black role models that you can look up to or black managers. I think in England now there is a bit of institutional racism and that makes it harder for black coaches and ex-players to become managers. And I think with that going on at the moment it will make it really hard for players like myself to find the enthusiasm. There needs to be someone to look up to and say [for instance] 'If Leroy Rosenior has done it' or 'if so and so's done it, why can't I be a manager?'

I personally haven't come across any racism in the game but I think the game has improved a lot. You might meet a few people that pretend to be your friend, and when your're not there call you racially abusive names. Funnily enough, after Sunday's game I was called a monkey [laughs] by a Chelsea fan. But before that I haven't really experienced anything.

I think we've really got to work hard at getting rid of racism. We've got to put more black people in high-profile jobs — more black managers, black chairmen, more black board executives — and really show that there are more black people that are capable of doing the job to a very high standard. But until we get more black ex-players and black people into high-profile jobs I don't think things will change.

Nigel's rise to the very heights of football has brought with it a plethora of achievements: leading West Ham United into the Premiership, captaining his country at Under-21 level and then the FA Cup final.

Like the rest of the West Ham Cup final team of 2006, Nigel was devastated by the result. But he was aware of being part of one of the greatest ever Cup finals, running the European Champions as close as possible, and he was called up as a reserve for the England World Cup squad. He went to Portugal to train with the side, but a stomach injury meant he had to withdraw; however, he was pleased to have been chosen and seen as potentially part of England's future.

For all this, the twins of experience, glory and disappointment, have not caused the Hammers' young skipper to forget those who have supported him or changed his basic principles:

I think I've been quite fortunate. There's been a lot of people around me. I'm not married and don't have a girlfriend right now. God, my mum, my family – they've been a great influence on my career and very supportive; they used to buy my boots for me when I couldn't afford it. My close friends have also influenced and supported me, and my agent, Tony Finnigan. Tony's been a bit of a father figure to me from a very young age [they first met when Nigel was 13]; *he's guided me wisely. We've made mistakes together, but we've learned. I don't really see him as an agent any more but more of a family member. Without his guidance and help, I don't think I'd be where I am right now. I'm also quite a religious person, so I'd have to say God comes first in everything, and if it wasn't meant to be I wouldn't be doing what I'm doing now. I've managed to avoid the wrong type of people in my career and I'm enjoying every minute of it now.*

Nigel's consideration for those nearest and dearest was exemplified when he visited his mum in Thornton Heath one afternoon. He asked her to go for a drive with him. Mother and son made their way south to Purley and parked outside a new house. He told Agnes he had a surprise for her and gave her the keys to the house. Of course she cried. That was a moment Nigel said he would cherish for the rest of his life. It made him feel good to let her know how much he appreciated all she had done for him, holding down two jobs so that his sisters could go to college and helping him to become the man he is today.

It seems Nigel is where he wants to be. Talking to him you get the impression that his commitment to the Hammers runs deep and that he sees his own ambitions intertwined with those of the club:

If I wasn't a footballer, I'd probably be a doctor. If not that, media studies or design. But I don't have any regrets about joining West

NIGEL SHOLA ANDRE REO-COKER

Ham. I think a life full of regrets is a life not lived. If I had to start my career all over again, I'd do everything exactly the same. I wouldn't change a thing, I've learned so much. Even at my young age, in such a short space of time. People that I know in the game say I know such a lot for my age that some people don't know until they're 30 or 40. So I wouldn't change a thing.

Listening closely to the Irons' on-field leader, one gets the impression that the current crop of players have worked out their own unique ethos as a team, reminding one of the great Celtic manager Jock Stein's view of the game at its best – 'a type of socialism':

At West Ham everyone gets on with everyone and there's no superstars. Everyone is seen as an equal.

JOEL JOSHUA FREDERICK MCANUFF

HAMMERS DEBUT: 7/2/04

'If we can keep sneaking up the table and get a few more good results, we can get even higher.'

On 1 July 2000 midfielder/winger McAnuff signed his first professional contract for the 2000–01 season with Wimbledon. The highly thought-of young player was one of a string of talented performers produced by the Wimbledon youth academy that included the likes of Nigel Reo-Coker. In his time with the Dons, McAnuff, who is a cousin of former Jamaica Olympic Bronze medallist sprinter (4x100 Relay) Nikole Mitchell, was voted Wimbledon's Young Player of the Year and was chosen to play for Jamaica against Nigeria in May 2002 (the Reggae Boys lost 0–1).

Admired for playing fluently on the left or right of midfield, driving defenders to distraction, Jobi commanded the admiration of many Premiership clubs and a bid was made by Portsmouth's Harry Rednapp. Although the club had gone into administration, the offer was rejected by Wimbledon.

But money was needed; Jobi went to West Ham for a fee of £300,000 on 2 February 2004, to be reunited with other ex-Dons David Connolly, Adam Nowland and Nigel Reo-Coker. A three-and-a-half-year contract suggested he was going to hang around Upton Park for some time but only six months and just four First Division starts and nine appearances from the bench later, at the start of the 2004–05 season, despite not wanting to leave London, McAnuff moved for £250,000 to promotion rivals Cardiff City. Few at Upton Park were happy at the departure of McAnuff. His goal against Crewe might be enough reason for this. He had run through a maze of defenders before slotting the ball into the bottom corner of the Alexandra goal.

Jobi scored 15 goals in 104 appearances for Wimbledon. He claimed three goals in 48 outings in South Wales, winning various Player of the Month awards along the way. He was transferred to Championship side Crystal Palace for a £600,000 fee in June 2005. He was now a mature and disciplined professional, and a potent threat at the heart of the Eagles' midfield, supplying skilful touches of trickery, feeding the forwards and well able to reinforce the attack.

As to the future when England played Jamaica in a pre-2006 World Cup friendly, Jobi was not at Old Trafford, although he most certainly would have been chosen to represent the West Indians, but early in that year he said,

> *It must be a world record for someone of my age to announce their retirement from international football … But if I didn't retire, Jamaica could call me up at any time and stop me playing for my club.*

It seems that McAnuff has put club before country but perhaps Jobi has ambitions on the international scene that might not be realised playing for Jamaica – as he has only played one friendly game, his options are open.

JOBI MCANUFF – CAREER RECORD				
CLUB	SEASON	COMPETITION	APPEARANCES (SUB)	GOALS
Crystal Palace	2005–06	League	32 (6)	8
		FA Cup		
		League Cup	1	
Cardiff City	2004–05	League	42 (1)	2
		FA Cup	2 (0)	1
		League Cup	3 (0)	0
West Ham	2003–04	League	4 (9)	1
Wimbledon	2003–04	League	25 (2)	5
		FA Cup	3 (0)	0

THE BLACK HAMMERS

CLUB	SEASON	COMPETITION	APPEARANCES (SUB)		GOALS
Wimbledon	2002–03	League	29	(2)	4
		FA Cup	1	(0)	1
		League Cup	2	(0)	1
Wimbledon	2001–02	League	22	(16)	4
		FA Cup	0	(2)	0
Total			166	(38)	27

ROBERT LESTER ZAMORA

HAMMERS DEBUT: 7/2/04

'Loved every minute of my career. Proper lucky!'

In January 2006 Bobby Zamora signed a new contract which would keep him at West Ham until the summer of 2010. He had celebrated his birthday on the previous Monday. Manager Alan Pardew said, 'It's fantastic news that Bobby has signed a new contract and I'm delighted that we have yet another of our young players committed for the long-term future … Bobby has made brilliant progress in the past 12 months and I'm very pleased with his contribution this season. He is a local boy who loves the club, and I hope he will go on to enjoy a lot of success with us in the years to come.'

Bobby was born in Barking Hospital in Essex on 16 January 1981. He told me,

> *My mum and dad lived in Manor Park, near Ilford. Mum's a teacher and Dad has done all sorts of jobs, but when I was born he was a social worker, working for the council. My dad's got many strings to his bow. I have two sisters, Michelle and Layla, and one brother, Michael.*

'Zamo', as he is known to his teammates, is a lifelong West Ham supporter and remembers his first live experience of the Hammers with some relish:

> *It was a game against Oxford. My mum and dad have still got the programme. I went with my mum at Upton Park. We were right by the*

tunnel. I felt lucky to be so up close to all the players; it was a right buzz for me.

It seems that Bobby had had a strong sense of his vocation from an early age. He recalled,

I was about eight when I started playing football for a couple of local sides. I played for a team called Lakeview. I first got to play for my district at senior school. My school wasn't really big on football. My mum, being a teacher, knew other people in schools and she found out about a trial for the district team, Newham. So the Monday after school I went along. Played a trial, had a few games; after that they called out the names that they wanted and I was one of them. It was only then I realised that the trial was for a year above me. But they said it was all right and that they could use me in that team as well. I went on and played for the county with John Terry, Stuart Taylor and Paul Konchesky, a lot of good players. Phil Rider [he was at Barking Abbey School] was the county coach at the time. Phil was a major part of my football coaching. I was at Little Ilford School – no disrespect, but it wasn't the greatest school in the world, Phil said, 'Do you want to come to Barking Abbey? We'll help you with your football, schooling etc.' Phil spoke to my mum and dad, and I decided to go there and it worked out really well. I concentrated on football and schooling at the same time. I was extremely lucky really.

Charlton was the first club I went to, then West Ham two or three months later. I was playing for the district and Frank Lampard Senior came along to the game. I was with my mate Frankie Nesbit; his dad, Danny, was there. He said Frank Lampard's here, he's come to watch you. I thought he was winding me up, 'come to watch me, yeah, yeah'. I was around 11 years old. After the game he said, 'We're really keen. We've watched you a lot, do you fancy coming over West Ham?' I thought, 'Yeah, definitely!' I went over to West Ham and I was there until I was about 14.

I'm a dab hand at picking up on any sort of sport. I'm just one of them sporty people, but in PE we did all sorts, basketball, table tennis, tennis, cricket. But football was my first love.

ROBERT LESTER ZAMORA

Bobby came to Upton Park via the legendary Sunday club, Senrab, who have a history of producing players of the calibre of David Beckham, Ledley King, Lee Bowyer and Jermain Defoe who once described Senrab as the youth equivalent of 'playing for Real Madrid'. With Senrab, Zamora played alongside John Terry (Chelsea), Jlloyd Samuel (Aston Villa), Paul Konchesky (Charlton) and fellow Hammers-to-be Joe Cole and Michael Carrick.

Bobby left Upton Park in 1996 after what might be called a 'breakdown of communications' within the club:

There was a West Ham group that trained at Chadwell Heath and another group that trained in Slough. Another group up North. The club were whittling down the groups and our group and the Slough group merged. We still played at Chadwell Heath on Thursday evenings. Ledley King was still there too. The Slough coach might have poached a team that played on a Sunday or a Saturday; a lot of lads were left out, including myself. I weren't best pleased. I was quite a good player in the area at that time, loads of clubs were interested. I just thought exactly the same as everyone else: 'I'll just go another way' as I didn't think the future was going to happen at West Ham.

Zamora was released on the same day as Jlloyd Samuel, Fitz Hall and Paul Konchesky (who would also return to the Hammers fold).

Zamora spent a brief spell with Chelsea:

I was good friends with John Terry. I used to go to Chelsea with John. We went down to Battersea together to train. But I had to deal with Osgood Slatters Syndrome, which put my sports activities to sleep really. I had to have six months off from playing sport, couldn't do PE or anything in school. I ended up knocking it on the head.

It says much for the young Zamora and the support of his family that he was able to get through what must have been a very demanding period for such a sport-loving young man. While it seems Chelsea more or less gave up on Bobby, the word about his talent had got around on the football grapevine:

THE BLACK HAMMERS

Norwich were on the phone constantly while I wasn't doing any football. I played for Norwich for about eight months and did well; they had a good youth team. But at that age I was tiny. Everyone that knew me would say, 'Little Bobby Lee, was really quick, a good player, but not really too big.' They released me because they said they didn't think I was going to grow; to be fair, their team were big, strong boys – Thomas Repkas at 15!

How wrong Zamora's Canary critics were. Now at 6ft 1in and 13st 8lb, Bobby is a powerful, talented and mobile forward, a stern challenge for any defence. After his spell in East Anglia, Zamo had the chance to return to his home county:

I got a phone call the day after I left Norwich asking me to come to Southend United: 'We'll offer you an apprenticeship, come and have a couple of games, we'll have another look at you.' They obviously knew about me. But Bristol Rovers were on the phone as well, the guy that used to work with Norwich, Richard Hexham, was working for Bristol Rovers. He phoned me up, told me he thought I was a good player and asked me to come down for a game. He said exactly the same thing to a good friend of mine who was at Norwich, Luke Williams. We both went down there together, played a game; first half I scored one, set Luke up, Luke scored one. At half-time he pulls us off and said, 'I want to offer you an apprenticeship, both of you.' Luke was probably my best mate at the time and we both jumped at the chance; 16 years of age, bit of adventure, play football with your best mate – it was perfect! If I'd have been at Southend I would have been living at home, probably would have been getting up to all sorts. I thought it was best to go and have a fresh start somewhere else.

After six outings and no goals with the Pirates, and a spell on loan to Bath in January 2000, Brighton and Hove Albion took Zamora on a three-month temporary stint at the end of the 1999–2000 season. However, following six goals in the same number of games, the Seagulls made the move permanent for a £100,000 fee in August 2000. Rovers wisely insisted on a 25 per cent sell-on clause. For Bobby, it felt like a make or break move:

ROBERT LESTER ZAMORA

At Bristol Rovers at the time, there was Barry Hayles, got the golden boot; Jason Roberts and Nathan Ellington were all there and I was probably number-five choice. Even though I was doing really well in training, I'd say better than a lot of them, when you come up through the ranks it's so hard for anyone to get in that door. Knowing what I could do coming back from loan and still not playing, not getting the opportunity to do anything, was a bit of a kick in the teeth. So when I went back pre-season I went into Ian Holloway, who was the manager at the time, with the youth-team manager Phil Baker, who was a great coach and a great player, he helped me out massively; I told Ian Holloway I wanted to move on. They weren't going to accept it but at the end of the day I thought I had my career and had to go when I wanted to go.

The young forward soon emerged as one of the brightest young talents in the lower divisions. When Brighton had to do without him, they were a lesser side. He scored 31 goals in his first full season as the Seagulls took the Third Division title, and then smashed another 32 in 2001–02, helping his side make First Division status. However, injury in the 2002–03 campaign halted Bobby's progress and was certainly a factor in the club's immediate relegation from Division One. Bobby looked back on his time by the seaside:

It was just one of them combinations that I think we've got at West Ham now as well. Everybody knows exactly what is required from everyone, everyone's willing to give 110 per cent, and a little bit of quality as well. We was lucky to win two Championships and the experience we had in Division One was quality to the last game of the season. I don't want to sound big-headed but I was out for 14 games, if I'd have played 10 of those games we might have pushed on.

During those two glorious promotion seasons on the south coast, Zamora had been voted PFA Player of the Year for Divisions Two and Three and had been the subject of huge attention from other clubs. Celtic, Monaco and a plethora of Premiership clubs were all said to be watching him. From the start of 2001, offers of between

£1.5 and £4 million were flying around. Early in 2001 Zamora was approached to play for the Trinidad and Tobago national team:

> *At the time they approached me, Peter Taylor was the manager of Brighton. He said, 'You are close to the 21s — it's a good opportunity to play for England.' It was just a couple of friendly games that Trinidad wanted me to play. It would have meant going away. We were going for the Division Two Championship. You're away a long time with Trinidad and we were so close to winning Division Two, I thought, 'No I'll stay — that'll happen again.' I've played for the 21s now. FIFA changed the rules, so for the last four years I've known I can't play for Trinidad. Unless they change the rules again, there's no chance.*

Amongst the continued rumours of multimillion-pound offers for Zamora, West Ham were said to be lining up a £4 million swoop. But in January 2002 Bobby's below-par performance for Brighton at Preston in the FA Cup reduced his market value, but speculation about Zamora and big-money transfer fees continued.

A possible move to White Hart Lane hit the headlines at the beginning of August 2002. Bobby was said to be disillusioned with the lack of ambition shown by the Seagulls.

While all this was going on, Bobby gained England Under-21 recognition. Reflecting on the experience of representing his country, he said,

> *To play for England is massive at whatever level. To get the recognition and to get picked for that team. I went to the European Championships alongside Alan Smith, Peter Crouch and Jermain Defoe and David Dunn; the team was unbelievable when I think about it now. We didn't do very well, but to be a part of that team and to play for England is a massive up.*

The burning ambition Bobby had to play in the Premiership could not be met by Brighton and he understood this:

> *They couldn't have got to the Premiership with the ground problems*

they've had. They've got a great foundation, it's a great part of the country to live in and the supporters are quality, but unless they can do something about the ground I can't see them progressing any further than just struggling in the First Division.

Bobby netted 77 times in 120 appearances for Brighton when Glenn Hoddle took him to White Hart Lane for a fee of £1.5 million in July 2003. The player's agent Phil Smith said the fee was 'a decent price in today's market for a Second Division striker. It has been a long time coming for Bobby but he is delighted to be going into the Premiership. It has always been an ambition.'

According to Bobby, he went to Tottenham because he

... loved 'em; Spurs are a big club with a big reputation. Glenn Hoddle was the manager, I thought, 'The experience he's had, played at the top level, if I go there and learn from the likes of Jamie Redknapp, Robbie Keane, Stephen Carr and Gus Poyet.' All the lads that were there were really good players, with great experience. I went along there, enjoyed my time there and learned a lot. The players that were there helped me and I loved playing alongside them.

His first appearance in a Spurs shirt came just two days after he signed for the club. He scored two goals in a friendly against Oxford United and was on target again in the 3–0 defeat of Norwich on 22 July.

However, Zamora's only goal in 18 League and Cup games with Spurs came against West Ham in the October 2003 third-round League Cup game at White Hart Lane – it put the Hammers out of the competition. His time at White Hart Lane had been difficult, with him never really establishing himself in the Premiership side. When I asked him what went wrong at Spurs, he told me,

Glenn Hoddle signed me and got sacked a couple of months down the road. David Pleat was in charge and I don't think me and David Pleat saw eye to eye.

THE BLACK HAMMERS

Zamora arrived at the Boleyn Ground, along with £7 million on the last day of the transfer window (2 February 2004). In return, Jermain Defoe got the bus to Tottenham. Bobby was happy to come back to Upton Park; for him,

> *West Ham is my team. I've followed them for years so to come over and put a claret and blue jersey on is something special – it's hard to say, it's hard to describe, there's a lot of feelings and I'm sure you can imagine exactly how it feels.*

In the same month Bobby scored on his debut at Valley Parade. It was an equaliser in the 2–1 defeat of Bradford City. Later in February, he netted the only goal of the game against Cardiff at Upton Park.

However, the following season, five goals in 20 outings, with West Ham missing out on promotion in the play-offs, beaten by Crystal Palace in the final, was not immensely impressive and for a year Zamora struggled to get a regular place in the first XI at the Boleyn Ground. He was beset by a number of niggling injuries and played more games from the bench than he did from the start, as Teddy Sheringham and Marlon Harewood were preferred up front.

From late 2004 through to early 2005, Bobby was linked with a number of Championship clubs and he almost signed for Palace at the end of that month, but he had no yearning to leave Upton Park:

> *I didn't want to go, they came in, I was told you can go if you want to, but with West Ham being my team … I knew that we had the ability to go on and play in the Premiership and that's what I wanted to do; so I just said, 'No, I'll stick it out, and get through this tough time.'*

However, West Ham's last-ditch qualification for the Championship play-offs gave Bobby the opportunity to shine. Against Ipswich Town (the third-place team that season that had finished 11 points ahead of the Hammers) in the semi-finals, he scored West Ham's second in a 2–2 draw, he also bagged both goals in the Hammers' second-leg win at Portman Road and it was Bobby's goal at the Millennium Stadium that defeated Preston North End, sending the Hammers back to the Premiership. For Bobby, even after being part of the West Ham side that shook European Champions Liverpool to their foundation in the 'greatest ever FA Cup final' in 2006:

> *That was the biggest game in my life. So many family and friends were there. Seeing the West Ham end packed out, and the misery of the year before. I know I've said it a thousand times already, but it really is like a dream come true. If I could have dreamed the end of that season I don't think we could have done it any better.*

Zamora netted his first top-flight goal in West Ham's 2–1 defeat at Manchester City in October 2005 and penned a fresh contract three months later to keep him at Upton Park until summer 2010. Just after West Ham had qualified for the last four in the FA Cup, Anton Ferdinand said of Zamora, 'Bobby is the funny one. He talks too much, but he's a great lad who is always buzzing. If you're on a downer when you come into training, he will make you think, "Oh yeah, I want to be here." He's a bubbly person who just cracks you up all the time and that makes work enjoyable. If you ask anyone in the camp who's the liveliest, they'll say it's him. He's the one who'll be cracking the boys up before the semi-final.'

For all this, there is a serious side to Zamora. He told me,

> *The ambition's always been there. I think every footballer wants to play at the top level and do as well as they can. To get recognition for your achievements in the game is a massive honour and an achievement that I love.*

This said, the end of the 2005–06 campaign was a disappointment:

> *Losing the Cup final was hard. It might sound strange with the penalty miss and stuff – in all honesty I think I hit that well, hit it in the corner – but the day was unbelievable. It was an absolute great day. The*

performance by every single one of the lads was exactly what fans could have wanted. It was heartbreaking for every single one of us but that is part and parcel of football and to lose on penalties is gutting but what an occasion and what an honour!

Bobby has moved around a fair bit, but has learned a lot from his travels:

Micky Adams [the manager that brought him to Brighton] *and Peter Taylor are both different characters, but I learned so much from the pair of them. With Micky it was about desire, winning and effort, that's what the Brighton team revolved around, that's how we won Championships. Peter Taylor, it was about tactics; he's a top man and taught me a massive amount. Anyone you speak to about him will only say good things.*

And it seemed that being at Upton Park has also had an impact on Bobby's continuing development as a professional:

At West Ham the player who has made the biggest impression on me is Teddy Sheringham. That don't need an explanation, he's a class act and to be able to do what he does at 40 years of age is something special. But also playing alongside Danny [Gabbidon], *who we signed last year, has been an education. He's a really intelligent player. I love playing with him. It's an honour to play with those two.*

This said, Zamora sees family and friends as being the people that have helped him most in his career and the people he admires most, with no one at West Ham coming close to the admiration and respect he feels for those closest to him. This seems typical of the man. Listening to Bobby reflect on his career and personal values, you are struck by his sense of fun and intelligence, but also his honesty and courage. His stance on racism seems to reflect his insight:

I've not experienced racism at Upton Park. You do hear things, not towards myself though. I think there has been a problem getting people into management and executive positions in football, but it's something that's changing all the time. It's only a matter of time. In my eyes racism is boring now; it's had its time. It's just stupid now. For me it would be just over my head, 'well done, mate, whatever.' I don't think there's any room for it now in the game.

Likewise, when asked about his relationship with manager Alan Pardew, he responded in a frank open way:

We didn't see eye to eye to start with. I'm a bubbly character and I like having a laugh and a joke. Don't get me wrong, I'm not a clown all the time; when he wants to talk and it's important stuff, I'm happy to do that. If you talk to Nigel [Reo-Coker] or anyone else, when we've lost a game, they'll tell you I'll come in and pick everyone back up and make sure we all focus for the next game. I don't know if the gaffer really liked that at first. He's definitely come on as a manager this year and he can get even better ... he's not bad.

He was equally sincere about his relationship with West Ham's passionate supporters:

I've had tough times at West Ham. The first play-off year wasn't the greatest start for me, but I managed to win the fans over and play some good football. But I'd like them to give the lads a little bit more leniency. The fans don't see behind the scenes; we do get pissed off and angry, we do get upset when we don't win. I'd like the fans to be right behind us all the time. It makes a hell of a difference; it's really hard to explain. The fans, when they're behind you, like the Tottenham game at the end of the 2005–06 season – they were so up for it, so behind us, it just gave us a massive boost. It was the last home game – that was a special game. Just the atmosphere of the day! The weather, the pitch, everything was perfect ... I like to win the London games.

Zamo is one of West Ham's most active players off the pitch and he seems to have strong feelings about this, but, indicative of the man, he expresses them in a humorous and fun-loving way:

Some people could do more for the community. I'm living in Canary Wharf – 10 minutes away from Upton Park, so I get roped into doing absolutely everything [laughs]. *I'll do 20 appearances in a week! I don't mind doing them, but when there are people who aren't ill, or saying, 'I got to take the kids,' that gets on my tits* [laughs]. *But it's good. When I go back to my old schools and so on every now and then, it's nice, just to show your face really.*

Although he has had a complicated path into top-class soccer, Bobby is a nice bloke, with a degree of humility that is endearing to anyone who talks with him. He says his favourite colours are claret and blue. He is aware that he is a person who appreciates neatness:

I don't like mess at all. I like to be neat, tidy and organised. My pet hate is anyone that is messy. The missus [Bobby's girlfriend Nicola] *gets it in the neck if she leaves anything about* [smiles]. *I don't know where I picked it up.*

Zamo has few other dislikes, although he told me,

I don't enjoy watching football on TV much. I watch it though and I went to watch Chelsea play Barcelona.

But he has plenty of likes:

Usher, Jamie Foxx, R'n'B is my sort of thing – just chill to them. I got an Aston Martin AMV8 and an Audi A3. I'm getting an RS4 Convertible next month [July 2006]; *I'm looking forward to that.*

Bobby has thought about coaching or management in the future:

I wouldn't mind being a coach. I'd definitely be the good cop out of the good cop, bad cop routine with the manager. It's something that would appeal to me but we'll just see what happens.

ROBERT LESTER ZAMORA

Micky Adams once said Bobby was a better striker at 19 than Alan Shearer at the same age. It is certain that at his best Zamora is an instinctive finisher with an eye for goal from any range. Bobby describes himself as

> ... quite intelligent. I can run, I'm not slow, I'm not lightning fast but I got enough to get about. I'm between Teddy Sheringham and Marlon Harewood. With a bit more about me [laughs].

However, according to the Boleyn Ground crowd, 'He comes from White Hart Lane, he's better than Jermain ...' and he definitely relishes big-time football, saying,

> This is the elite, it's what we live for ... I have no regrets playing for West Ham or any of the games or anything. I've absolutely loved every minute. Even at the tough times. I think those times just make you more of a man. That's an experience in itself.
>
> It's hard to explain playing for a club that I've always thought of as mine. It's proper weird [laughs]. I'll be playing in a game in the Premiership and I'll be singing 'I'm Forever Blowing Bubbles' along with the fans. It's an absolute buzz.
>
> I wouldn't do anything differently with my football; loved every minute of my career. Proper lucky!

SÉBASTIEN CAROLE

'I would hope to stay beyond the summer if possible.'

A two-footed, highly talented player, able to cover the right- or left-back positions or on either side of central midfield, Carole came to Upton Park on loan from AS Monaco during February 2004 initially for the rest of the 2004–05 season with an option of a permanent move to East London. He had been with the French Ligue 1 club for three seasons, but had played just 20 games, scoring five goals. On arriving in the Docklands, he commented,

> *I am glad to be here; I would hope to stay beyond the summer if possible; I love the English game, there is a lot of space, and it is passing football.*

The French Under-21 made his senior debut for the Irons in a Boleyn Ground encounter with Crewe Alexandra as a substitute late on in the game. That was Sébastien's only appearance in the West Ham first team before returning to Monaco to be part of his club's training for the European Cup final against FC Porto.

Carole, who was born in Pontoise, France, on 8 September 1982, had another loan spell, this time with Chateauroux in the second rung of the French game, before signing a two-year contract with Brighton on 12 August 2005 in time to start their ill-fated campaign in the Championship, and he was rarely out of the side.

In the summer of 2006 there seemed to be a strong chance that Carole would join Championship side Leeds United.

CHRISTOPHER GEORGE ROBIN POWELL

HAMMERS DEBUT: 14/9/04

'We live in a society of people of different colours, creeds and cultures, and we've got to try to live together.'

Chris Powell, able to play as an orthodox left-back or as a left wing-back, having good pace, excellent timing in the challenge and no hesitation in marauding forward to make an impact in attack, was born in Lambeth, London, on 8 September 1969. He began his career with Crystal Palace, playing his first senior game for the Eagles in December 1987, but with just a few first-team games to his name, and an 11-match loan interlude at Aldershot, a free transfer took him to Roots Hall.

Powell had made 292 appearances for Southend (most as the Shrimpers' skipper) when, in January 1996, the bald eagle Jim Smith swooped into Essex with a £750,000 transfer deadline bid that took Chris to First Division Derby County. Subsequently, the rampaging Rams rumbusted their way into the Premiership. Chris was to miss just a handful of games between 1996 and 1998.

Having played 101 games with the Pride Park posse and having supplemented his contribution of intelligent and accurate passing with a couple of goals, Chris returned to his home city in September 1998 to join Charlton, who, splashing out £825,000, broke their transfer record to bring him back to South-East London.

Following the disappointment of relegation in his first season at the Valley, the creative full-back became part of the backbone of the side that enabled the Addicks to bounce straight back into the top flight, winning the First Division Championship in the process.

Chris scored his first goal for Charlton against Tottenham

Hotspur in the 2000–01 FA Cup but was unable to prevent the Addicks crashing to a 4–2 defeat.

A doyen of the wide run, finished off with a dangerous centre, Powell made his mark in the Premiership, and was called up to play for England against Spain in February 2001, as part of Sven-Goran Eriksson's first-squad selection. His forward runs caused numerous problems for the Spanish but unfortunately Powell picked up a knock and did not complete the game. For all this, Eriksson retained him for England's World Cup qualifier against Finland in March and he was again in the squad for the friendly against Mexico in May, coming on as a second-half substitute. Chris also turned out for the World Cup qualifier against Greece in June. In all, Powell won five England caps, a record for a Charlton player, filling the problematical left-back role for his country. Chris was only the third Addicks player since 1946 to play for the full England side. At an age when most top-class professionals are reaching the twilight of their playing days, Chris was at the peak of his game. On 2 May 2004 he gave his approval of the England manager:

Sven? I love him. In fact, I now love all things Swedish, from Dime bars to Volvos.

Of his Indian summer of international football, he said,

Looking back, it seems surreal, but it was a great achievement. People look at you differently, thinking you shouldn't make mistakes on or off the field.

But when his contract finished at the conclusion of the 2002–03 season, the Charlton board offered no more than a stingy one-year extension. With some justification Chris wanted a two-year deal. Fulham were ready to take Powell to Craven Cottage but again to the extent of no more than a one-year deal. Premiership new boys Portsmouth were also interested but Powell signed a 12-month contract extension at the Valley in July 2003 and made another one-year deal in the summer of 2004. However, not wanting to remain in the shadow of Hermann Hreidarsson in September 2004, Powell joined West Ham in League One on a month's loan. His five appearances in claret and blue were impressive enough to get his stay at Upton Park extended for another month and, following his release by Charlton in December 2004, he committed himself to the Hammers until the end of the season.

More glory followed when Powell was instrumental in West Ham's dramatic 2004–05 return to the Premiership. Irons supporters will always remember his jig of delight with the young Mark Noble long after most of the players had returned to the dressing rooms at Cardiff.

In June 2005, turning down an attractive offer from Queens Park Rangers, Chris returned to Charlton on a one-year contract, with a view to developing his coaching skills, having made 41 appearances for West Ham.

Powell started the 2005–06 season as Charlton's left-back following the transfer of Paul Konchesky to West Ham after Chris recommended him to Alan Pardew before leaving Upton Park. Ironically, Powell had kept Konchesky out of the Charlton side for a number of years.

In November 2005, Powell was appointed chair of the Professional Footballers Association, but it seems he has no intention of hanging up his boots. With over 600 League games behind him, he recently commented,

> *Teddy* [Sheringham] *is still playing so why can't I do the same? He loves football. People tend to say he plays in a position where he is not using his legs much but he enjoys playing, he enjoys training, and that's the key to it all. I look at Nigel Winterburn and Stuart Pearce, who were both left-backs who played until they were 39 or 40. I know I have to take it year by year as I won't get a three-year contract but at the moment I feel fine. I have been fortunate with injuries too and that plays a big part in it.*

Still a skilful, unflappable, consistent and cultured player, Chris continues to be a good man-marker and a decent passer of the ball. His all-action approach has made him popular everywhere he has

THE BLACK HAMMERS

played but he is known as one of the friendliest faces at Charlton's Sparrows Lane training complex. He is a tremendously likeable person and is remembered with affection at Upton Park. After appearing in the FA Cup at the Boleyn Ground in 2006, he said,

> It was lovely to come back and get a decent reception … I'd like to think the West Ham fans appreciate the part I played last season, and I'll always remember the time I spent at Upton Park … It was a shame to leave, because I was looking forward to being a part of the challenge back in the Premiership, but I'm delighted to see how well the team have done. They've exceeded everything people expected of them, but I always felt the players had it in them and it was just a case of how they would handle the step-up.

In June 2006 Chris joined newly promoted Watford for another season in the Premiership.

In November 2004 a BBC poll of Southend United supporters voted Powell their all-time cult hero. One supporter described Chris as 'a very skilled, left-footed defender, who could quite possibly be considered one of the nicest men in football, a true gent'.

That's probably about right.

CHRIS POWELL – CAREER RECORD			
Crystal Palace	24.12.1987	30.08.1990	
Aldershot	11.01.1990	18.03.1990	L
Southend United	30.08.1990	31.01.1996	
Derby County	31.01.1996	01.07.1998	
Charlton Athletic	01.07.1998	17.12.2004	
West Ham United	10.09.2004	10.12.2004	L
West Ham United	17.12.2004	30.06.2005	
Charlton Athletic	11.07.2005		

DARREN DAVID POWELL

HAMMERS DEBUT: 21/11/04

'You just realise where you're at and just get on with the job.'

D arren, born in Hammersmith, London (Wednesday, 10 March 1976), came to Upton Park on loan from Crystal Palace. A strong 6ft 3in, 13st defender, he made his debut for West Ham on 21 November 2004 at the New Den, a game that ended in defeat for the Hammers.

Powell began his football with Hampton & Richmond in the Isthmian League, before, in July 1998, joining Brentford, who had recently been relegated to Division Three, for a fee of £15,000. He won a Division Three Championship medal in his first term with the Bees and was also voted as Player of the Season by the supporters at Griffin Park. The big centre-half forged a powerful partnership with Ivar Ingimarsson, an Icelandic international, at the fulcrum of the West Londoners' defence that took them back to the Millennium Stadium for the LDV Vans Trophy final, but Port Vale finished strongly to secure a 2–1 victory that day.

In the semi-final of the 2001–02 Division Two play-offs, the Bees met Huddersfield Town. It was Powell who headed home the goal that drew Brentford level with the Terriers, laying the ground for a 2–1 victory. Under manager Steve Coppell, Brentford lost out to Stoke City in the play-off final despite having been just minutes away from automatic promotion on the final day of the season.

In August 2002, after four years, 156 games and eight goals, a £700,000 fee took Powell from Brentford to First Division Crystal Palace. He was back at the Millennium Stadium in 2004 with Palace thanks to his vital goal, after coming off the bench, in the play-off semi-final, again in the second leg; this time the opponents were Sunderland. His effort in the dying seconds of the match obliged the Black Cats to play extra-time before matters were settled by way of a penalty shoot-out. This took Palace to Cardiff, where Darren again took the field as a substitute (after an hour of play) and subsequently into the Premiership, ironically at the expense of West Ham.

Powell played little part in the Eagles ill-fated term in the Premiership and spent a month on loan at Upton Park at the end of 2004. In July 2005 he was out of contract and signed for Harry Redknapp at Southampton on a 'Bosman' free transfer, having played 55 games for Palace and netting twice. Powell made his debut for the Saints on Saturday, 6 August 2005 in a 0–0 draw at home to Wolverhampton Wanderers. He scored his first (and at the time of writing only) goal for Southampton against Ipswich Town. To date, he has played 25 times for the St Mary's crew.

At one point, it looked as if Powell, girlfriend Syreta and their three-year-old daughter, Jademe, might settle in the East End area, as he and manager Pardew had some background. While studying Sports and Recreation, Powell had lined up alongside a former FA Cup finalist for a weekend kickabout with Morden Nomads, a good Sunday-morning side, not long after the then reserve team manager at Reading had finished playing. After seeing his on-loan Eagle head home an equaliser in the hard-fought 3–2 win over Watford on his debut as a Hammer at the Boleyn Ground, Pardew said, 'Darren's not the most cultured player but he's a warrior and the opposition don't like coming up against him.'

But Powell was only to play five games and score one goal for West Ham.

Darren had never planned to become a Premiership professional. Right from the very beginning, he was happy enough to be kicking a ball around. When he was at school he was quite content to be playing semi-professionally for Croydon and then Hampton, his main focus being the Sport and Recreation course he was doing at college.

SHAUN O'NEIL NEWTON

'Do you remember when we played in Spain in the Anglo-Italian?'

Shaun started his football career with Charlton as a trainee and, after 243 games for the Addicks between 1992–93 and 2000–01, scoring 19 times, he moved to Wolves, where from 2001–02 to 2003–04 he turned out in the old gold on 130 occasions, contributing 12 goals to the cause of the men from Molineux, who laid out £850,000 (plus a possible further £300,000 depending on appearances) for his services in August 2001.

Newton, known as 'Beetle' and 'Newts' to his teammates, scored on his debut against Portsmouth and made 28 Premiership appearances in 2003–04, creating the Wanderers' first ever Premiership goal. But this didn't save Wolves from an instant return to the Championship.

Newton, who first saw the light of day in Camberwell on 20 August 1975, is a right-sided midfielder, with three England Under-23 caps (gained in the 1996–97 term) to his credit. He scored for a Football League Under-21 representative side in a 1–1 draw with an Italian Serie 'B' XI in February 1998.

Shaun was brought to Upton Park on loan from Wolves in March 2005 to help with the bid for promotion. Alan Pardew paid £125,000 for the dynamic player, who seems to manage to cover the whole pitch. Newton was to make his presence felt in the two-leg play-off semi-final defeat of Ipswich Town, showing his experience in the Wolverhampton midfield alongside former Hammer Paul Ince to good effect. He kept his place for the final and consequently celebrated his fourth promotion from the First Division, having been involved twice previously with Charlton and once with Wolves.

Shaun is noted for his pace and ability to go past opponents on the outside and for his fine delivery of crosses; he has produced some spectacular goals during his career. He scored his first goal for the Hammers in April 2006, the only goal of the match that saw Manchester City leave Upton Park pointless.

When the Irons returned to the Premiership, many of Shaun's appearances came by way of the bench, but he rarely failed to perform when called upon and he is not shy of letting the likes of Anton Ferdinand know when the Hammers' star defender has done well and when he hasn't. In Anton's words, 'He doesn't beat around the bush.'

DANIEL LEON GABBIDON

'We were involved in one of the greatest finals of all time.'

Having represented Wales at Youth, Under-21 (17 appearances) and full international (19 caps) levels, Danny signed for West Ham just after the Hammers' return to the Barclays Premiership in July 2005 for a fee of £2 million. Danny played a pivotal role in the success enjoyed by Alan Pardew's men upon their return to the English elite and the Hammers boss was able to count upon his reliable consistency perhaps more than on any other player in the squad.

Born in Cwmbran on 8 August 1979, Gabbidon started his career as a trainee with West Bromwich Albion in 1998. He graduated to take his first steps in League football in 1998–99, when he made two appearances. He started the following season as Albion's first-choice right-back, where he performed with distinction before a loss of form, coupled with a nagging shin injury, cost him his place. For all this, West Brom gave Danny a contract that tied him to the Hawthorns until 2003. However, after 27 outings for the Baggies, in August 2000 he was transferred to Cardiff City for £175,000 and quickly established himself as a key figure in the Bluebirds defence, as he went on to forge an outstanding central-defensive partnership with young (also a Hammer-to-be) James Collins, going on to become a consistent element in Cardiff's promotion season, playing in all the outfield defensive positions.

Former Hammer and England international Neil Ruddock

expressed his admiration for Gabbidon and urged the then Wales boss Mark Hughes to give Danny experience at international level. Ruddock saw a resemblance between Gabbidon and another former West Ham player, Manchester United and England's Rio Ferdinand, who had been a role model for Gabbidon since his earliest days.

Danny made his full international debut in March 2002 against the Czech Republic, but, following Wales' exit from the Euro 2004 Championships, which he felt deeply, he suffered a loss of form.

Selected in the PFA's First Division Team of the Season in 2003–04, Danny continued to flourish at club and international levels, showing great awareness and a composure on the ball, demonstrating his suitability for a higher grade of football. The central defender scored 10 goals in 219 games during his five years at Ninian Park.

According to Anton Ferdinand, 'Gabbs keeps himself to himself. He's a quiet lad, but he can have his moments with the banter. He's one of these lads who likes to sit back and take it while cracking up and laughing everywhere.'

Gabbidon was voted Welsh Footballer of the Year on 3 October 2005, and proved an instant success at West Ham. He gained over 50 per cent of votes in a poll to choose the club's best performer for the first half of the 2005–06 season on the leading Hammers website KUMB and was selected Hammer of the Year at the end of West Ham's glorious campaign that took them so near to defeating the Champions of Europe in the FA Cup final. He is only the third player in West Ham United's history to win the coveted Hammer of the Year award in his debut season at Upton Park.

Danny spoke for the rest of his teammates when looking back on the 2006 Cup final:

It was a great game to be involved in but the way we lost makes it all a bit hard to swallow. We were so close to winning the game and all I keep seeing in my mind is that goal from Steven Gerrard.

I headed it out and I think Yossi [Benayoun] tried to take another swipe at it but missed. The ball carried on rolling out and, when I looked up and saw him running on to it, I was a bit worried. As he hit it, I kind of knew it had half a chance, but it was an unbelievable strike and something that only he was capable of.

He was the difference on the day, there's no doubt about that. If he'd been playing for us, we would have won convincingly and, if he hadn't been playing at all, I think we still would have won.

It was going to take something special like that to beat us, and then we still had chances to win it, with the ball hitting the post and then falling to Marlon on one leg! I suppose it's that kind of drama that makes the FA Cup so special, and there's definitely some consolation that we were involved in one of the greatest finals of all time.

DAVID BELLION

'There is so much to learn about football in England but I want to learn.'

Born in Sevres, France, on 27 November 1982, Bellion made his mark with AS Cannes in the French Second Division. The fast-moving forward had been with the side since the age of 14 and was at the club at the same time as Patrick Vieira. The south–coast side has a distinguished history, having also produced the likes of Zinedine Zidane and Johan Micoud.

Bellion turned down a number of clubs in Le Championnat before being snapped up in July 2001 on a Bosman free deal by Peter Reid for his Sunderland side. David was quickly hailed as the 'new Thierry Henry'.

Bellion made his League debut in a 2–0 defeat at Fulham in the opening month of the season. He played 10 games in his first season at the club but failed to get on the scoresheet, his only start coming against Sheffield Wednesday in the Worthington Cup. A number of injuries effectively ended Bellion's season (he spent much of the year in France getting treatment).

As Sunderland collapsed and were eventually relegated, David brought the number of games he played for the Black Cats up to a couple of dozen, scoring his only goal in a 1–0 win over Aston Villa in September 2002. Surprisingly, Manchester United made a bid of £1.5 million for his services in the January transfer window. This, even more surprisingly, was turned down, but Alex Ferguson eventually brought Bellion to Old Trafford when his contract expired on 1 July 2003. Bellion signed a four-year deal at Old Trafford, but as he was only 23 years old at the time the fee would be set by a tribunal at £2 million.

DAVID BELLION

Bellion promptly scored on his debut for United, a fine finish against Celtic on the club's pre-season American tour. He made his League debut for the Red Devils on 27 August 2003 in an Old Trafford game against Wolves. His first competitive goal came at Leeds United in the Carling Cup. United fans were impressed by David's speed and dribbling ability, although he did seem to be easily out-muscled by defenders.

In his first season with United, his appearances were mostly limited to substitute roles and, by the start of 2004–05, with few goals to his credit it was clear Bellion had become frozen out of the first-team picture.

The 6ft striker and French Under-21 international came to West Ham on a one-year loan deal starting in August 2005 on the club's return to the Premiership. He was to say,

In Manchester it was difficult to achieve my ambitions, even though I believe in my qualities … Firstly, I spoke with the Manchester United manager who thought it would be better to have me 'within sight' at West Ham. When Sir Alex Ferguson advises you to do something, it's hard not to listen.

He scored on his debut in the 4–2 League Cup win at Sheffield Wednesday as a 65th-minute substitute for Marlon Harewood. But competition for a strike spot at Upton Park, with Harewood, Teddy Sheringham and Bobby Zamora in form, left Bellion with just seven matches for West Ham. According to Bellion,

The Hammers were back in the Premier League, they had good results early on with the players who took them up, and I arrived there injured, and so it was hard to win a place.

However, Ferguson allowed Bellion to bring an early end to his stay in the East End of London and, in January 2006, return to his native France to see the season out on the Cote d'Azur with Nice in Ligue 1. He saw his move to West Ham as a mistake.

HOGAN EPHRAIM

HAMMERS DEBUT: 20/9/05

'I want to go as far as I can.'

After coming through the academy system, Hogan joined West Ham in 1999. This Islington-born (31 March 1988) forward has represented England at Under-16 and Under-17 levels and has scored a number of important goals for his country. Particularly memorable was his performance for John Peacock's Under-17s v Russia wherein he hit four goals. At the time of writing, he has scored seven goals in 14 Under-17 internationals.

An intelligent player, knowing when to challenge for a ball and when to hold back, Hogan was prominent in the Hammers' 2004–05 FA Youth Cup run. He played in the UEFA European Championships for England in Italy in May 2005, netting twice in three matches.

After making an impact in Kevin Keen's reserve team, Hogan made his senior debut in a Carling Cup game at Hillsborough on 20 September 2005, coming on as a substitute in the 87th minute of the 4–2 defeat of Sheffield Wednesday.

Also able to play the role of attacking midfielder, Hogan is highly thought of at Upton Park and is expected to make an impact in the first team in years to come.

KYEL REID

'West Ham is a great club.'

A talented midfielder/left-winger, Kyel was born in South London (26 November 1987) and signed professional forms with West Ham shortly after his 17th birthday, having joined the club as an academy scholar in the summer of 2004. A regular in the reserve team during 2005–06, he has represented England at Under-17 and Under-19 levels, scoring his first goal for his country on 4 May 2004 in an Under-17 European Championship qualifier v Norway.

Reid made his Barclays Premiership debut in the 1–0 victory at the Hawthorns.

CONCLUSION

A book needs a last word, but then again, in the case of this book, there probably shouldn't be any final statement. Maybe it would be better to see the narratives and biographies that have gone before as a start of something, 'a better world' perhaps? Certainly there will be more *Black Hammers*, but we are possibly coming to a time when there will be only *Hammers*. Just as Black History is not something separate from the rest of history (and to make it so would be a very subtle form of apartheid), the reality is that all the Hammers are one. As one of the *Black Hammers* told me,

> At West Ham there are only two colours, and they are not black and white, they are claret and blue …

However, although, to some extent, the myth that West Ham fans are inherently racist has been undermined, *The Black Hammers* suggest that something far more subtle or even more insidious than overt racism on the terraces has been going on in football over the years. One is left with a sneaking impression that the focus on supporters has acted as something of a diversion from forms of institutional racism that have limited opportunities for black players when their playing days are done. But there are also the honours conferred by the authorities that run the game; why, for instance, have so few black players been given the captaincy of England compared to say the Dutch or French teams? Other questions arise from such queries. In the 2006 World Cup, the first names on the lips of the

CONCLUSION

Motsons of this world were Rooney (Fat Boy Slim), Beckham (Thin Boy Flat), Crouch (Tall Boy Slack) and Owen (Short Boy Short); how long has the English line been led by blue-eyed, blonde-haired white boys? Where the fuck was Jermain Defoe in July 2006? How many fans in England clenched their fists and said 'Yes!' when 'Mr Dynamic' Steve McClaren replaced Sven the letch? Germany have got Klinsmann, Barcelona have Frank Rijkaard and Marco van Basten is in charge of Holland; England have the man who for the majority of his career played for Hull City mostly in the Second and Third Divisions! Ask yourself, would you have been more interested if Paul Ince had been involved? Would the team play more interesting/attractive football if Ian Wright had a role? Would you prefer your elder statesmen of the English game to be 'Sir' Les Ferdinand or Bobby 'Whatisname' Robson?

What listening to *The Black Hammers* did for me was answer one question, however, as is the case with education, answers generally give rise to wider questions but also provide a clearer view of the nature of reality and the means by which this is often hidden from us.

BIBLIOGRAPHY

Barnes, J. (1999) *John Barnes: The Autobiography*, London: Headline

Belton, B. (1997) *Bubbles, Hammers and Dreams*, Derby: Breedon Books

Belton, B. (2004) *Burn Johnny Byrne – Football Inferno*, Derby: Breedon Books

Belton, B. (1999) *Days of Iron*, Derby: Breedon Books

Belton, B. (2003) *Founded on Iron*, Gloucestershire: Tempus

Belton, B. (2003) *Johnnie the One: the John Charles Story*, Gloucestershire: Tempus

Belton, B. (1998) *The First and Last Englishmen*, Derby: Breedon Books

Belton, B. (2005) *The Men of 64: West Ham and Preston North End in the FA Cup*, Gloucestershire: Tempus

Belton, B. (2006) *West Ham United Miscellany*, London: Pennant Books Ltd

Blows, K. and Hogg, T. (2000) *West Ham. The Essential History*, Swindon: Headline

Fenton, T. (1960) *At Home with the Hammers*, London: Nicholas Kaye

Ferdinand, L. (1997) *Sir Les: Autobiography of Les Ferdinand*, London: Headline

Greenwood, R. (1984) *Yours Sincerely Ron Greenwood*, London: Willow Books

Groves, R. (1948) *West Ham United*, London: Cassel & Co.

Helliar, J. and Leatherdale, C. (2005) *West Ham United: The Elite Era – a Complete Record*, Essex: Desert Island Books

Hogg, T. and McDonald, T. (1995) *1895–1995 Hammers 100 Years of Football*, Independent UK Sports Publications

BIBLIOGRAPHY

Hogg, T. (2005) *West Ham United Who's Who*, London: Profile Sports Media Ltd.

Hugman, B. (1998) *The PFA Premier & Football League Players Records 1946–1998*, Hertfordshire: Queen Anne Press

Inglis, S. (1988) *League Football and the Men who Made It*, London: HarperCollinsWillow

Irving, D. (1968) *The West Ham United Football Book*, London: Stanley Paul

Irving, D. (1969) *The West Ham United Football Book No. 2*, London: Stanley Paul

Korr, C. (1986) *West Ham United*, London: Duckworth.

Leatherdale, C. (1998) *West Ham United from Greenwood to Redknapp*, Essex: Desert Island

Lyall, J. (1989) *Just Like My Dreams*, Harmondsworth: Penguin

Mallory, J. (1997) *Football League Tables*, Glasgow and London: Collins

Moynihan, J. (1984) *The West Ham Story*, London: Arthur Baker Ltd.

Northcutt, J. and Shoesmith, R. (1993) *West Ham United. A Complete Record*, Derby: Breedon Books

Northcutt, J. and Shoesmith, R. (1994) *West Ham United. An Illustrated History*, Derby: Breedon Books.

Oliver, G. (1995) *World Soccer* (2nd ed), Bath: Guinness

Shaoul, M. and Williamson, T. (2000) *Forever England – A History of the National Side*, Gloucestershire: Tempus

Stiles, N. (2003) *Nobby Stiles – After the Ball*, London: Hodder and Stoughton

Thompson, P. and Hale, S. (2004) *Shankly – From Glenbuck to Wembley*, Gloucestershire: Tempus

Turner, D. and White, A. (1987) *Fulham A Complete Record 1879–1987*, Derby: Breedon Books

Turner, D. and White, A. (1998) *Fulham Facts and Figures 1879–1998*, Hants: Northdown

Ward, A. (1999) *West Ham United 1895–1999,* London: Octopus

Journals/Newspapers
Daily Mail
East London Advertiser
Ex-Magazine
Hammers News
Newham Recorder
Soccer History
Stratford Express
The Times